"In this well-written, well-researched story, the reader lives with a solitary little Jewish boy in the house of a German family in World War II, dressed in rags, often bitterly cold, always hungry, doing heavy work in the fields or lying alone at night in the dark, totally ignorant of the outside world. The constant fear of the unknown, the arbitrary punishments, the minuscule pleasures that could brighten a whole day, the complex relationships with his captors are all there, but above all there is the will to survive as an upright man—as he so triumphantly did."

— **Reg Green**
author of *The Nicholas Effect: A Boy's Gift to the World*

"To meet Mitka Kalinski and to hear his story, the hurdles and horrors he overcame, is to understand that love once in a while triumphs over hatred—that perseverance, hard work, compassion, and more than a dose of boyish good luck help one survive a World War. Mitka's story is amazing and, in the end, beautiful. His ability to forgive, to move forward, to raise a family and build a life in the West is just as profound. His courage to confront the painful past of his youth, to share it all with his wife Adrienne, and to return to the hell from which he escaped so many decades ago—this carries lessons for all of us. We must bear witness; we must never forget."

— **Jacob Wheeler**
independent journalist in Traverse City, Michigan

"The moment I heard Mitka's story, I immediately knew I needed to write music for it. How often do you get a canvas like that of Mitka Kalinski's life? It has been an absolute honor to be involved with every aspect of his life, and this project and getting to know him has made me a better person—more grateful, kinder, and more willing to be patient with others. This is a story that everyone needs to hear, for it will absolutely change the life of all who are touched by it for the better."

— **Jordan S. Roper**
film composer and creator of the symphonic composition
"My Name Is Mitka"

Mitka's Secret

A True Story of Child Slavery and Surviving the Holocaust

Steven W. Brallier
with Joel N. Lohr and Lynn G. Beck

WILLIAM B. EERDMANS PUBLISHING COMPANY
GRAND RAPIDS, MICHIGAN

Wm. B. Eerdmans Publishing Co.
4035 Park East Court SE, Grand Rapids, Michigan 49546
www.eerdmans.com

Although the publisher and the authors have made every effort to ensure that the information in this book was correct at press time and while this publication is designed to provide accurate information in regard to the subject matter covered, the publisher and the authors assume no responsibility for errors, inaccuracies, omissions, or any other inconsistencies herein and hereby disclaim any liability to any party for any loss, damage, or disruption caused by errors or omissions, whether such errors or omissions result from negligence, accident, or any other cause.

27 26 25 24 23 22 21   1 2 3 4 5 6 7

ISBN 978-0-8028-7916-5

Library of Congress Cataloging-in-Publication Data

Names: Brallier, Steven W., author. | Lohr, Joel N., author. | Beck, Lynn G., author.
Title: Mitka's secret : a true story of child slavery & surviving the Holocaust / Steven W. Brallier with Joel N. Lohr and Lynn G. Beck.
Description: Grand Rapids, Michigan : William B. Eerdmans Publishing Co., 2021. | Summary: "The remarkable life story of Mitka Kalinski, who, while still a child, survived the Holocaust and seven years of enslavement to a Nazi officer, then began a new life in the United States and revealed his secret past decades later"—Provided by publisher.
Identifiers: LCCN 2021003752 | ISBN 9780802879165 (paperback)
Subjects: LCSH: Kalinski, Mitka. | Jewish men—Ukraine—Biography. | Holocaust, Jewish (1939–1945)—Ukraine—Personal narratives. | Holocaust survivors—United States—Biography.
Classification: LCC DS135.U43 B73 2021 | DDC 940.53/18092 [B]—dc23
LC record available at https://lccn.loc.gov/2021003752

Biblical quotations follow the New Jewish Publication Society translation unless otherwise noted.

*Dedicated to the children of the Holocaust
whose stories will never be told*

Contents

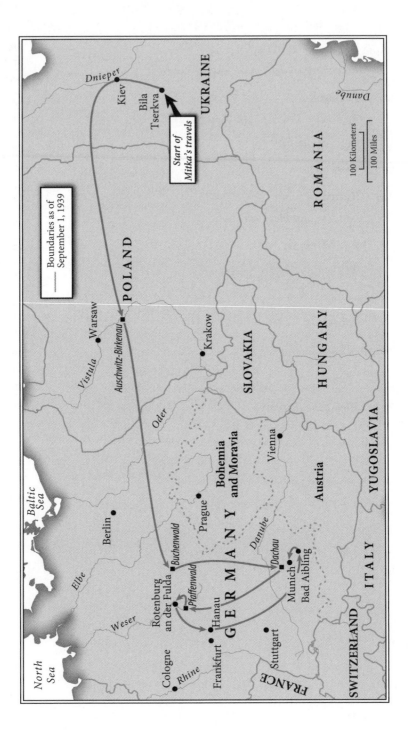

Preface

On Twelfth Street in the Nevada town of Sparks sits a dwelling so modest it surely attracts no attention save for the tchotchkes that decorate the exterior. In the front yard, songbirds fly in and out of a stunted tree to feast on seeds, and a homemade sprinkler contraption irrigates the postage-stamp patch of grass between the house and a chain-link fence. Two plastic replicas of Jack Daniel's statue guard the door to the enclosed front porch.

There stands an old man prepared to greet us. Ramrod straight, he looks larger than his six-foot frame and younger by a decade than his eighty-plus years. The brim of his ball cap is unable to conceal the aura of easy, contagious joy that radiates from his sky-blue eyes. He leans forward with a smile.

"My name is Mitka," he says as he extends a broad hand with fingers that feel like hammer handles. "Come in, come in."

He turns and opens the door.

We make our way across the cramped porch, filled with solar-powered toys ("our grandson, Stephen—he gives those to us"), hackneyed axioms on posters, and boxes. Inside the living room, an Elvis clock, legs swinging as the seconds pass, hangs beside a picture of Jesus. One menorah sits atop a bookcase; another adorns the mantle. Photographs are everywhere.

Mitka gives us a tour, item by item, each with its own story. Often he recalls the person who gave it to him. Sometimes he describes how he purchased a piece on a trip with family. As he talks, the objects become more than just trinkets. They hold personal memories, connecting Mitka to people and places.

Lynn Beck and Joel Lohr—my writing partners—walk with me into the wide but shallow room that is both a dining and a living area. We find chairs around a four-top table. Adrienne, Mitka's wife, sits at one end with Mitka at her side.

Two weeks ago Joel, a professor and friend, approached me with a fantastic story. Over a casual dinner with Lynn (who is also my wife) and me, he shared the broad outline of Mitka's story. It was a story that his neighbor Robert Lucchesi had doggedly tried to bring to the big screen for some twenty-five years, ever since he met Mitka while camping in Bodega Bay. Prospective deals came and went, but Adrienne steadfastly held to her belief that a book needed to be written before any movie could be made.

Joel, a published author, took an interest and had begun exploring how to get Mitka's story written as a book.

But he had questions. He knew this was a big story. It was my experience as a onetime agent for the William Morris Agency that prompted Joel's inquiries. After answering Joel's questions, I took a chance— "Would you and Robert consider me as the writer of Mitka's story?"

After reading some writing samples I sent him, Joel called a few days later. "Can you schedule a trip to Sparks to meet Mitka and Adrienne? Could it be next week?"

Joel explained that the trip was necessary for one reason alone. If I— with the help of Lynn and Joel—was going to be the writer of Mitka's story, then it would come down to a simple question: Could Mitka and Adrienne trust us with their story?

And so there we sat in a house that for six decades has been the home of Mitka and Adrienne Kalinski, two improbable people whose lives were shaped by one of Western civilization's greatest crimes: the Holocaust. Each one of us gathered around the table realized that now, at last, Mitka was ready to have his story told.

Mitka and Adrienne had purchased this house in 1961, two years after they moved from North Tonawanda, New York, to Sparks. It was in Nevada that Mitka found year-round work and, with it, the satisfaction of supporting his family. However, Mitka carried a secret. He kept memories of his childhood—a childhood of train cars and death camps and slavery—buried, hidden even from his wife and children.

It was on a day in 1981 that the horrors of Mitka's early life, horrors that had for years smoldered within him, burst into flame. And then, like a wildfire, his need to tell and retell his story could not be extinguished.

From that day forward, Adrienne documented everything Mitka said. Then, painstakingly, the two of them followed every lead they could to validate Mitka's memories and to find the truth. Mitka's memories begin around 1939, when Hitler was in the early stages of bringing death and destruction to Europe.

Slavery

CHAPTER ONE

Kinderheim

Bila Tserkva and Kiev, 1939–1941

"One . . . two . . . three . . . four . . . five . . ."

A boy—five or six years old—counted as the bombs fell.

From the oilcloth-covered table in his Sparks, Nevada, home, Mitka Kalinski recounts one of his earliest childhood traumas. His fists contract to punctuate words, of anger, pain, longing, joy.

"During the night, five bombs. You ask me, how do I remember five? A five- or six-year-old kid can count to five—so five—one, two, three . . ." He counts with his fingers. "So five bombs—and I was scared."

Six-year-old Mitka wore a nightgown—a heavy one, he remembers, as it was one of the few garments he owned. He cowered in his bed, the first in two long rows. Plaster crashed from the ceiling.

"My sheet fell on the floor and I was scared to pick it up and I was curled up like this." He pulls his arms into his chest and lowers his head, cringing.

It was dark. The boy looked around as best he could. He saw no adults, which had been the case for several days. Only children—young children—surrounded him. The older ones slept in another room. A month earlier, a teacher had told the children that everything would change in the coming weeks.

"So five bombs. That's probably what she was talking about. The bombs came."

The morning after the bombs fell—the morning after he lay counting, without covers, on his cot—he remembers hearing an inaudible voice telling him to flee. Mitka trusted the voice and obeyed. Barefoot and wearing his heavy nightgown, Mitka and another child, a boy whose name he cannot recall, ran from the building. The boys fled across the Ros River, which at that time of year was low enough to ford. The potato and wheat harvests, the shallow river, and Hitler's offensive push into Russia help to establish the time frame as late summer or early autumn.

After knocking on the doors of several homes and being turned away, the boys came to a forked road. They argued about which way to take and, both being strong-willed, chose differently. Mitka pressed forward, alone, into the woods.

Two years earlier Mitka had arrived at the *Kinderheim*, a boarding school for young children, in Bila Tserkva, Ukraine. Marigolds were blooming, he recalls, though at the time he didn't know the word for the flower. Decades later, brushing his hand across yellow petals, he recognized the pungent scent and was immediately transported back to his arrival in Bila Tserkva. And to a woman whose face he cannot see or remember, but who held his hand.

"I remember being on a horse wagon with people with black hats and long shawls, and I remember fleeing. Later I found out that the Nazis invaded Poland in 1939. I think we might have been fleeing from Poland to the Ukraine. So that was the year this all happened. It was 1939."

The recollection of a flight in a horse-drawn vehicle is one of only a handful of memories Mitka has of life before his arrival at the *Kinderheim*.

"I remember a man. He came to a house. He had a nice little sports car with a wheel, a spare tire, in the back, and he carved me a boat for the water with a knife like this." As he speaks, Mitka mimics carving, paying great attention to the details of the remembered toy boat. He continues, "And he had a patch over his eye."

The man with the patch set the boat on water, and the two watched it float.

Several beats pass before Mitka says, with plaintive tenderness: "I think that man was my father." He continues, his voice unusually soft and halting, "My father—I can hardly say those words. I'm not even sure what they mean."

A less vivid but nonetheless cherished memory is of a woman with dark hair who was affectionate toward him.

"I remember a lady, and, one particular time, I was in the crib, so I had to be very, very young. She had a rubber band that she gave to me. I remember taking the rubber band like a string to make music . . . *ping, ping, ping.*" He makes a rhythmical twanging with his voice, his hands miming the plucking of the band. "She gave me the rubber band, and she gave me a hug and then walked away. I was in the crib standing, and I watched her walk out the door. She had long hair. She closed the door. That's the last I saw her. I believe she was my mother."

He wants desperately to remember more of this woman. He cannot.

His next memory, he believes, is from a time shortly after the flight from Poland. "I remember playing with two little girls, and my father had to go into the war. . . . I bet he left me to go to the war."

At this point in the telling Mitka breaks from memories and tries to make sense of what happened next. He believes he was most likely living with someone other than his parents, possibly placed there by his father. "And that's when the people I was staying with probably had the idea—and this is me now speaking—to put me out of their house and to put me somewhere else. And that woman"—not the rubber-band woman, but his intermediary caregiver—"took me to the *Kinderheim.* And now I put two and two together. Do you know why they put me out of the house?"

The look in his eyes makes clear that this is an important question for Mitka. It's one of many that has haunted him. Acknowledging that he doesn't know a sure answer, he offers his best guess: "I think they learned what I was—a Jewish boy."

Mitka pauses. There is something important for him in this realization.

"They figured out that if the Nazis found out, the whole family would have been wiped out. I don't know if it is true or not, that if they were harboring a Jew they would have been wiped out. I don't know if it was true, but I came to that conclusion.

"I always thought that because I wasn't wanted, I was sent to the boarding school. I wasn't wanted. I always knew that I was different because of what I was and the language I spoke—that I was different and I wasn't wanted. I never saw the woman who put me there again—the woman who took me by the hand and put me there."

As Mitka continues, his jaw tightens and his voice gets firmer.

"She put me in Bila Tserkva," he says matter-of-factly but with an anger-tinged tone. "She put me in that boarding school and left me there. I do know that I did not want to be there. I carried on, and they put me in a corner. I did not know what was happening. I just knew that I did not want to be there. I was a bad boy, and they made me stand in a corner."

Mitka often repeats the phrases "they put me in a corner" and "I was a bad boy" as he remembers the *Kinderheim*. They reflect, it seems, both the shame and the isolation he felt.

As quickly as it comes, the anger leaves. Mitka pulls his shoulders in and wraps his arms around his body. "When I think about it now, right now, I am that little boy. I don't think I ever grew up. I'm still six years old in my mind. I'm still there."

Two winters passed while he was at the school. He is certain about this detail. Seasons were the way he recalled the passage of time.

Other fleeting impressions stuck with him. He knew the *Kinderheim* was a place he did not want to be, but not all his memories are hurtful. He remembers liking the chicken he was fed for meals. And playing with a tricycle, a pedal car, and a hoop and stick.

He recalls gazebos around the yard, or as he describes them, "umbrellas built of wood." He sketches a simple yet detailed drawing of the boarding house and points to the four gazebo locations. Within the building he identifies an office, dormitories, a laundry room, and a kitchen. On his drawing he shows where the outhouse stood and where the Ros River flowed adjacent to the grounds. He also shows where the school's resident peacock roamed—he collected its feathers and talked to it. "I always talked to animals. They talked back. I could hear what they said," Mitka proudly declares. He remembers giving one teacher a peacock feather. To this day he keeps a peacock feather close by, standing in a tall vase in the corner of his living room.

A field trip into town is another memory. The city's name, Bila Tserkva, means "white church," and there was such a church. At the time Bila Tserkva could be described as a religious city, home not only to Christians but also to a large, active, and sometimes persecuted Jewish community. The church Mitka remembers may or may not have been the church for which the town was named, though this is unimportant to Mitka. He'd been to the church with other children. He describes statues—lots of statues—but not in the area where Mass was said. On this same outing Mitka saw his first movie.

As he remembers people from this time in his life, he recalls a "night watchman," an "office lady," other unnamed adults, and especially the woman who dropped him off at the *Kinderheim*.

Mitka sees no faces in his memories of this time, only bodies. This experience of not remembering faces, just bodies, gnaws at him. He struggles to comprehend why he sees no eyes, noses, mouths, and ears. "Maybe it was because I was so little. I don't know." He wishes he could remember more—especially of his life before the *Kinderheim*.

In mid-August 1941, on the day bombs fell on Bila Tserkva, Mitka and the other children were forced to contend with Hitler's devastating vision. In pursuit of racial purity and of *Lebensraum*, or "living space," where the master race could propagate, Hitler and his men spent the spring and summer of 1939 preparing for war. Germany attacked Poland on September 1, 1939. France and England responded on September 2, declaring war against Germany.

On June 22, 1941, in direct violation of a nonaggression pact signed by Hitler and Stalin in 1939, the Nazis raised the ante considerably by invading the Soviet Union. Under the code name of Operation Barbarossa, Hitler moved from a war of domination to a full-throated *Vernichtungskrieg*, or "war of annihilation."

Bila Tserkva was one of the towns in Hitler's path.

In their march through Ukraine in summer 1941, the Nazis targeted for arrest and execution all Jewish men between the ages of seventeen and forty-five. In July Higher SS and Police Leader Friedrich Jeckeln approved the inclusion of women in massacres. In mid-August, Jewish babies and toddlers whose parents had been killed were transported to and locked in "a schoolhouse in Bila Tserkva."

Before the bombing that prompted Mitka's flight, he remembers soldiers arriving in "big green trucks" at the front of the *Kinderheim*, and children being unloaded. Mitka points to a place on his rough drawing about three quarters of the way down one side of the building and says with satisfaction, "And I could see it from here. In front of the office— that is where the trucks came." He cannot explain why, but those green trucks bearing children somehow portended bad things. "Maybe it was what the teacher told us. I don't know. I just felt like something bad was going to happen."

Something bad did indeed occur. And not just the bombing.

On August 21 and 22, General Walther von Reichenau, commander of the Sixth Army of Nazi Germany, ordered the slaughter of Bila Tserkva's adult Jewish population, an act carried out by the Einsatzgruppen, elite Nazi killing squads, with the help of German soldiers and Ukrainian allies. Only children, stranded and locked in a school building, were left. Next, orders were given that stated, unequivocally, that the actions taken to stamp out "Judeo-Bolshevism" must, of necessity, include the killing of Jewish children.

The order was a hard one, even for disciplined and war-hardened soldiers. It was especially troubling to two military chaplains, Catholic priest Ernst Tewes and Lutheran minister Gerhard Wilczek. These chaplains attempted, with some success, to persuade a German officer, Lieutenant Colonel Helmuth Groscurth, that the murder of children was a step too far. The colonel brought the concerns to senior military officials, and the massacre was postponed while they were addressed. Ultimately, though, Groscurth came to agree that "alternative accommodation for the children was . . . impossible . . . and that this breed has to be exterminated."

One soldier, a witness to the murders on August 22, described them with these words:

> I went to the woods alone. The *Wehrmacht* had already dug a grave. The children were brought along in a tractor. I had nothing to do with this technical procedure. The Ukrainians were standing around trembling. The children were taken down from the tractor. They were lined up along the top of the grave and shot so that they fell into it. The Ukrainians did not aim at any particular part of the body. They fell into the grave. The wailing was indescribable. I shall never forget the scene throughout my life. I find it very hard to bear. I particularly remember a small fair-haired girl who took me by the hand. She too was shot later. . . . The grave was near some woods. It was not near the rifle range. The execution must have taken place in

the afternoon at about 3:30 or 4:00. It took place the day after the discussions at the *Feldkommandanten*. . . . Many children were hit four or five times before they died.

Many years later, looking at photographs of Bila Tserkva, Mitka recognized the school building that housed the orphaned Jewish children. "That was it. That was the *Kinderheim.* Those children who were killed—they were the children that the trucks brought." His other memories align with events preceding this massacre.

Mitka escaped execution by deciding to run from the school where he had lived for two years. Now a different and very real struggle for survival confronted the boy. He recalls walking and walking, for days and nights, always alone. Sometimes he trekked through forests, but more often it was through fields. In some fields he found potatoes beside furrows, potatoes missed in the harvest. "I always say no matter how good you plow, always one potato comes out. It always does that. And I walked on the field and I ate raw potatoes on the field."

He continues. "In other fields I saw rows of golden 'teepees.' That is how I remember that it was fall. There was—what do you call it—this stuff that grows that they cut and they tie it together—like what you make bread of—wheat. And when it was tied together it would make a little teepee and you could sleep inside. It was like a little tent, and I slept inside."

These standing grain stalks not only formed a shelter in which Mitka could sleep, they also gave him another food source. From the head of a stalk he broke off the husk and somehow released the kernels of wheat from it by rubbing. He also ate sorrel, a bitter-tasting plant he knew as *Schavel.*

Despite potatoes, wheat, and sorrel to eat, he was always hungry. "Hunger like this no one can understand. Five days, at least, with no food. When you're hungry to death you find out what's edible—raw potatoes and wheat."

After days of walking and knocking on doors as he found them, his luck turned for the better, at least temporarily. At one of the houses an elderly woman said she would give him some food and let him sleep there if he would watch her cow until her son returned, and that when her son returned, he would have to leave. "I slept right at the back of the [entry] door . . . on some rags . . . some bundle of rags or something."

How long he was at this farm, he can't say. He does recall that when the woman's son returned, "I was forced to leave." As he started walking down the road, a German military convoy picked him up. (Mitka believes the woman or her son turned him over to the Germans for reward money.) The trucks were loaded with people, but he didn't see other children, just adults. During the ride Mitka heard lots of talking, and he kept hearing one word: Kiev. "I never heard that word before, 'Kiev,'" he says.

"All of a sudden the truck stopped and I hear 'Everybody out!' Almost immediately . . . *tat-tat-tat*." Mitka fires an imaginary rifle, mimicking the sound of gunfire.

"I remember the noise. Oh, that noise. It was not pleasant to hear that noise. People were lined up and then they started falling. I fell too. People fell on top of me and pushed me along with them. Bodies buried me. I always say, I must have been buried a hundred feet."

When the executioners stopped shooting and all was silent, Mitka wriggled his way to the top of the body heap. He had avoided being shot. It was getting dark now, and the soldiers had gone, leaving corpses behind. Still wearing the nightgown he had worn when he left the *Kinderheim*, Mitka was cold, hungry, filthy, and scared. No living person was in sight. "Quiet, quiet, quiet . . ." is all he heard.

Mitka sketches the scene and points to the killing site, to the position where the gunfire came from, and to what was most probably the Dnieper River.

Watching the History Channel years later, Mitka learned of Babi Yar, a massacre so named because it was at the Babi Yar ravine near Kiev that the Nazi killing squads and local collaborators shot more than thirty thousand Jews and an unknown number of other people over the course of two days. Features of the Babi Yar massacre closely match Mitka's experience, so much so that he is convinced he did indeed survive this specific mass shooting by being buried beneath the bodies of the murdered. As with the Bila Tserkva massacre, it's impossible to verify if Mitka was in Babi Yar or if his near death occurred in one of the many other slaughters that were a part of Operation Barbarossa.

After escaping the mass grave, Mitka remembers walking out of a gulch and toward the river. He had walked a distance, though he cannot say how far, when he saw trucks and activity ahead. He points to the position of the trucks on the simple map he has drawn. Wanting to find help, he walked to the trucks, putting himself into the hands of more German soldiers.

The soldiers held rifles and were loading people into a train car—a cattle wagon. Mitka remembers only adults with him, crammed into the car so tightly that no one could sit down.

"I forgot the messy part," he says. "When I was inside that cattle wagon, if I wanted to fall down I couldn't have. And if you had to go to the bathroom, you had to go where you stood. Some people said there was a bucket there, but I never saw one. There was no bucket. You just went to the bathroom where you were. And while the train was moving, people died."

Reaching for one of the many books about the Holocaust that fill the shelves in his home, Mitka finds a grainy photo of a cattle wagon that transported prisoners to the camps, a wagon that is on display at the United States Holocaust Memorial Museum. "That cattle wagon there seemed smaller than the one I was in." Mitka then points to a small compartment—he calls it a *Häuschen*, meaning a small house—built on top of one end of the wagon. With his finger he traces in the air a narrow structure covered by a slightly steepled roof.

"Do you know what is in the *Häuschen*? There is a wheel to stop the train. I'm probably the only one who would tell you that because I was in it. I bet nobody else has been in one."

What led to Mitka climbing up into the *Häuschen* was an incident in which some prisoners attempted an escape. The soldiers "got us off the train sometimes. I don't know why, but maybe it was to give us a little soup or something. All of a sudden there was a lot of shooting. Now I know that *tat-tat-tat* sound was machine guns shooting at us.

"Somehow people were running from the train. People were running in the bushes. And I could see people lying on the side of the tracks. And where is that machine gun coming out of? That little *Häuschen* there. They closed the big door"—where Mitka would have entered—"and the train started to move, and I didn't want to be shot.

"The train was moving . . . slowly, slowly." He pumps his arms to mimic his running. "I had a hell of a time climbing up on that cattle wagon. The running board on that thing was so damn high.

"I didn't know much because I was so small. But I did know that I was afraid to fall underneath the train." Now he reaches up for imaginary ladder rungs, one after the other. "So I climbed up that ladder on the *Häuschen*, and that was how I learned there was a wheel inside. And if anyone asks you—now you know there is a wheel inside."

The fear leaves his voice, and he says these last words with a smile and the pride of a young boy who took a risk and succeeded, a boy who knew something about the inner workings of a vehicle that held him captive.

Mitka does not know how long he was on the train. He speculates it was days. With a wry chuckle he recalls another stop where people were picnicking in the grass across from the prisoners' soup line.

"I had a tin cup. I don't know where I got that tin cup. And when we went out of the train, some man had a crust of bread. He came to me and said he would give me the crust for that tin cup. And we had more conversation, and we traded. I gave him the cup, and he gave me the crust. And then, before I ate it, he grabbed the crust back. Because he took the cup for soup, I had nothing. When the soup came, I put my hands out. I had to put hot soup in my hands."

Mitka reaches for a tin cup he received years later as part of a promotion at a strip-mall steakhouse, which hangs on a hook in his kitchen. This prize—a promotional trinket of no real value—holds great significance for him, reminding him of his past. He cradles it in his hands as if it were an archaeological relic of inestimable value.

The train came to another stop. It had been a "long time" since the previous stop. Everyone was taken off the train at a wheelhouse, where locomotives were turned back in the direction they came from. All were loaded onto a different cattle wagon. Through the slats in the new railcar, Mitka saw the cattle wagon he'd been on moments before.

"When I looked back, they took hands and feet and threw dead bodies out."

On this second cattle car, crammed just as tightly as the first, Mitka heard a new word. *Birkenau.*

CHAPTER TWO

Camps

Birkenau, Buchenwald, Dachau, and Pfaffenwald,
Autumn 1941–Winter 1942

It was the autumn of 1941. Mitka had traveled by rail on several cattle cars from the banks of the Dnieper River in Kiev to Birkenau, a distance of approximately six hundred miles. Like millions of Jews, prisoners, and other deportees, he was loaded onto a train not knowing what was happening to him or where he was going.

Cattle wagons and freight cars had a practical advantage for transporting prisoners. Easily locked and windowless, these railcars needed fewer troops to transport human cargo. And the wagons could accommodate large numbers. Official SS regulations proposed 50 deportees per car; however, it was not uncommon for 100, sometimes even up to 150, persons to be packed into each railcar. Food and water were not supplied; neither was a toilet. Sometimes the floor was layered in quicklime; other times a bucket latrine was thrown onboard. Mitka says of the smells of urine and excrement, "It's all we knew, so you got used to it."

The highest priority for the Nazi war machine was to move personnel and armaments. Therefore, Holocaust trains were regularly shunted aside onto spurs where they waited, often for days, sometimes weeks, before being allowed to move. While they were idled, "passengers" were left in the cattle wagons with no ventilation, no food or water, and exposure to extreme cold or heat. It was not uncommon for guards to find that, when the doors were opened, everyone inside was dead.

But not all died in the trains. Sometimes, as in the case of Mitka, the cars became a mixture of corpses and those clinging to life, bodies pushed tightly together. Often in interviews, Mitka talks of the association between the trains and seeing bodies—"so many bodies." His voice grows soft as he says, "It didn't mean nothing to me."

Again and again, Mitka comes back to the idea that death meant nothing to him. "People died," he says wistfully, "but I don't remember feelings when that happened—no feelings." He seems bewildered and embarrassed by the idea that he did not comprehend the finality of death. Though he doesn't make the conclusion, it's hard to escape the idea that the trauma Mitka experienced while trying to survive, coupled with his young age, protected him from understanding the death all around him.

As he describes his journey from Kiev to his first camp, Mitka talks of changing cattle wagons, of "moving all the time." In the last cattle car before arriving at the camp, he recalls hearing that their destination was Birkenau. "Yes, Birkenau," he says. "I never remember hearing 'Auschwitz.'" As an adult he had learned that Birkenau was one of many subcamps in the complex that was Auschwitz.

Auschwitz-Birkenau was located near the border between Poland and Germany on a site that had, according to historian Nikolaus Wachsmann, functioned "as a temporary settlement for seasonal workers" during World War I. Later, before being transformed into a massive concentration camp, it functioned as a holding place especially, but not entirely, for Polish prisoners.

When Mitka arrived at the camp, he entered a world where starving prisoners were brutalized physically and psychologically as they were forced, at Auschwitz and its subcamps Birkenau and Monowitz, to build officers' homes, barracks for prisoners, and buildings to store equipment, as well as gas chambers and crematoria for their own executions.

Mitka expresses regret that he doesn't remember more details about his time in this camp. He then returns to a powerful impression: "The only memories I have are of being hungry. When you are hungry, you forget everything else. I only remember hunger. I could sit on a dead body and eat a meal—because dead bodies didn't mean nothing to me in those years. Nothing at all."

The next and only other story he shares from his time at Birkenau is being assigned a job in a brickmaking operation. He describes a conveyor belt on which blocks of clay came down.

"I held this thing with four wires on it. Just picture this—a thing with four wires on it that cuts brick." He forms a square with his hands to indicate the frame he held and continues, "It was a thing to cut brick, and they put me on that job, but I couldn't do it. I was too young to do it."

Mitka turns his attention, next, to the work he was able to do. "So they put me on a round pit. Picture this round pit. Those bricks came out of a pit. And out of that round pit is a shaft going like this." Here again, he gestures, placing his left hand on his right elbow and using his right forearm to demonstrate a lever. "And there is a horse over here."

The presence of a clay pit at Auschwitz-Birkenau is one of the only details from Mitka's memories that neither he nor others have been able to confirm. It troubles him. There are pictures of clay pits and brickmaking operations at camps other than Auschwitz-Birkenau, especially Sachsenhausen and Buchenwald. And there is clear evidence of a *Maurerschule*, or masonry school, at Auschwitz I in Barracks 7, within which "relatively healthy young men were taught the craft of fashioning and laying bricks." When Mitka arrived at Birkenau the camp was just being built, and there was a need for construction materials. Perhaps such a pit was there. There were unquestionably rock quarries at Auschwitz. Based on descriptions of drainage projects, it is more than likely that there was clay at Auschwitz as well, clay that prisoners were forced to dig by hand. But it is also possible that Mitka worked in brick production during his time in Buchenwald or Dachau.

Whether at Birkenau or another camp, Mitka remembers a pit that was like a giant mixing bowl. It was filled with clay. In its center was a paddle that could be turned. At the top of the paddle shaft a wooden beam extended and was connected to a horse's harness. The horse pushed the beam around the pit to mix the clay.

Because the six- or seven-year-old Mitka did not have the strength to push the four-wire frame through the clay, he was assigned a task that was a source of some pleasure for the small, curious boy. "They made me sit on the beam next to the horse and go round and round to mix that clay."

Moving on from his specific recollections, Mitka speaks haltingly, stopping then restarting, as he considers that the bricks he helped make could have been used to build gas chambers where the "Final Solution" was carried out. He believes this to be so. He tries to communicate his guilt. Looking away, he speaks with a pleading timbre. "Could these hands have helped build the ovens? But I did not know."

The moment passes without further comment.

Mitka does not know how long he was at Birkenau. He does know that "after days and days" he was put on yet another train car, which took him to Buchenwald, some four hundred miles west. Why he was moved he does not know.

Like his other rides in cattle cars, the train to Buchenwald was packed shoulder to shoulder with adults. Other children are not a part of his memories. Once more, he knew no one and felt constant hunger. When the train stopped and Mitka and the others were herded into the camp, the camera in his child-mind captured a photograph in perfect focus. The image would never leave him. However, at the time he had no frame of reference for what he saw.

"When I went to Buchenwald, they hung them people like this on a pole—a pole going way down the back. They were hung there till they died. I saw hundreds, maybe thousands of dead people, but I didn't know what it meant."

Mitka goes on to describe men and women whose hands had been tied behind their backs and who were then "hung maybe ten feet above."

The hanging Mitka remembers was one of a number of signature tortures of Oberscharführer Martin Sommer, a sadistic camp official at Buchenwald between 1938 and 1943, known as the "Hangman of Buchenwald." This particular form of torture elicited agonized screams from the prisoners who endured it, which led to that part of the camp being called "the singing forest." Sommer, with full support from Commandant Karl-Otto Koch, functioned as "the unofficial camp executioner." Noting that Sommer's "cold-bloodedness was re-markable even among the SS," historian Nikolaus Wachsmann de-scribes him thus:

Sommer was a man of exceptional cruelty. He dispensed the official punishments like whipping, and took part in other outrages, starving and choking prisoners, sexually abusing them, and crushing their skulls; on some days, he later admitted, he had dished out more than two thousand beatings in the bunker.

Mitka has no memory of Sommer or Koch or, indeed, any of the perpetrators of the crimes he witnessed and experienced. He does, however, clearly recall evidence of the torture and sadism that characterized Buchenwald. Mitka also remembers that it was around this time when he wore a yellow star, "for a little while." Curiously, he says, "I never told anyone I was a Jew. That was something I didn't even realize myself." Later he would find a way to remove it, noticing that prisoners who wore the star were treated with particular hatred and brutality.

From Buchenwald Mitka traveled on another train to Dachau. It was upon entering "a tree-lined, big arched gate" to Dachau that he saw the iconic sign that has come to symbolize Nazi concentration camps. The three-word motto, made of metal and suspended above the gates of many concentration camps, read

ARBEIT MACHT FREI

"Work makes free." This iconic slogan, simple and notorious, was part of an elaborate Nazi propaganda effort to represent the camps as, in Heinrich Himmler's words, "strict but fair" and "an actual control measure"—a perverse promise, holding life and freedom out as a fair exchange for inmates' hard work.

Historians like Wachsmann, Otto Friedrich, and others who have studied the camps argue that some Nazis likely believed this "mystical declaration that self-sacrifice in the form of endless labour does in itself bring a kind of spiritual freedom." Most, though, including SS camp officers, caught the irony of the phrase. In fact, guards in Sachsenhausen, a camp in Oranienburg, Germany, turned the slogan on its head when they pointed prisoners to the crematorium and declared, "There is a path to freedom, but only through this chimney!" Certainly most prisoners, at least those who lived long enough to experience life in the camps, recognized the monstrous farce of "Arbeit Macht Frei."

To the boy Mitka, who understood Yiddish, Russian, and Polish but could not read, these words held no meaning. However, he recalls that "someone, in my own language"—he believes it was either Polish or Yiddish—"told me what the sign said."

The sign stuck with him. As an adult when he saw a photograph of the sign again, the moment of recognition struck like a lightning bolt. It all came back. In an instant he returned once again to Dachau's gate.

When the train stopped and all—the living and the dead—were taken off, the women were separated from the men. Mitka was made to stand in the line of women. He doesn't remember being told to undress, but he does recall knowing that he and all the women stood naked before the guards. "Can you believe it?"

It is a question he repeats often during interviews. He speaks it in an altered pitch. His hands move up from his thighs and drop back to his knees in a slap. "Can you believe it?" he declares, as if he's talking about someone else.

He was marched, together with the women, to a building where he "climbed steps down into a large room." He saw shower heads pointing down from the ceiling, and pipes. Mitka speculates, "That spray— I guess it was to delouse. They sprayed us with something that burned, and it hurt really bad."

Mitka tells of how at one point he cowered in a corner, driven there by his embarrassment at being stripped, exposed, and vulnerable among "so many naked women." His cheeks redden as he relives the humiliation.

For the greater part of a year, Mitka had lived in three concentration camps. Sometime around September 1942, for reasons unknown, he was moved again. As with previous moves, yet another cattle wagon carried the starved, thirsty, filthy, sardine-packed prisoners down a track. This time the destination was Lager (Camp) Pfaffenwald.

The stop for Lager Pfaffenwald was unlike previous ones. When the train braked to a halt, Mitka and the others stepped onto the platform of a town's train station. He remembers a sign at the station. He couldn't read it, but he had heard those around him talking about it: Asbach.

"Everybody out of the wagon," Mitka says of the arrival, his tone indicating that it was an order he heard.

"Now we start walking." Together, all the prisoners walked "into a forest" to the camp, a distance of slightly less than two miles. Looming just beyond the forest was a large bridge—a bridge that forced laborers who had previously inhabited Pfaffenwald built as a part of the Autobahn. For the child Mitka, the sight of the bridge towering above the forest was "a memory you do not forget."

As they approached an entrance building, Mitka saw barbed-wire fences, guard towers, and soldiers. At this point in the trek, a woman held onto Mitka and shielded his eyes. She didn't want Mitka to see the corpses stacked in a pile before them. She was too late. The sight had no particular meaning to Mitka. Though the woman, who spoke Yiddish, hadn't been able to spare him from the gruesome scene, her act of kindness had a great impact on Mitka. He never forgot it. For a moment, he did not feel alone.

Established in 1938 as a *Reichsautobahnlager* (RAB), Pfaffenwald was a forced labor camp built for the specific purpose of constructing the Asbachtal Bridge on the Autobahn, today the A4 motorway, between Kirchheim and Bad Hersfeld. By the autumn of 1942, when Mitka arrived at the camp, the bridge had been completed and the camp had been repurposed. No longer did it house the many laborers compelled to build a bridge. At the onset of the war, bridge laborers were removed and replaced by a succession of Czech, French, Polish, and Russian prisoners and other forced laborers. Usually because of illness or some physical limitation, these inmates were unable to work at the expected levels. Pfaffenwald opened a hospital ward, of sorts, to isolate tuberculosis sufferers, and to abort fetuses of pregnant prisoners. Until the end of the war it continued as a foreign labor and abortion camp. Those who did not die at Lager Pfaffenwald were transported to a nearby euthanasia center, Tötungsanstalt Hadamar (Hadamar Euthanasia Center), to be murdered.

At Pfaffenwald, Mitka saw things he has never been able to tell anyone. "Oh—the things that I found out in Pfaffenwald. When I tell you about it, I am still there, and I do not know why, but I am still there. And believe me, it scares me."

When pressed about it, he says that someday, maybe, he can say what happened. For now, it's just too difficult. If he ever does, he says it would be only in the presence of his wife. He's told no one in seventy-five years.

Mitka relates mostly snippets of memories from his three or so months at Pfaffenwald. Sometimes what he retained is connected to a narrative of experience, but often it is free-floating. Even these tidbits, such as seeing the Asbachtal Bridge, match the known record of what occurred at Pfaffenwald.

Once in the camp, Mitka and the others were placed in a large building. "Where I slept, there was a roof—it was only half there." From his portion of the floor he looked up through rafters to the sky.

He remembers other buildings—dormitories, a dining hall, a kitchen, an office building, and guard towers. One structure—the latrine—he describes as a long trench with a plank suspended above the ditch. Seeing people trying to balance themselves on a board, lined up one after another, with no privacy—this bothered Mitka. He said he got used to it but always felt embarrassed.

While at Pfaffenwald, Mitka was made to drink something that made him "very, very sick" and gave him "constant headaches." Then "they put a tube up my nose and they pumped something up my nose." He remembers "being locked outside, naked, in the cold, for a long time," and then "they put something on my back—hot glasses on my back—like fire."

Years later he learned about Hadamar, which also contained a national hospital, and ventures that, when other "experiments" happened to him, "I must have been at Hadamar." He had been in a hospital setting, he thinks, that didn't remind him of Pfaffenwald.

While at Pfaffenwald, Mitka witnessed murders and other horrific events that would stretch credulity were there not corroborating records. In one instance he describes a procedure he saw performed on women.

"I will try to demonstrate." Mitka clenches an imaginary knife and raises it to his sternum, then runs it downward to the bottom of his belly. "They cut the stomach up and then they throw something against the wall."

The seven-year-old didn't recognize that the women he had seen and heard screaming in pain were pregnant. Until sometime around 1981, he had thought that he had seen something like "puppies" being taken from the women's bellies and thrown against the wall to die. It was only when his wife Adrienne explained that what he had seen were fetuses that he came to realize abortions were being performed in this way at Pfaffenwald. He also believes the incisions were made with nothing more than "pocketknives," something confirmed by others.

"And then they try to put them back together with something like glue, instead of sewing it up . . . but they died anyway."

Paradoxically, Mitka's slightly more positive recollections of all his camp experiences come from Pfaffenwald. Through smiling lips he talks about how a small boy could crawl, undetected, under the barbed-wire fence enclosing the camp. "There was a tree that was way tall, and the *Bucheckern* (beechnuts) would fall. And you know what time of year it is when the nuts fall. I was the only one who could crawl under. And I would hand the nuts to the people. We were starving, and we were so glad to get the *Bucheckern*."

When he first began collecting the beechnuts, they were still green, not ripe. Regardless, the nuts supplemented a diet of thin "yellow soup, or maybe it was beet soup."

Mitka had a job while in the camp, a job he enjoyed. He recalls that two girls worked with him and "we stacked bread that a baker brought twice a week. Every three days I got a piece of it."

Occasionally the baker let Mitka ride on his cart to deliver bread around the camp. "I never forgot."

Sleeping with what seemed like "hundreds of others," Mitka tried, as best he could, to stay warm. One night toward the end of his time at Pfaffenwald he wrapped his leg around the leg of the woman lying next to him. "I had to get up to relieve myself. When I came back, she didn't move, and she was cold." He realized she was dead.

Mitka talks about a woman who befriended him and spoke Yiddish. She was one who also spoke with guards, perhaps as an interpreter. He believes she knew he would be taken out of Pfaffenwald. One day she pulled him aside, spit on her hands, straightened his hair, and, speaking Yiddish, told him, "Sei gut, sei gut" (Be good, be good).

Laughing, Mitka says, "My hair—imagine—I had hair in those years."

A new chapter in young Mitka's life was about to begin. A man came to the camp, selected him, and took him to a town called Rotenburg an der Fulda.

"And if that Nazi did not take me out of there in 1942, I would have been slaughtered in Hadamar. That Nazi didn't do it to save my life. He knew I was Jewish. He did it because he needed a little boy."

Improbably, the orphaned, now seven-year-old Mitka had survived four Nazi concentration camps. He was, however, not free.

CHAPTER THREE

Iron Gustav

Rotenburg an der Fulda, December 1942

On Monday, the fourteenth day of the twelfth month of 1942, Mitka Kalinski left the camp of "birth and dying"—Lager Pfaffenwald. He became, if not the only, then certainly one of just a handful of survivors of this place of death. To arrive at Pfaffenwald doomed one to die there. Mitka's death sentence was stayed, but for what?

On that Monday, two significant milestones happened to the boy. First, he was given a name: Martin (pronounced *Marteen*). It was a name that he would be known by until 1949. Second, he was assigned a date of birth—December 14, 1932—making him, by diktat, exactly ten years old, the minimum age for conscripted labor according to German law. Two fictions—a name and a birthdate—now identified the lad.

The morning had been like any other for Mitka, until a woman who spoke Yiddish pulled him aside, arranged his hair with her spittle, and told him to be good. Shortly thereafter, two men singled him out and took him out the entrance of Pfaffenwald. They walked, with Mitka following, to the train station at Asbach, the same station he had arrived at a few months before.

The dominant man, a German named Gustav Dörr, led the way, followed by Eduard Gruschka, a Polish POW who had been conscripted by Dörr to serve as a laborer, translator, and factotum. Gruschka, who spoke Polish, communicated with Mitka since the boy understood only snippets of German that he had picked up at the camps. They boarded the train and rode to Rotenburg an der Fulda, a short ride of roughly sixteen miles. At the train station in Rotenburg, Gruschka left the party, and Mitka walked with Dörr across a bridge over the Fulda River, then through the center of the town to a large house at Badegasse 14.

Unbeknown to Mitka, he had been selected by Gustav Dörr to be a child laborer at a house located on his small farm. Living in this house were Gustav's parents, Christian Georg Dörr and his wife; Gustav's sister, Anna Dörr Krause, and her companion, Herr Holke; and Anna's daughter, Rosemarie. (The home of Gustav, his wife Lisa, and daughter Anni was a short distance away from the farmhouse.)

When Mitka arrived at his new dwelling, it was late in the day, and he was hungry—which was not unusual for him. The first thing he remembers is being scrubbed by Anna, scrubbed so hard that "it hurt," leaving abrasions on his skin. Years later, Gustav noted that Mitka arrived "filthy." Mitka thinks it likely that he had not washed since the delousing shower he had had upon arriving at Dachau. "His head was shaven bald and he was called, like the other alien workers, '*Stoppelrusse*'—Bald Russian." He was put back into the dirty rags he had worn, and he remained barefoot. Having never worn underwear, he wore none now. Indeed, he had no idea what it was.

The so-declared ten-year-old, who, in fact, was likely a child of six or seven, was locked in a room for the night without food or water.

Like his beginning at the *Kinderheim* in Bila Tserkva or fleeing to forests and fields or crawling out from under corpses in Kiev or riding in cattle wagons to camps, once more Mitka faced places, people, and experiences that were entirely new.

The town of Rotenburg an der Fulda sits in a narrow place in the Fulda Valley in the Hesse region of Germany. It dates to the first half of the thirteenth century. Old Town, where Mitka was brought to live, hugs the left bank of the Fulda River. In architecture typical of old structures in Germany, "half-timbered" houses dominate the narrow, cobbled streets. A red stone church rises near the town center.

From its beginning, the picturesque village was home to Jews. Between 1731 and 1880, the Jewish population grew from 133 to 390 people (12 percent of Rotenburg's population). Its members built a synagogue in 1738, then built and dedicated a larger synagogue in 1924. The small Jewish population knew, by experience, the town's reputation for active, and at times violent, anti-Semitism. Ann Beaglehole, in her book *A Small*

Price to Pay: Refugees from Hitler in New Zealand, 1936–1946, describes
one incident that played itself out in Rotenburg during the 1930s:

> Ester Einhorn was born and brought up in a small town, Rotenburg
> (Fulda). . . . It was in small towns like hers that "much of the cruelty
> and pushing round of Jews happened first." When Ester Einhorn's
> father was beaten up, the family decided to move to Berlin. While
> the family's furniture was being packed in a van, the person who
> had bought the house grabbed a table from the van saying, "I'll have
> that." The day before, this man had tried to push Ester's father down
> a flight of stairs.

Because of mistreatment such as this, most Jews elected to leave Rotenburg after the Nazis came to power. The few who remained paid a heavy
price years later.

One town citizen at the center of Rotenburg's anti-Semitic activity
was Gustav Dörr. Like his father, Gustav made a living in and around
Rotenburg as a junk dealer. During the war, concentration camps were
a source of salvage that he and others sold. Often he acquired clothing,
shoes, and other personal effects that had been taken from Jews and
other forced laborers at camps. Also for income, he rented some of the
rooms at his Badegasse 14 house; sold products from his farm, such as
milk, eggs, pork, beef, vegetables, and grain; and hired out his horses
and wagons as a "carrier" to make local deliveries. He was also involved
in butchering and taxidermy.

In the course of his many activities, Gustav often attended to matters
at his Badegasse 14 address, though he lived on his farm outside the
central part of town. There he oversaw as many as twenty-six French,
Polish, and Russian forced laborers, whom he kept with the blessing of
prevailing German law.

Rotund and barrel chested, Gustav had a large frame and, even so,
a seemingly oversize head, as photos show. When his mouth was open,
his lips formed a kind of rectangular hole that conveyed a cocksure
implacability.

Gustav was an active member of the Sturmabteilung (SA), a para-
military wing of the Nazi Party. "Founded in Munich by Hitler in 1921

out of various roughneck elements that had attached themselves to the fledgling Nazi movement," the Brownshirts, as they were commonly known, were exceptionally ruthless. The SA's role and influence were greatly reduced after 1934 as Himmler and his Schutzstaffel (SS) grew in power. Its members, however, continued to operate beyond the control of any official government apparatus. Militarily organized and led by officer veterans of World War I, members lived in virtually every town and city throughout Germany. Unaligned, unaccountable, and fiercely loyal to one another, the SA had their own mission, which happened to be in perfect concert with Nazi ideology. It featured, especially, hatred of Jews.

In order to understand the man who claimed Mitka as a slave, it is essential to look back in time to the events of November 7, 1938.

On that Monday night, and stretching into the wee hours of Tuesday morning, calamity rained down on Jews in Rotenburg and nearby Bebra. SA storm troopers, Nazi Party members, and townsfolk began by throwing rocks through the windows of all Jewish homes. And it didn't stop there. They entered the homes, ransacking rooms, breaking furniture, and destroying china and anything they didn't want to take for themselves. The mob destroyed everything in sight—"not a single pane of glass nor any window crossbar remained"—all in the presence of mothers, fathers, children, and grandparents. Fires were started while firemen and police tacitly encouraged the destruction by their passive presence. Especially painful for the long-standing Jewish communities of these two towns was that their synagogues were desecrated and destroyed.

A seemingly unconnected event in France, also occurring November 7, would play an important part in the unfolding drama. In Paris, a Polish-born Jew, Herschel Grynszpan, attempted to assassinate German diplomat Ernst vom Rath. When vom Rath died of his injuries on Wednesday, November 9, Nazi Minister of Propaganda Joseph Goebbels used the assassination to light the fuse on the tinderbox of German anti-Semitism. In an inflammatory speech, he specifically singled out and praised the events that had occurred two days before in Rotenburg and Bebra. His words discharged a shock wave of violence and destruction against Jews throughout Germany. Thus, infamously, November 9,

1938, became known as *Kristallnacht*—the night of broken glass. What Goebbels had engineered, the Nazi Party, along with the German state, executed to perfection.

The next day, Germans saw downtown sidewalks littered with debris, debris the Jews were forced to clean up. Jewish-owned businesses, homes, and synagogues were destroyed. Not visible was the theft of their personal and sacred property. Though they had been poorly treated for years, this was a major turning point for German Jews. Home ceased to be a safe place for them.

Much of what is known about Nazi practices came to light because of the diaries, letters, and personal accounts of Jews. One such letter describes the evil that happened in Rotenburg on November 7, 1938, the day this small German town became the template for Kristallnacht.

Henrietta (Henny) Rothschild and her husband, Manheld, her young son, Joseph, and her extended family were residents of Rotenburg when their family home was destroyed and their personal property demolished or stolen. Almost a year later, while in exile, she wrote a still-raw letter to her relatives describing the atrocities that began November 7. One of the only perpetrators Rothschild identifies by name is Gustav Dörr.

> Around 3 p.m. Lotte came by and told us that Gustav Dörr had been at Aunt Lina's and had wanted to extort money from her—now he is at Vicktor's. He came to Aunt Lina just when she wanted to eat, and demanded her jewelry and money; naturally she refused him, and so he overturned her table, together with all the tableware and food that was on it.

Pages later, in Rothschild's long letter, she describes the Kristallnacht in Rotenburg. "During the night they heard—as we had—furniture being hacked to pieces & chinaware and all kinds of other things being thrown out onto the street." She then, again, indicts Gustav:

> You can imagine all that was stolen during this operation. Plenty of people managed to stuff their pockets full; a lot of the supposedly respectable citizens there were not too pious to keep from enrich-

ing themselves with Jewish belongings. When they were finished and drunk from all the wine, etc., that they had come across in the cellars, Gustav Dörr drove a horse-drawn buggy through the town, dressed in a *Sargeneskittle* [a burial shroud], a top hat on his head, and a big *Chumash* [Pentateuch, the five books of Moses] in his hand—you can imagine the fun of it.

This letter was first published in the article "'Like Hunted Animals'" by Heinrich Nuhn. Nuhn notes that others corroborated Rothschild's account of Gustav Dörr's actions, including a Lutheran pastor:

After the war, dean Hammann of the Rotenburg-Neustadt Lutheran congregation made an entry in the church records in which he stated: *"Two ruthless Rotenburg Nazis . . . were not ashamed of driving through the town in a horse-drawn carriage in a triumphal procession in which they carried holy utensils/gadgets from the synagogue with them. One of them was presenting himself like a king on his throne, the other was playing the role of a coachman with a big cigar in his mouth. Apparently not aware of the blasphemy they were committing, every time they were passing by the house of a Jewish family, the 'king' would shout: 'All of you who feel troublesome and aggrieved, would you please come here to me.'"*

An SA leader also offered testimony:

Horst Mainz, the chief SA squad leader in November 1938 and main defendant in the district court trial against the trespassers of 1938, in his judicial interrogation commented . . . *"I met Gustav Dörr driving around in his carriage clad in a top hat and a shroud. I rebuked him for . . . being something ignoble. I received the reply that, on a holiday . . . even then these things should be allowed."*

That Kristallnacht in Rotenburg was particularly violent compared to that in other German towns and cities can be seen in the words of Rothschild later in the letter. Because Gustav was an instigator and a key perpetrator, her words offer a glimpse into his character. "A lot has happened everywhere in these days, but what all transpired in Rotenburg was the absolute worst of all that took place. I can only say that no matter where we went, as Rotenburg Jews we were greeted with special *rachmones* [Yiddish for 'pity,' 'compassion,' 'mercy']."

Additional bits of information about Gustav Dörr supplement and solidify the Kristallnacht portrait of the man. Although he was only one among many wreaking havoc on Jews in Rotenburg, he was, it seems, a force, indeed "the biggest Nazi in Rotenburg."

Locally, Gustav was known by the sobriquet "der Eisene Gustav," or, as English speakers would say, Iron Gustav. But this nickname seems insufficient to portray the nature of Gustav Dörr. His role in the events before and after Kristallnacht, documented for history, defines a particular kind of man. It is the spectacle of Gustav Dörr, mocking Jews with their purloined sacred objects, that introduces us to Mitka's master.

CHAPTER FOUR

Moly

Rotenburg an der Fulda, 1942–1943

When Mitka awoke on his first morning in Rotenburg, ten days before Christmas, he might have seen houses festooned with garlands, window-panes glinting in firelight. The pastoral village, however, would become, for Mitka, nightmarish over the course of his seven-year enslavement.

Yet at this moment in time, Mitka's world was neither idyllic nor hellish. He had no basis of comparison to a normal childhood; neither did he have expectations. It had been a thousand days since he had been dropped off at the *Kinderheim* in 1939. On this day, just as he had on every other day, he woke ready to do whatever he needed to do—to live, to endure, to survive.

When the door to his locked room opened, Mitka saw darkness. Beyond the fact that it was before dawn, two other realities prevented him, he says, from seeing and sensing what surrounded him: hunger and cold. The ache in his belly pushed out any thought other than food, and the shivering of his body eclipsed any possibility of comfort.

"Did you cry?" and "When did you cry?" and "Why did you cry?" I ask. He pauses. Moments pass. He fumbles to answer the questions. First, he simply responds, "Yes." Mostly, he can't place crying with events in time. As to when, he replies, "All the time." As to why, he can't answer the question. He does talk about the tug of longing, though he isn't sure what he longed for. He conjectures that he wanted "my parents, but I didn't even know that."

The previous night, Mitka endured Anna scrubbing him in a metal washtub while others in the kitchen stared. Naked in front of strangers, he felt embarrassed. He put on his dirty rag-clothes and Anna escorted him to his room. On this first night, Mitka slept on straw placed on a wooden board encased in a frame. He covered himself with a horse blanket. By morning he had wet his straw mattress, something he did every night until he left Rotenburg. Today he cannot conceal his shame when talking about this experience, and yet telling it seems his only antidote to the humiliation. "Each morning I took the wet straw out and brought in dry straw."

The room had no other furniture. It did, however, have a window. Soon after he arrived someone installed bars on it, making the prison secure.

That winter morning, December 15, Mitka wore pants held up by string, a shirt, and rags tied around his feet. He believes he must have received other clothes as he grew, but looking back, he remembers none until 1945. He does recall having "those Hollander shoes" in the winter. "You know your feet are going to get cold. But wooden shoes does not last you very long, and they split longways. I tied a rag around them. Otherwise, they pinch the skin. So I walk with rags tied around my feet, mostly. And I got used to it."

When Anna unlocked the door to Mitka's room that morning, she took him on a tour of the house while instructing him on the work he was expected to do. "I went around two, maybe three times so she could tell me over and over. The biggest problem when I went to the Nazi family . . . I had to learn everything on the farm."

The Badegasse 14 property covered one town block from front to back. It was three stories high and had a barnyard at its back. Describing the house, Mitka pauses and reaches for paper and pen. He finds it easier to sketch the floor plan. As he draws, he relates details about the kitchen, the bedrooms, two upstairs apartments, a smokehouse, a slaughterhouse, the attached stable, the lofts, a locked room on the third floor that he was forbidden to enter, his own room, and the two-story outhouse. "That's a funny one. Have you ever seen a double-high outhouse?" He leans back on his chair, slaps his knees, and laughs. "Pretty good joke, huh. Somebody below gets a big *Scheisse* surprise from the guy on top."

Removing "crap from the outhouse" became one of Mitka's many jobs. "There was double people. That's why it filled up so fast." The human waste was collected in a vat in the ground. "I take the cover off, and I have a ladle to put it in a can, and then I dump the can in a round tank on the wagon." He then rode to the fields, where he spread it for fertilizer. "It must have stunk like hell, but it didn't bother me in those years. You got used to it, the smell and all."

From the outset, hard work and long hours characterized Mitka's daily routine. His tasks encompassed every aspect of the Dörrs' in-town subsistence farm.

Among piles of collected junk in the backyard, sheds had been built to house various animals. Mitka learned to feed chickens, ducks, geese, turkeys, rabbits, pigs, goats, horses, cows, pigeons . . . "oh, and there were lots of rats." He milked Lotte, the cow, and the goats morning and night. He groomed the two horses, cleaned stalls, and pitched manure into a waste pit in the yard. Every two, sometimes three, days, when the manure pit was full, Mitka hitched the horse called Schimmel to a manure wagon and drove south, out of town, to farm fields owned by Gustav. With pitchfork in hand, "I would load the manure onto the wagon." Pointing to a map, he continues, "And I would take the wagon from here to here and put it in piles and spread it out on a field."

Over and over, Mitka reminisces about time he spent alone on the manure wagon. Quite unwittingly, he makes it one symbol of his experiences at the Dörr farm. "I was sitting on the wagon. And I was so sad, and that was when I would cry. That's when the loneliness sits on me."

One time after Mitka returned from the fields, Anna saw his red, tear-stained cheeks. She called Gustav. In Mitka's words, "she told Gustav, 'Take this *Jude* back to the camp!' And I understood that because Yiddish and German are similar, you know. And I had to spend the night with that. . . . And I didn't want to go back to the camp.

"Now, Gustav came the next morning," and Mitka got on his knees in front of him. "I had to put my hands on his boots and I had to kiss his boots. . . . I begged, and he did not take me back to the camp."

There was a lesson in it for the seven-year-old: "No more this crying with the manure wagon." Every weekend after that, Mitka recalls, he was made to shine those same "tall black boots."

Two large guard dogs—Moly and Asta—also lived at the Dörr house. Moly—"he was a good size." Mitka gestures to indicate a dog just above his adult knees, about two feet tall.

At some point early on in Mitka's time there, Moly attacked him, making a deep laceration on the inside of his upper left thigh. The cut was not cleaned, nor was it bandaged. No doctor was called. Mitka was told to lie on straw in the hallway for what he thinks was a day and night. Afterward he went back to work. A wide, jagged, three-inch-long scar remains with Mitka as a reminder of Moly.

That first winter, Mitka worked outside in snow, rain, or sunshine, without a coat. At the end of each day he was locked in his room without heat. In frigid weather he put cow manure and horse urine to use. He learned that if he stood in fresh *Kuhscheisse* (cow manure), he could warm his bare feet. If he put his hands under the horse or cow, he could warm his hands with *Pisse*.

"Who in the heck would watch me? It was God and me. When the cow did the job down there, I don't know what made me do it, but it felt good. Same thing when the horse or cow urinated. But my hands was so cold that when the warmth hit, I thought my hands would fall apart. It hurt so bad, but once I got over it, my hands got warm."

Mitka became resourceful in other ways too. The pigs ate a concoction of vegetables—beets, carrots, potatoes, and "stuff I didn't know"—cooked into a slop by Gustav's parents, whom Mitka would learn to call Oma and Opa, meaning "Grandma" and "Grandpa." To feed himself, Mitka scavenged whatever he could from the animals' feed. Without self-pity—without any emotion, really—he says, "I had to carry the slop to the pigs, but I got into it first, then I give it to the pigs. This is my life story right here."

Mitka can't recall how he learned to milk Lotte, but it's likely that Opa taught him, since he taught Mitka many of his chores. After each milking was done, Mitka poured the pail of milk into "a big can with a heavy thing on top to close it."

A typical metal milk can of the era was two feet high, one foot in diameter, and held ten gallons. Such a can would contain eighty pounds of milk and, in total, would weigh about one hundred pounds. It seems

probable that Mitka had help loading these containers until he grew
strong enough to handle one alone, though his recollection is of doing this work on his own. Some milk cans he carried on a hand-pulled
wagon to a location just across from the red stone church in the city
square, not far from the house. Other times he loaded the milk cans
onto Gustav's truck to be delivered to market in the neighboring town
of Bebra. He remembers that Eduard Gruschka, the Polish prisoner who
was, seemingly, Gustav's right-hand man, usually drove the truck and
that he rode in the back with the milk. At the church location he would
set the cans on a rack where they were checked in and accounted for by
a government official. "They had to give it to the government—milk
and eggs. Nazi time."

On one occasion when Mitka's throat was sore, he filled a milk can
and then, "I don't know what possessed me . . . I drank and drank,
I drank so much, and then I put water in it and sealed it." He lifted the
full can of diluted milk onto Gustav's truck for delivery as usual. Sometime later, "they got the answer back: the milk was no good. And that
was some beating I got, but I tell you, it was worth it."

There were eggs to collect each day. As with the milk, Mitka delivered some eggs to the government collection depot at the church.
Because the chickens laid a predictable number of eggs, on one occasion
when the count came up short, Mitka was blamed for stealing the missing eggs. Mitka knew what would happen next. Anna made him stand
bent at the waist, his hands stretched out to grip a sawhorse in front of
him. Then she beat him across the back with a *Peitsche* (horsewhip),
counting while she did so. As he tells it, when he took beatings from
Anna, which was often, it was never one lash . . . or two; it was always
more. Sometimes she counted to twenty-five.

Later that day Mitka climbed the ladder to the barn's uppermost
hayloft. He spotted a chicken there, outside its coop. "The chicken sees
me and flies down. I'm curious and I look around, and there is a big
nest up there. And I took the eggs and gave them to Mrs. Deist, the
neighbor lady." Having found the missing eggs after taking a beating,
Mitka made a choice. As the neighbor woman, Mrs. Deist, commented
years later, "Mitka was like Robin Hood. He took from the Nazi family
to give to me."

Mitka was not allowed in the Dörrs' living quarters except when they needed something. Sometimes he brought them food items, other times firewood and coal for the stoves. When something needed to be removed, such as the stove's ashes, a family member called him.

On one occasion, Mitka happened to be in the kitchen when Anna was reading a letter. He overheard the conversation taking place around the table about the letter's contents. Anna had learned that her and Gustav's brother Georg, a German soldier, had been missing in action or captured on the Russian front. Having been called by Anna for something, Mitka was in the right place. It was, however, the wrong time. Anna lashed out, "My brother is missing in Russia, and I have to feed this *Judenfresse*!"

Mitka says, "You could see the hate in her eyes." He took a beating with the whip.

"I would say Anna beat me the hardest. There is a hit, and there is a *hateful* hit. She hit me with a hateful hit—badly, badly. She liked me dancing, screaming, and hollering."

Often when Mitka got beaten, the reason for the beating was unclear to him. However, he tried to learn from these episodes. Don't cry, listen, avoid contact with others as much as possible, and, if it seems like trouble is coming or if there's bad news, "I was out of there."

One of Mitka's favorite hiding places was in the haylofts. He knew these lofts well because of daily work that took him into them. It was one of his jobs to keep them full of hay and straw that were brought to the house by wagon from Gustav's remote farm. Distinguishing the remote farm from Badegasse 14, he says of the latter, "This is just a house, with animals in it."

Bedding for the large animal stalls, and Mitka's own mattress, came from straw in the first loft. The second loft stored feed hay for the cow, horses, and goats. Mitka describes the chopping machine he used to cut some of the hay into one-inch pieces. He would then mix the chopped hay with oats for feed. Using an auger system, Mitka loaded straw or hay onto a large screw to move it from the lofts to the barn floor. The third loft served as an attic where miscellaneous household and farm things were kept.

To access the lofts, Mitka climbed a wooden ladder attached to the wall of one of the hallways inside the house. Up and down he climbed, often

several times a day. It was by climbing to the third loft that Mitka found a
refuge—a place that he could escape to, a place he could call his own.

While working in the yard, Mitka was aware of townsfolk, especially other children, staring at him. Sometimes he recognized that they
laughed at him. They made no attempts to get to know the *Stoppelrusse*,
and in his early years he was too afraid to say anything to them.

Mitka did find friendship, however. When he discusses this, his
eyes light up. He smiles with pride. "Oh the animals . . . they were
my friends."

Caring for the animals gave Mitka "someone" to talk to, and talk
to them he did. And each day, an audience that did not talk back "listened" to Mitka. As he describes the trust he shared with a barnyard
full of animals, the inflection of his voice shifts, his confidence rising
with each syllable.

Mitka singles out Lotte, the cow, and his favorite of the two horses,
Schimmel, for special recognition. One meaning of the German word
Schimmel is "white horse," or "whitey." "Even the horse had meaning
to me. . . . He would pull the wagon. . . . I worked with him all the
time." Looking at a published photograph of one of Gustav's wagons,
Mitka points to one of the horses on the team: "That's Whitey, I'm
sure of it."

Mitka is especially gratified by one incident in which he believes
Schimmel took his defense. He had been in the kitchen doing some
chore when, for a reason he cannot recall, Oma beat him with the whip.
Her husband, Opa Georg, seeing the severity of the whipping, threw a
shoe at her, telling her, "Enough!" Mitka took the opportunity to run.
He ran down the hall toward the stalls with Oma right behind him.
They both ran into the stall, and she, again, struck him. At that moment, "Schimmel turned around and kicked Oma in the leg." The kick
was powerful enough to break her leg. Mitka was "so scared" when that
happened, fearful that he would get into more trouble. But he was also
thrilled. "Whitey was a strong little horse. She was beating and beating
me, and he stopped her. Now you tell me that he was not my buddy."

Among the animals, there was one he loved above all. Moly and
Mitka had not gotten off to a good start. Yet Mitka, even after Moly
had viciously bitten him, never speaks of being afraid of either Moly or

Asta, which he knew to be guard dogs. Both dogs slept in and around all the other animals but usually in one of the stalls. Mitka fed, watered, and cared for them, as was expected. He doesn't speak about how they became close, implying that of course, why wouldn't Moly be his friend?

Then one day Mitka found himself in the barnyard with Gustav and others in the family. Between him and the family members stood Moly. "When that Nazi found out that the dog was friendly with me, he told me, 'Martin, you call Moly.'" Before Mitka could open his mouth to follow Gustav's instruction, it became obvious to all that Moly had become his pet. "I didn't even have to call him. He just came to me, and I was so happy."

The moment passed and Mitka went about his work. He took the manure wagon to the field, and when he returned he put the wagon away and returned Schimmel to his stall. Finished with his work, "I had to get water from the faucet."

Mitka proceeded to the water spigot at the entrance to the slaughterhouse. About to fill a pail with water, he looked down and saw Moly's hide at his feet.

"It was in the slaughterhouse. They killed him and left the skin right where I would see it."

Tears well in Mitka's eyes and his voice cracks. "My Moly—my beautiful Moly. He was my friend, my good friend. I wish he had not been my friend. He would be alive if he had not been my friend." He pauses and then adds, "But he lives with me today. I carry his scar."

CHAPTER FIVE

The Voice

Rotenburg an der Fulda, 1944

When translated, *Der Maulesel* means "mule." Sarcasm fills the air when Mitka says the word. He singles it out of the German phrase "Er fiel vom hinteren Ende eines Maulesels," meaning "He fell from the backside of a mule."

Mitka explains, "Opa, my grandfather—or at least I called him my grandfather—when people naturally asked him, 'Who is that boy?' he would say, 'Oh, we found him when he fell from the wrong end of a mule.'"

That Opa Georg chose not to reveal the circumstances by which Mitka was taken could imply that he simply didn't want to bother explaining the matter or, alternatively, that he wanted to conceal it. It seems most likely that joking about Mitka's sudden arrival was Georg's way of deflecting attention from it. Giving Mitka a German name heightened the deception. Indeed, this became a pretext to pass him off as a foster child of sorts. Taking in a foster child had an added advantage for the Dörr family: it enabled them to score moral points for selflessness and nobility on the cheap.

The sting of how Georg had dismissed Mitka troubles him. "All that happened to me, the Nazi family never knew. Gustav's mother, father, sister, they never knew the life I lived before I lived with them—never talked about it, never asked."

Without a past, Mitka was more or less forced to accept the identity that was thrust on him. "Anna said I never had a name until they named me Martin. I think I kind of forgot if I ever had a name before then. I was called Martin for seven years."

Keenly, Mitka now recognizes that, when the Dörrs made it seem as if he just appeared out of thin air, his history—*his story*—was erased. In a certain sense, this truth does not surprise Mitka; he understands that he was something less than a person to Gustav. Gustav knew Mitka was a Jewish child and, therefore, felt he was not deserving of human rights. That this negation disturbed Mitka can be seen in his next thought. "At that time, I did not want to know anything about Jewish people, nothing—nothing. Because they were there one day, and the next day they were not. You saw people with that yellow star disappear. And I even wore that yellow star once. But I didn't want to have nothing to do with 'Jewish.'"

In all of this, work became one source of self-esteem for Mitka. "What made me happy was, you give me an order, I carry it out. You ask me to take something to the baker, and I do it." Throughout his time in Rotenburg, he was always eager to please those on whom he depended. On the one hand, he wanted approval; on the other hand, he was terrified of being returned to Pfaffenwald and of Anna's frequent threats to "nail his tongue to the wall." This particular threat most often occurred when Mitka, unable to communicate well in newly learned German, resorted to speaking Yiddish.

Mitka's need for acceptance and for avoiding peril ultimately became a positive in his mind. Without irony he observes, "They taught me to work."

Upon learning the conditions under which Mitka lived and worked, someone might very well ask: Why didn't he run away? Mitka certainly had ample opportunity to do so. His work was largely unsupervised and took him away from the Dörr household daily. He could be seen around town driving a wagon to the Dörr farm or to the neighboring town of Bebra. Despite being locked in his room each night, he came to realize greater independence as the months and then years passed. Still, he says, the thought of escape didn't occur to him.

Once when the adult Mitka was speaking at a school, an elementary student asked him directly, "Why didn't you run away?" After a moment of thought, he responded with a question: "Where would I go?" Indeed—for a boy with no connection to anyone or any place, with no discernible protection from the danger he saw around him, with limited ability to make sense of his unnatural world, and with no home save Badegasse 14—where *would* he go? Further, Mitka's record of running away was poor, to say the least. He usually ended up on cattle wagons or in concentration camps.

But there is a second answer that Mitka offers, a simple statement that gets at another important aspect of his circumstance: "It's all I knew."

By any definition, Mitka was a slave. Yet he was called Martin and was, at times, referred to by the Dörrs as their foster child. He called Gustav's sister Tante Anna, meaning Aunt Anna. As already mentioned, Gustav's parents he knew as Oma and Opa, the familiar and affectionate way to refer to grandparents. So it was that Mitka had a substitute family of sorts. However, he did not have real membership in the family.

Mitka did not run away. In fact, contradictory though it seems, he formed an unusual and complicated bond with the Dörrs. The bond he had with Gustav was particularly strong, perhaps because Gustav was the one who rescued him from Pfaffenwald. As well, he knew that Gustav denied Anna's demand to take him back to the camp. Tante Anna, Oma, and rarely Opa, not Gustav, meted out the beatings, the humiliations, and other cruelties. But he also feared Gustav. "You don't dare talk about him or you wouldn't be around the next day. If I had any brains at all I could have gotten out. But I didn't dare. Something like that better not enter your mind."

Mitka recognized another characteristic in Gustav. Derisively, he refers to him as a *Schmitzt*. "That's a nasty name in German. It means he was a conniver. He was a sneaky guy." It's likely that the word *Schmitzt* was a slang term to him, derived from the German word *verschmitzt*, which means clever, cunning, sly, or shrewd. Mitka succinctly adds, "And he was a son of a bitch."

Mitka never speaks directly about the bond he had with his captor, but it is one thread that runs through the whole of his story, even though his avoidance of the subject suggests he does not fully grasp the connection.

In part, Mitka's relationship with the Dörr family might have been a necessary strategy to survive. In this, it seems likely that aspects of "capture bonding" or what has been labeled Stockholm syndrome, together with insights derived from the psychology of attachment, help explain Mitka's relationship to Gustav Dörr and, to a lesser extent, Dörr family members. He endured beatings and threats, was denied food, was forced to toil, experienced cold without a means to become warm, was isolated, and was regarded as less than human. These abuses would seem to be powerful reasons to escape, certainly to have profound hatred for one's captor. Yet to this Mitka says, "But I was just a child."

So Mitka worked on. It was the work Mitka did and the relative independence it gave him that put him in contact with other forced laborers like himself, albeit adults. Gustav kept up to twenty-six men—prisoners of war—of various nationalities. These prisoners lived in a large barn at the remote farm where Mitka took manure to the fields. He remembers Poles, Russians, and one Frenchman.

Mitka was supposedly a "foster child," and as such, his life should have been qualitatively different from the lives of those conscripted to work on the farm. His life, however, had far more in common with the others' than with that of the children in the Dörr household. Indeed, his life had all of the characteristics associated with slave labor. He lived and worked under deplorable conditions and was beaten regularly. These realities and the fact that Gustav deliberately assigned Mitka's birthday as December 14, 1932, so that he would be within the legal parameters for conscripted labor in Germany, confirm that he was, in fact, a forced laborer—not a foster child—and that the Dörr family viewed him as such. Interestingly, though, there is, to date, no evidence that Mitka was ever registered with a labor office or given an *Arbeitsbuch*, a workbook required for all laborers as a way to document and regulate them. He also, unlike other forced laborers, was given the Dörr family name.

It was at Gustav's farm that Mitka, during the harvest season, would go out to cut hay and wheat alongside other workers. He cut the hay with a scythe. When the hay had dried on the ground, he would return to turn it with a wooden rake for further drying before it was baled.

Wheat, too, was cut and threshed. The wheat was then taken to a mill to be ground into flour. From the threshed wheat, Mitka gathered straw and put it into storage in the large barn until it was needed for the animals at the house. Most of the harvesting Mitka did in the company of Gustav's other workers. However, sharpening the scythes was something Mitka did alone at the house.

Slaughtering hogs, cattle, sheep, goats, and various fowl became a less frequent, though important, part of Mitka's work. In this, he assisted Opa. The work had curious aspects, the reasons for which Mitka did not piece together, though he remembers them well. One of these aspects was that Opa hid his butchering knives and other tools in a locked compartment in his apartment at the house. When he needed them, he was secretive about retrieving and returning them. Another was that many times, when assisting Opa, Mitka was kept up late at night for the work even though it could have been done during the day. Before these nighttime slaughters, blankets were carefully placed at the bottom of the slaughterhouse doors so that no light escaped.

A likely explanation for this clandestine work can be found in wartime law regarding all agricultural products and meat in particular. Beginning in August 1939, the German government developed protocols and systems for strictly controlling agriculture, structures that were at odds with time-honored practices in rural areas. Historian Jill Stephenson elaborates:

> In addition to rationing, these systems included . . . periodic animal censuses, and attempts to control and monitor the numbers of live and slaughtered farm animals in villages and on individual farms. In particular, there were stringent regulations to restrict the slaughter of livestock, so that only limited amounts of meat would come to the market at a time, to prevent the possibility of an immediate superabundance being followed by a severe shortage.

These regulations did not sit well with many farmers, and they frequently found ways to operate outside the law, oftentimes with the tacit assent of the *Burgermeister* or mayor. Food that was not under the control of the central government could be consumed by individual families, shared with the community, or bartered for goods and services. Most likely, Opa concealed slaughters to follow this common, albeit illegal, practice.

As occurred in other wartime economies, sometimes the animal to be killed was a horse. As Mitka describes it, Opa would place a canvas bag over the horse's head and then strike a blow with a sledgehammer to its head, rendering the horse unconscious before slitting its throat and letting it bleed out. A covertly slaughtered horse produced for a family added meat that was palatable but—unlike, for instance, a cow— escaped the notice of officials.

On other occasions Mitka would accompany Opa to neighboring homes and farms in and around Rotenburg to butcher livestock and tan hides. Often this work was done at night too.

So it was that Mitka knew about meat and hides, knowledge that served him well. For instance, when he returned from butchering, with hides loaded in the wagon, Mitka was tasked with salting, rolling, and tying the skins. However, before he salted a hide, he would scrape away bits of meat left on the skin. His hunger was such that he ate the scraps of raw flesh even though, he says, they often had maggots on them.

There was another occasion, less stomach-turning, in which Mitka's knowledge of the meat stores played a role. "I went to work one day, near Gustav's barn, and I heard this beautiful music. I dropped everything I had in my hand and went to where the music was. A prisoner had a beautiful accordion, and I had to have it." The accordion was a small, four-button instrument that Mitka speaks of as if he were reciting poetry to his beloved. Mitka wanted the accordion so badly that in the course of conversation he found the courage to ask for it. "The prisoner told me that if I got him a half pound of speck—what you make bacon out of, salt pork—then I could have the squeezebox."

However, to complete the transaction meant considerable risk for young Mitka. "It never entered my mind that I might get into trouble. But what is trouble?" With a sardonic smirk he adds, "I didn't know trouble!" He would have to steal the pork, conceal it for delivery, and then get the accordion back to a safe hiding place. His motivation had never been so great.

To steal the salt pork, Mitka had to find a way to get into the locked smokehouse. Fortunately, the worker thought he could help. "He showed me how to make a key. You take a good-sized wire—a heavy gauge wire—and you flatten the end with a hammer. You flatten it like this." Mitka demonstrates with a hammering motion as he speaks. "And you bend it like this, and over here you make a little loop so you've got something to hold on to. And you put that thing in a lock."

Mitka had his plan, "and it worked. I went into the smokehouse and I got that piece of meat. My heart—it was beating." Mitka places his hand over his chest and gives an exaggerated double pat, making a thumping sound. He continues, "I put the meat under my shirt and I went for that squeezebox and he gave it to me. That was a happy time for me, to steal the bacon, because I knew I was going to get the accordion."

Mitka returned with his prize and climbed the ladder in the hall to the uppermost loft, his refuge. He hid the squeezebox under straw. For the first time, Mitka had something he could call his own: an accordion that he was determined to learn to play.

On some days Mitka could slip away from his work and retreat to the attic loft, which was above a part of the house removed from the main living quarters. "I knew when the family was far away and they could never hear you. I would have time when I fed the animals, and believe me, I would know there was safety when the Dörr family was not around."

Mitka acquired the accordion early in his time in Rotenburg, probably as an older seven-year-old, perhaps as a young eight-year-old. He describes teaching himself to play. "It took a long time. I would say it took me years. But once I got to know the accordion, then I could do it. An accordion is not a simple instrument. You do this," as he demonstrates with his fingers, "and there is one sound, and you do this, and there is another sound—kind of like a harmonica."

After learning all he could about his instrument, he made another leap forward. "Late in the afternoon I would hear the soldiers marching when they came into town." Here Mitka assumes an erect, military posture and extends his right arm, mimicking the *Heil Hitler!* salute. He then brings both hands down on the table in front of him, making a rhythmical *brmph, brmph* sound. "And there was singing," he continues.

"And I learned that Nazi song—four different notes. You need to learn the song, and then you can learn to play it." He was referring to the so-called Nazi national anthem, the "Horst-Wessel-Lied."

During his time at Badegasse 14, fun and laughter—never mind play—had no place in Mitka's daily life. Perhaps, then, it's not surprising that music sparked something potent in him. So strong were his impulses that despite the risk of making a deal for the accordion, and despite the ongoing risk of concealing and playing it, the child would not be thwarted. He took the accordion to his castle, and there, he was sovereign over his kingdom. It was just him and his squeezebox.

Mitka still plays the "Horst-Wessel-Lied" on an accordion quite like the one he had as a child. First he plays it as a march, and then he plays it as a polka—just as he had taught himself more than seven decades before.

Mitka's aptitude for learning music matched his talent for fixing things—though that didn't always work out well for him. On one occasion, Mitka was sent by Opa to a jeweler to get his eyeglasses fixed. "When I got to the shop, the shop was closed, so I figured out how to fix the glasses. And I was so proud." When he returned, he was asked, "How much was it?" He answered, "Nothing." Opa Georg, presuming Mitka had lied to him, beat him. "I got beat because I fixed his glasses."

Mitka had another occasion to use the skeleton key he had fashioned under the tutelage of the prisoner. Ever curious, he one day decided to attempt entry into the strictly forbidden, locked third-floor room at Badegasse 14.

On this occasion, he believes that the Dörr family was away from the house. "I don't know. Maybe Opa was working outside, and Anna and Oma must have been gone somewhere." He crept up the stairs and, just as he had done with the smokehouse door, put his improvised key into the lock. With only a few jiggles of his small hand, the lock gave way.

Pushing the door open, the boy ventured into the dark room and, at first, faced an open window. He then turned toward the door to leave. What he saw both astounded and terrified him. "There were these heads hanging near the door. It felt like their eyes were looking at me."

The pace of his telling quickens. "I didn't stay long, but I know what I seen there. I turned and ran, and I never went back."

It is hard to imagine what the young boy saw that day, but his memories of seeing heads are firm. "I know what I seen." He feared the room and its contents; even more, he believed that his owners were, in some way, responsible for the terrors within it. This fright never left him.

Often when speaking about his time in Rotenburg, Mitka refers to his handmade drawing of the layout of the house. He points out the kitchen and speaks of being called a *Fresser*—a German word for a glutton, a "gobbler" (usually associated with animals), a big eater. He says the word again with a derisive tone and look, as a slur, recalling that he was a skinny kid with a ravenous appetite. The drawing brings to mind that he never ate a meal in the kitchen. "They never fed me, but occasionally I go on a wagon with Opa and they make a sandwich for Opa. Opa gave me part of the sandwich with *Schmalz* [lard] on it. The bread is solid bread, not like you got here. But the whole time I was with them, I was on the hungry side."

Mitka was aware that the pig slop he ate contrasted sharply with how the family ate. "One time I picked up a cake at the baker. I take it back to the house for a birthday party for Rosemarie. I wanted some of the cake, but I had to leave." Wistfully, he adds, "But I was so happy for Rosemarie."

It was around this time that Mitka began to experience despair, or, as he puts it, "I guess I kind of thought that this was going to be my life. I couldn't see any way that things would ever be different."

But something happened that transformed Mitka's way of thinking and gave him the confidence to go forward.

Mitka points on his sketch of Badegasse 14 to a room away from the kitchen: "Over here, there's another little room. That's where I was when I heard a voice. I went here"—he points again—"and I could see through the window. There were trees. I could see the leaves. I was in this position, and I stopped. I couldn't see nobody. I could hear a voice speaking and I had goose bumps, and I didn't know what it was."

Spellbound, Mitka listened. The moment is one he recounts over and over, one that is clearly life-changing. He heard a voice say, "Am Ende findest du dein Ziel."

He peered through the glass, looking for the speaker, but saw no one.

For a few moments Mitka seems to be in that small room. Then he returns to the present, to his home in Sparks. He is a touch emotional as he explains that the words he had heard that day "gave me the strength to last for seven years. That is my feeling."

Today Mitka believes God spoke to him that day. As Mitka narrates his story, what comes across is the sense that he had been depressed before the voice spoke to him. Depression is not a word he would use, though it describes as well as anything what seemed to be going on inside him. When he heard the words from the unseen source, he felt rescued. God had made a promise to him. He clung to this assurance. He clings to it still, to words that have carried him through the whole of his life.

Am Ende findest du dein Ziel

In the end you will find your purpose.

CHAPTER SIX

A White Flag

Rotenburg an der Fulda, Spring 1945

Hearing the voice say "Am Ende findest du dein Ziel" (In the end you will find your purpose) had punctuated an otherwise dull march of time for Mitka. He had heard the voice speak to him and him alone. The extraordinary experience would mark him indelibly, yet it changed nothing of his day-to-day. As Mitka's time at the Dörrs grew into months and then years, a cadence settled on the days. He plodded through the seasons—feeding the animals, cleaning stalls, moving hay and straw, and carrying out sundry tasks assigned by Dörr family members. These were routines that, as he grew, gave him little other than the satisfaction of accomplishment.

Staying fed was a constant preoccupation. Mitka ate mostly what the animals ate, though when possible, he would steal bread, eggs, or salt-cured meat. He grew accustomed to cold in winter, never quite shaking a chill. During summers he wore no shoes, and so his feet developed calluses that enabled him to walk easily on cobblestones and fields. He welcomed warm days that gave him an extravagance of sorts. He could slip away to the Fulda River to wade in the shallows, bathe, and rinse some of the filth from his clothes.

Though not actually caged, Mitka lived each day hemmed in by boundaries just the same. One privation exceeded all others, though at the time it caused him no pain. Not once since he left the *Kinderheim* in Bila Tserkva did he attend school or receive any kind of educational lessons. In Rotenburg he saw children going to and coming from school. He wondered what happened there. He longed to participate. He had no idea that at school students learned to read and write. That opportunity was denied him. He was, after all, a Jew-boy—not quite human, more like a talking, walking mule, exceptionally useful for work.

One grace in all of this was his accordion. Unwittingly, through music, Mitka had tapped into something surprising. His transforming the leaden beat of a military march tune into a lively dance tune rather poetically revealed that, despite his circumstances, he possessed a sunny disposition. This disposition, and the skill Mitka developed of simply living in the moment, looking neither forward nor backward, enabled him to cope.

In some cases "cope" was an understatement, as time and again, Mitka escaped death. Improbably, he did not freeze, nor did he starve. He recovered again and again from illness and untreated wounds. Miraculously—and against all likelihood—he stayed alive.

Corralled apart from the world at Badegasse 14, in the Hessian town of Rotenburg an der Fulda, Mitka did not, nor could he, comprehend war, even though he saw it, felt it, heard it, and smelled it in little ways each day.

"One particular time, I see the planes. When the guns start shooting it looked like a black pancake in the sky. They shot one plane down. It was right where I take my manure wagon."

Mitka watched the ejected British flier parachute to the ground and get taken prisoner. The drama of the event evoked a passing interest in him, nothing more. For Mitka, as for millions of others, the abnormal state of war had become normal.

During these years, some of Mitka's chores had a macabre element to them, of which he was unaware at the time. For instance, he recalls a regular errand to a neighboring town. He would harness Schimmel to a wagon for the four-mile trip from Rotenburg to Bebra. Upon reaching his destination—a warehouse—he would load the wagon with clothing, cameras, eyeglasses, paper, other miscellany, and . . . skulls and bones. He would then drive back to the house, where he sorted the articles. After arranging them by type, he'd put them into a baling press, tightening the chain mechanism at each end of the machine to compress the piles into cubes. For him it was a job, like any other, that held no particular significance. He learned, years later, that these objects had come from the camps, that they represented lives extinguished in the Final Solution.

As Mitka talks about handling the possessions of the dead and, indeed, of carrying their bones, the cadence of his sentences, the tone of his voice, seems to move from amazement to grief and, finally, to shame. He repeats, again, a statement that seems to help him make sense of his time at the Dörrs. "I did not know what was going on. They got a perfect guy to do that job—me."

Another prominent sign of the war that Mitka encountered was flak guns—the antiaircraft artillery developed by Germans after the Versailles Treaty of 1919.

"Guns were put in trenches around Gustav's field where I took the manure," Mitka says. "And there was a nearby barn where they had heat, where they thresh the wheat. And I played with that thing. And I tried to pick up that big shell. It must have been three feet long. If I could, I would have shot that gun, but it took two or three people to operate." He remembers "ten or twelve, maybe more" flak guns positioned at the farm. He has vivid memories of hearing sharp explosions and of watching airplanes break from their formations as the artillery guns shot their rounds into the sky.

In 1939 the Nazis commandeered the Jakob-Grimm-Schule, a girls' school established in 1924 in Rotenburg, turning it into the prisoner-of-war camp Oflag IX A/Z. This prison was a subcamp of Oflag IX A/H in Spangenberg. The Rotenburg POW camp housed primarily British Commonwealth officers, but as the war progressed, Polish and American officers were imprisoned there too. Because of its location, Mitka was often near the camp, and he'd stop to watch prisoners as they exercised in the yard. Unlike concentration camps, POW camps afforded prisoners reasonably humane conditions. They were provided with adequate food, cold daily showers and hot showers once a week, and opportunities to produce plays and musical revues. Mitka remembers hearing talk around town about the prisoners housed there. One time, he recalls, he heard that prisoners had escaped. "That's what I heard—forty prisoners escaped from the Jakob-Grimm-Schule. That's the number I heard. And they told the Hitler Youth to shoot to kill. Those are the words they used."

Records from Oflag IX A/Z do, in fact, show that prisoners escaped, but there is no mention of such a large group. Nor are there records of

Hitler Youth playing a role in any captures. It is not unlikely that what Mitka heard came from either alarmed citizens or proud young members of the Hitler Youth, the Nazis' mandatory youth organization for all Aryan boys between thirteen and eighteen. It seems entirely plausible that the story was the product of young members who were boasting, likely with some exaggeration, about their important role in pursuing enemy prisoners. Regardless, it made an impression on young Mitka. As he tells of the incident, he repeats, "They told them to shoot to kill." What happened to the prisoners—whether they were successful in their escape or were shot or recaptured—Mitka doesn't know.

Whatever Mitka heard about prisoner escapes from local youth almost surely came from Willi Deist, a neighbor and the only child with whom Mitka interacted during his seven years of enslavement. Willi lived around the corner from Badegasse 14 and was a member of the Hitler Youth. Mitka had no idea what it meant to be a member of the group. He just liked their uniforms. Once, in an effort to impress Willi and his friends, Mitka raised his arm in the familiar *Heil Hitler!* salute. Looking back, this embarrasses him, but he understands his motivation. He was lonely and eager for friends.

Mitka's eagerness proved to be a problem when, one afternoon, he ventured into a cluster of boys. "The Hitler Youth were talking, and I got in there. And I said, 'What's so special about Hitler?'" Mitka's question was sincere, but the Hitler Youth cell believed he was mocking Der Führer.

"Maybe they didn't like the way I said it. They put me down and kicked me and called me a *Scheisskopf* [shithead]. Willi was one of them."

After the beating, Mitka says he was marched to the *Rathaus* (city hall), where he was thrown in a cell. Though it's hard to imagine youth persuading local officials to lock up a boy for such an infraction, history tells us that seemingly small acts of disloyalty in Nazi Germany, like not performing the Nazi salute, could land ordinary citizens in jail. If failing to give the salute was punishable, it's not unreasonable that Mitka's questioning Der Führer resulted in him being detained. He found himself not only humiliated by his fellow youth but also in jail. "They gave me bread and water," he recalls. Worse for Mitka than the pain from the beating was the thought that he would be sent back to Pfaffenwald. "Oh I was scared—so scared." The stay in jail seemed to him an eternity; he believes now it was a few days. It was Gustav Dörr who came to the *Rathaus* and arranged his release. Ironically, the slave master had, once again, saved him.

As Mitka trudged on, day piled onto day as the years rolled forward. Nothing distinguished the drudgery of Sunday from Monday. It was only in the seasons and the changing weather that he perceived the passage of time. The relentless physical labor never abated, and in fact, as Mitka matured, new tasks were added to his workload. Expectations of him increased, which found him often working alongside Gustav's adult forced laborers.

Now and again, Mitka got to do something outside the humdrum. Usually this involved a trip away from the house and farm. One such time, he and the Polish laborer, Eduard Gruschka, accompanied Gustav to Kassel, where the house of Gustav's uncle had been destroyed in a bombing raid. The three had gone to Kassel to salvage furniture from the bombed-out structure. With Gustav's truck heaped high, they headed back to Rotenburg. The sound of bombs exploding around them brought back memories for Mitka, of lying in his bed at the *Kinderheim* in Bila Tserkva.

In another instance, Mitka had gone to Kassel with Tante Anna and Oma for a reason he doesn't recall. What sticks in his mind are the air-raid sirens that suddenly blared out in rapid succession. It was a familiar sound to all in those years. Bombing raids in Bebra and Kassel occurred frequently, and though Mitka doesn't recall direct bombing of Rotenburg, he remembers frequent warnings of raids. He knew to seek shelter. On this day, when the sirens sounded, Tante Anna stopped the truck. The three got out and hastily searched for safe cover. Anna wanted to run to a nearby building. Mitka disagreed and insisted the women go with him under a trestle beneath nearby train tracks.

"I argued with them and got a slap. Because I argued, there was no time to run to the building."

They dashed under the trestle and stared as the building where Anna had wanted to run collapsed. It took a direct hit from the bombs. Mitka's stubborn and inexplicable—even to him—sense that they needed to seek shelter under the trestle had saved their lives. "I saved them, and all I got was a slap," he says dejectedly.

Mitka speculates that Rotenburg was spared from Allied bombing because of the imprisoned British fliers housed at Jakob-Grimm-Schule. "Boy, God even looked after me on that too—being in a city that was not bombed—because they would not bomb their own men."

By 1945, it had been a little over three years since Mitka was first enslaved, at Birkenau. The Allies were in the final stages of bringing Germany and its Nazi war machine to its knees. The Russians were marching from the east toward Berlin; the British and American forces were coming from the south and west. German soldiers were fleeing, pushed from every remaining defensive stronghold.

Although he didn't understand what was happening, Mitka could see changes in Rotenburg. He remembers that food was scarce, and that troops and tanks filled the streets. The Dörrs "must have known what was coming. I didn't know, but they knew."

As Mitka tells of the days around the end of the war, he adds a new detail to his story. For the first time, Mitka attaches dates to his memories.

"It was Thursday before Good Friday, 1945."

Maundy Thursday held no religious significance for the boy. For citizens of Rotenburg, who would usually be celebrating the Christian Holy Week, 1945 was different. The perceived invincibility of the vaunted Third Reich had evaporated, and "even Nazi true believers had to see that the war was lost." Hitler's war machine was reduced to retreats and defensive redoubts. Nazis on the run had arrived on Rotenburg's doorstep.

General George S. Patton's Third Army was tearing across the German landscape, taking one town after another. Rotenburg an der Fulda was merely another town on Patton's march from Frankfurt to the strategic objective of Kassel, a much larger city with significant munitions factories and a concentration of Nazi personnel. Mitka didn't perceive why pandemonium gripped Rotenburg. He did understand that something had shifted. He'd heard talk that the enemy—the American soldiers, referred to by the Germans as "Amis"—were coming. For Mitka, the Amis evoked fear.

But there were more immediate fears. On that Thursday, March 29, 1945, a Nazi soldier came to the house and was ushered into the kitchen.

Mitka remembers standing in the corridor near the kitchen. It was the same spot where he had heard a voice utter unforgettable words that gave him courage when he was at his lowest.

"I saw him take off his coat. He sat down and he took his revolver out of its holster and he set it on the counter. He saw me when he moved to the kitchen door.

"I was sneaky and I snuck like I normally do. I wanted to know what was going on, and I had learned how to listen and watch." Mitka laughs with a hint of self-congratulation as he tells on himself.

As he recalls the Nazi soldier who had entered the home, the image of "long black boots" lingers. "He had his legs crossed, and his gun was on the counter. And he was sitting this way and he uncrossed his legs." Mitka, with a bit of a flourish, exaggerates the soldier's movement.

His voice goes up a notch, and his pace quickens. "And I grabbed his gun and run down the hallway to that stationary ladder."

Mitka knew that the SS soldier and Dörr family members were following right behind him as he ran. At the base of the ladder, he reached high and grabbed a rung with one hand. His other hand held the pistol.

"It was heavy, pretty heavy." Here, again, Mitka mimics the motion of climbing, reaching upward with one arm while the other hangs by his side. "That was hard, climbing by one hand. I made the monkeys look crazy, and I just ran up there. And finally they came to where the ladder was. And I could hear their voices."

In the third loft Mitka, silent save for the pounding of his heart, listened to the perplexed soldier below him declare, "Er konnte nicht es dort das schnell zusammensetzen. Er konnte nicht dort sein." (He could not make it up there that fast. He couldn't be up there.)

What prompted Mitka to scamper off with the SS soldier's gun? To this day, even he isn't sure. "Don't ask me what or who made me grab the gun." He only knows that he felt compelled to act.

Today he believes that the Nazi had come to kill him—that he had become a burden to the Dörrs, a liability, and that a quick execution had been planned, something that in the chaos surrounding the war's end would have likely gone unnoticed. "The SS man came with his uniform, and he came to do away with me because the Americans were coming." Given Mitka's experiences, his logic makes sense, whether or not his conclusion is true.

In this instance, hiding in the loft, Mitka avoided detection.

"I waited out until the air was clean. The Nazi officer left, and I don't know what happened, and then I come down."

When Mitka descended the ladder, he expected a beating. It did not come. He left the house and walked to the Hoberück neighborhood many blocks south and west, where he buried the gun. When he returned to Badegasse 14 that afternoon, to his surprise, the chutzpah he had shown when he pilfered the SS officer's gun seemed to have been forgotten.

Standing at the front of the house, Mitka saw a truckload of prisoners rolling by. One prisoner pointed to him and yelled out, "'Stay there!' They were telling me to stay with the family. It's confusion now, and nobody knows what the hell they're doing. Gustav was not around. But later on I found out. I heard that he run away.

"That next day—Good Friday—now I participated in that. Anna told me to go with her." With astonishment he adds, "On bicycles!"

Among the junk Gustav and Opa salvaged were bicycles and bicycle parts. Mitka had learned to repair old bikes and from salvaged parts build "new" bikes, another of his duties.

"Martin, get the bike!" Anna barked. In front of him stood an adult-size bicycle, which presented a problem. The seat was too high. To further complicate matters, Mitka was not a skilled rider. "And there was a big bar, and I went underneath with my feet. I was too short to sit on the seat and reach the pedals. 'Come with me,' Anna said, and I did."

Positioned under the triangular frame of the bike, Mitka pedaled. He followed Anna, riding toward town down a cramped lane called Brückengasse, which sloped downward to the bridge that crossed the Fulda River. Mitka's bike picked up speed, careening forward toward a group of people waiting to cross the bridge, which was clogged with tanks leaving Rotenburg. Mitka furiously pumped the pedals in an attempt to brake, having no idea that the British-style bike had hand brakes.

"There were tanks everywhere, and I was riding that bike lying down because I couldn't sit on the seat and reach the pedals. I had to make a decision: Do I run into a tank? It would probably kill me right there. Or do I run into a guy on a bike?"

Here Mitka starts laughing. "I run into the bike and the wing nut hit the tire and it went *pshhhhhh*. I popped that guy's tire. He had a flat tire right there."

The column of tanks and soldiers continued rolling along in retreat, over the river, unconcerned with the crash of a boy and his bicycle.

"It was the Germans, the tough guys running away."

Anna gave an order: "Walk with me." Mitka crawled out from under the bike and laid it aside.

They continued southeast on foot to Lispenhausen, a small town halfway between Rotenburg and Bebra. It was there, by a set of railroad tracks, that Mitka looked down on a group of people standing shoulder to shoulder.

"That's when I saw the SS shooting."

He does not recall recognizing the targeted people, but he notes, "I was up above, looking down." He continues, "I didn't know 'Jewish.' I just know you have a star, and the next day you are not there. Maybe it was Jews, but it could have been the prisoners I saw the day before. So the Germans were shooting. She made me watch them be executed. Baddest thing. I'll never forget it. Soldiers just shot everybody."

Mitka was no stranger to death, but what happened next shocked even his benumbed senses.

"One SS man stepped on the bodies. He went and shot each one again. They were already dead, but he shot them. You don't forget blood coming out of those heads. I was scared."

Soldiers threw the corpses onto a flatbed truck. Anna, with Mitka in tow, turned and walked back to Rotenburg. They crossed the bridge and made their way to Badegasse 14. Soon thereafter, he, like everyone else in town, heard an explosion.

"I remember when the bridge blew up—the sound—you could hear it everywhere. And I can almost tell you the exact time. It was about 1:30 in the afternoon."

Before their retreat, German soldiers had set explosives and detonated the Fulda Bridge.

"I bet I was the last person to cross that bridge before it blew up."

A gaping hole was all that remained, bookended by intact steel edifices on either end. Moving east with tanks and artillery, retreating Nazi troops likely destroyed the bridge in obedience to Hitler's March 19 "Nero Order" to leave nothing for the enemy, but also to slow pursuing American forces.

Meanwhile, at Badegasse 14, Mitka was told they were going to a vacation house that Gustav had under construction in the "mountains" not far beyond Hoberück. They set off on foot and arrived before nightfall. Gustav did not join them.

Mitka eventually fell asleep on that Good Friday night. Saturday passed unremarkably for him; he has no memory of the day.

On Easter Sunday, Mitka woke to the sounds of mortar fire. Sometime that morning the Dörr family, with the exception of Gustav, returned to Rotenburg. Mitka, not knowing what was going on, wandered his way back to Rotenburg alone. As he walked, one sight made a particular impression, both because he'd never seen anything like it and because he didn't know what to make of it.

"An old man was walking to town waving a white flag."

CHAPTER SEVEN

Amis

Rotenburg an der Fulda, 1945–1949

A turn in Mitka's life marked the midday of April 1, 1945. He had spent the previous night at a house he had never been to before. People moved about frantically, and he had seen and heard unexpected things throughout the weekend. As he walked down the mountain back to town alongside the old man carrying a white flag, he was alone. He can't recall how or why he was separated from the Dörr family. He was merely returning to Rotenburg.

When he arrived in town, he encountered Amis—American GIs—seemingly everywhere. He had previously heard that these men were the enemy, people to be feared. As he wandered, he loitered here and there, passing soldiers who filled streets in the town center. He happened on one GI sitting in an army truck. The door was open, and the American's booted foot was propped against the doorframe. Although Mitka didn't understand English, he distinctly recalls the words, "Hey, kid." The Ami gave him a chocolate bar—the first he'd ever had—and a citrus-flavored, powdered candy. A smile comes to his lips as he remembers, "It tasted like lemonade."

Although he had been conditioned to fear Amis, the fact that American GIs replaced German troops didn't faze Mitka. Looking back, he says, "I just wish one of them had told me the damn war was over."

One sight, however, left him wonderstruck.

"So there was no bridge to cross the Fulda because the Germans blew it up, but all of a sudden, out of nowhere, the Amis made a cockeyed thing that I've never seen. It was this bridge where you float things. And you could walk over it—not drive, just walk." He continues, "It was like a *Tom and Jerry* cartoon." Here Mitka moves his right index and middle fingers in a scurrying motion across the table. "*Bap . . . bap, bap . . . bap*—they put up this pontoon bridge . . . and fast."

On his return to Rotenburg, Mitka did not go back to Badegasse 14, the only place he thought of as home. Instead, he stayed with the American troops. He's not sure how long he did this. "It could have been a couple of days. It could have been a couple of weeks." His memories of that time (he was about ten years old) are few but distinct. One memory is of helping the GIs haul fresh water, since "they would not drink the water in Rotenburg."

When most of the American troops had pulled out of Rotenburg, Mitka returned to Badegasse 14. "Where else would I go?" To his surprise, the Dörrs treated him as if nothing unusual had happened. There were no beatings from Tante Anna, and no one said anything about his absence; he simply resumed his work as before. The panic and fright that had permeated Rotenburg receded, and Mitka settled back into his routines.

The German state of Hesse, which included Rotenburg an der Fulda, fell to Patton's Third Army in late March 1945. As troops moved through the region, some remained behind to impose martial law on cities and towns from Frankfurt to Kassel. Hesse was a part of the American zone of occupation following the war (the other three zones in Germany were occupied by Great Britain, France, and the Soviet Union, respectively).

That American GIs would befriend a boy like Mitka was not unusual based on anecdotal stories and film portrayals of soldiers' actions during the war. Yet Mitka's staying with the soldiers for such a prolonged time is surprising. Since December 1942, he had lived at Badegasse 14. It was the only home he had. However, he moved with ease into the world inhabited by people he had once believed to be enemies.

Sitting back in his chair, his arms crossed over his chest, Mitka radiates serenity. "I kind of liked the Amis. I liked being with them."

Mitka's words indicate that a new reality had taken hold of him. His time with the Amis had given him something to compare to his experiences with the Dörrs. For the first time, he started to think about how others treated him and how he regarded them in turn.

Beginning April 1, 1945, twenty-eight months after he had come to Rotenburg, Mitka's life changed. The old order of things in Rotenburg was gone. His address was the same and he still worked for the Dörrs, but some things were different.

As Mitka's life changed, so did the world. Throughout the month of April, dramatic events were unfolding. The Allies' victory over Axis powers was imminent. On April 12, President Franklin D. Roosevelt suddenly and unexpectedly died at his home in Warm Springs, Georgia. Not three months before, on February 4, Roosevelt, Prime Minister Winston Churchill, and Premier Joseph Stalin had convened at Yalta in Crimea, Russia, to set the terms of postwar peace and to formulate a plan of self-determination for the people of a liberated Europe. Upon Roosevelt's death, Harry Truman became the newest member of "the Big Three"—leaders representing the United States, Great Britain, and Russia. On April 29, Italian partisans executed Mussolini and his mistress, bound their feet with wire, and hung their bodies upside down at a gas station in Milan. On April 30, Hitler took cyanide and then shot himself in his *Führerbunker*, committing suicide with his longtime mistress and wife of one day, Eva Braun. Days later, on May 7, at 2:41 a.m., Germany surrendered, unconditionally, to the Allies. Germany's dream of racial purity was dead, as the nation, for the second time in less than thirty years, bowed to its enemies.

With the end of the war, Mitka's relationship to "the Nazi family," as he calls the Dörrs, shifted—at least legally. The laws that had allowed them to take and enslave the young boy died along with Hitler and his regime. That said, in practical terms, little changed. Mitka was one of the "lost children," a relatively small group within the larger tribe of displaced persons (DPs) after the war. These children had no family, no one to claim them or to help them. Freed from Nazi domination, they were nevertheless trapped by the sheer lack of options. Mitka's circumstances, his utter aloneness, bound him, thus, to the Dörrs, the only family he knew.

In the early months after the war's end, Mitka overheard a story. On Holy Thursday, March 29, 1945, Gustav had provided laborers and carts to assist in the evacuation of Allied prisoners from Oflag IX A/Z, the prisoner-of-war camp at the Jakob-Grimm-Schule. Apparently, Gustav left Rotenburg with the evacuation team and did not return. The chatter was that he had been hiding in the Russian zone until he decided that he would be better off returning to the American zone. Gustav, as Mitka recalls, snuck back into Rotenburg with another man, and they hid in the *Schloss*—an ancient, repurposed castle in the old part of the city, not far from the bombed-out bridge. Belgian soldiers discovered the two men and proceeded to beat them severely. The beating killed the companion, and Gustav was badly injured. Men in white helmets, likely Allied military police, intervened, pulling the Belgians off the badly injured Gustav. Mitka heard from the Dörr family that Gustav had nearly died and that he had been hospitalized as a result of the beating.

Around the same time, after Mitka had returned to the Dörr household and while Rotenburg was under martial law, Anna gave Mitka a slip of paper and told him to go down to the Fulda River, where a man with a boat would meet him. He was instructed to deliver the note to someone on the other side. He doesn't recall the person to whom he was sent but speculates that it was "maybe the baker whose shop was over there."

Mitka went as he was told and met a man waiting on the old-town side of the Fulda. They got into a skiff and pushed off into the current. In the middle of the river, the small boat overturned, dumping both the boy and the man into the water. Not surprisingly, Mitka couldn't swim. When you're flailing and frantic to stay afloat, he quips, "Boy, you learn fast." He "dog-paddled," as he tells it, "for my life." As he thrashed about, he heard shouts coming at him from sentries stationed on either end of the destroyed bridge and looked up to soldiers lining the remains of the bridge, all with rifles pointed at him. He didn't paddle long before more soldiers waded into the river and dragged him from the water.

What happened next calmed the frightened, soaked boy. An American soldier spoke to him—in Yiddish. He asked Mitka what he was doing and where he lived. Also, the soldier read the note that Anna had written. Mitka got a warning about the rules of martial law, after which the soldiers took him back to Badegasse 14. As for the Dörrs—"they got into trouble. They shouldn't have sent me out during martial law." He never knew the reason he'd been sent to deliver the note. He believes, though, that this might have been an attempt, on Anna's part, "to get rid of me." He explains, "You see, I knew a lot about the Nazi family. Maybe—and this is just me talking now—they were afraid of what I would say. This would have been a great way to make sure that I never talked to anyone about what they had done."

Mitka's conjecture may or may not be accurate, but it makes some sense. The war's end brought enormous privations to Germany and its citizens, and Gustav's injuries and absence from his home and family surely created great stress for the Dörrs. All of this may have led to an increased sense of paranoia on the part of Anna.

By the summer of 1945, Mitka's work at the Dörr house and farm had settled back into a regimen much like before, except he no longer made the trip to Bebra to pick up the relics and remnants of the victims of the Nazis. His life outside work had changed somewhat in that strictures placed on his movements diminished, and he learned he could roam throughout Rotenburg without being punished.

One newfound freedom was going to the movies at a theater located in the *Schloss*. He usually bartered for tickets with potatoes he had stolen (potatoes were prized at the time). At the *Kinderheim* he had seen his first movie sometime between 1939 and 1941. He describes the hand-cranked projector and his amazement at seeing "moving pictures." At the *Schloss* before the end of the war, he had seen a handful of movies, though it had always been a secretive excursion. When the German surrender came, he went to the theater far more often and no longer tried to conceal it.

More than any other activity, seeing films opened the outside world to Mitka. The stories captivated him. He imitated characters, and he saw places and people outside the narrow confines of Badegasse 14.

Another benefit came to him through film. He heard music that was new to him, and he memorized melodies. The two songs that comprised his repertoire up to this point were military marches. But Mitka's repertoire swelled to many songs with each new movie soundtrack he heard. Back in the loft, he learned these on his accordion. Still, he took precautions to play only for himself, fearing the repercussions that an audience might invite.

One of the movies Mitka saw sometime after its release in 1946 was *The Magic Bow*, the British musical based on the life and loves of the Italian violinist and composer Niccolò Paganini. The love story, but especially the music, made a lifelong impression on him. So, too, did the performance of Stewart Granger as Paganini. Movies would, over the coming years, be Mitka's foremost classroom.

Interestingly, as Mitka was exploring the possibilities of life beyond the confines of Badegasse 14, outside agencies, unknown to him at the time, were beginning work to provide him a chance at such a life.

At the war's end, the conquering Allied forces faced a devastated Europe. The destruction of major cities was matched and, perhaps, exceeded by the destruction of virtually the entire infrastructure that provided both economic and social stability. Germany, of course, provided the greatest set of challenges, including purging the country of Nazi influence in a process called "denazification," identifying and prosecuting war criminals, rebuilding physical and economic structures, managing the interests of the four victorious nations, and coping with millions of displaced persons—"4.5 million of whom were roaming the Western Zones of Germany alone." In order to manage what was clearly a humanitarian crisis, military governments turned to "international relief agencies to take on the enormous task of providing the recently liberated DPs [displaced persons] with shelter, food, and other services. Founded in 1943, the United Nations Relief and Rehabilitation Administration (UNRRA) was the largest organization of this kind, an international super-agency representing over 40 countries."

It's not clear how Mitka came to the attention of UNRRA. He was, after all, someone who might have been easily overlooked, given the enormity of UNRRA's mission. Perhaps American GIs who befriended him tipped off UNRRA workers to his situation. When the boat had capsized in the Fulda River, maybe the soldier who inquired of him in Yiddish told someone. Another possibility is that neighbors of the Dörrs, some of whom had shown him pity, played a role. Or it could have been that Gustav's notoriety in Rotenburg, his ignominious participation in Kristallnacht, and his use of forced laborers drew attention to Mitka. However it happened, some official in UNRRA's massive bureaucracy decided to consider the well-being of one cast-off child: someone

began an administrative investigation, which had Mitka's best interests
as its goal. Unaware of what was happening, Mitka now—for the first
time in his life—had advocates.

On Saturday, September 21, 1946, Mitka distinctly remembers
wearing shorts, suspenders, a shirt, socks, and new wooden shoes—the
first "real" clothes he can ever recall having. He bathed, his hair was
combed, and he was told exactly what to say for an appearance before
officials at the *Rathaus*. Oma took him by the hand and walked him
into city hall.

On September 21, 1942, four years earlier, Mitka was starving,
barely clothed, and facing death at Pfaffenwald. But for the fate of becoming Gustav's slave, Mitka, too, would have died, like almost all at
Pfaffenwald.

Now, four years later, two events occurred that Mitka places on the
same day. These events were important to him because they corroborate
his memory. First, the Fulda River crested above its natural level, and
the high-water mark left on the bombed-out remnants of the bridge
was memorialized with a plaque. Second, Mitka was gussied up for his
public appearance and coached with words for those who would judge
the Dörrs' treatment of him. That pivotal Saturday in September of 1946
began a process that would set Mitka on a trajectory with far-reaching
consequences.

If a picture had been taken of Mitka that day, it would have shown
a smartly dressed boy whose appearance belied his actual life. It was
all a facade. Mitka was groomed to bear the patina of a child formed
in a caring family. Mitka's words, as he remembers them, likely gave the
same impression, as he repeated what Anna and Oma told him to say.
It would fall to UNRRA investigators to determine the truth about the
boy's circumstances. The reality was that the end of the war had changed
the way the Dörrs treated Mitka—but only in small ways. He was still
beaten, albeit less often. He still slept on straw with bars on the high
window of his room. He was cold in the winter and always hungry. And
once he completed his *Rathaus* testimony, the pressed shirt and pants,
the suspenders, and the vest were taken away. He dressed himself in his
usual fashion, putting back on what could only be described as rags.

The first known documentary evidence of an examination of Mitka comes from UNRRA's Bureau of Documents and Tracing, US zone, and is dated November 30, 1946, two months after his *Rathaus* testimony. Signed by one F. Przyluski, chief of branch, this memo makes two simple points. First, the "subject," "Dymitro Kalinsky," was an "unaccompanied child . . . living now in Rotenburg a. d. Fulda, Badegasse 14." And second, "so far, no other information is available and it is suggested that someone from the child tracing service investigate this case." A second, follow-on document, from the same office, is dated December 10, 1946. Addressed to the attention of an UNRRA "Child Welfare Officer," this memo states that a field tracing officer had examined "KALINSKI, Mitke (Demitro)." It includes the following brief:

> This is to advise you that the case of above child has been examined by our Field Tracing Officer and the following information secured:
>
> Age of child 14 years. Born in Bialacevkiew, Russia. Came to Germany in 1942. Since December 14th, 1942 he is working in Rotenburg a/F for the German family Christian Dörr, Badegasse 14, Rotenburg a/F. The boy is in very poor condition and he needs badly clothing.

Of his life up to this time, the rare and scant records about Mitka were those possessed by Gustav Dörr. Some of these may have been created by Gustav to legitimize to German authorities his taking of Mitka from Pfaffenwald and using him as a laborer. Also, the *Kinderheim* in Bila Tserkva (Bialacevkiew in the UNRRA memo) was the first place Mitka can recall, but this Ukrainian town is, almost certainly, not his birthplace.

In the meantime, Mitka's life at Badegasse 14 continued with its usual challenges but also with a continued uptick in adventures—including stealing money from Opa and Oma, a tale he tells with equal shares of guilt and glee. He pulled off the larceny by hiding under their bed. When they came to bed that night, he remained motionless and hushed until he was sure they'd fallen asleep. Mitka laughs in the retelling, and makes a snoring sound. "I got them that time. I got them good."

From under the bed he snuck in the dark to find a wallet in Opa's pants pocket, from which he helped himself to *Reichsmark* banknotes. He had no idea how much he'd taken until he showed the paper money to Willi Deist. One turned out to be a *Hundert Reichsmark* note. Willi had no trouble convincing Mitka that they should strike out on an adventure with Mitka's newfound wealth.

Whatever the amount that Mitka stole from Opa, it was enough for Willi and Mitka to go the short distance to neighboring Bad Hersfeld to have a jolly time at the Lullusfest, a carnival of sorts, which continues even today. They bought things—Mitka remembers some silver rings—and rode the rides. It was one of Mitka's happiest memories of his time in Rotenburg. The Hitler youth who had beaten and kicked him when he asked, "What's so special about Hitler?" was now his first playmate.

Throughout 1947 and 1948, investigators worked on Mitka's case. During this time the International Relief Organization (IRO) replaced UNRRA. As he reflects on his life, Mitka frequently expresses frustration that the Dörrs held him for such a long time after the war's end. He had not known that leaving was an option. Nor did he know that his was, apparently, one of a relatively small number of extremely challenging cases. Indeed, the phrase attached to Mitka by UNRRA—"unaccompanied child"—carried weight in that it referred to children "16 years of age or under; outside of their countries of origin or that of their parents; orphans or children whose parents have disappeared or whose parents are unattainable or who have been abandoned; not provided with a legal guardian; [and] not accompanied by a close relative."

In all but the earliest of the reports detailing the investigation into Mitka's situation, the accompanying forms contained spaces for usual biographical information: name, sex, nationality, date of birth, weight, hair color, height, religion, and so on. There were also spaces for additional biographical information to be filled in regarding the displaced child's family members. Every time a space was provided for the names of the displaced person's mother, father, brothers, sisters, and any other relatives, Mitka's papers contained a single word: *UNKNOWN*. On page after page, this word was repeated, serving as a stark reminder that, indeed, Mitka had no known family history. The biographical details attached to Mitka had been derived from the available evidence, thin as it was. Such things as a birthdate of December 14, 1932, a birthplace in Bila Tserkva, Ukraine, and his name, Demitro Kalinski, were among the "facts" passed from document to document.

Notably, even though the name Demitro or Demitri (for which Mitka is a typical nickname) Kalinski was, in fact, Mitka's name, he believed his name was Martin. He does not remember hearing his real name until 1949.

Mitka saw Gustav only two times after 1945. The first time, Oma went to see her son at an institution with Mitka in tow. Mitka believes they went to a jail or perhaps a hospital. When he talks about this trip, once again, the complicated nature of his relationship with Gustav is evident. The boy who wants to please his master can be heard in Mitka's retelling.

Sometime before the end of the war, Mitka had acquired a cigarette-rolling machine. Where or how he came into possession of the device he doesn't know. What he realized, after learning to roll cigarettes, was that he possessed a commodity for barter or gifts. Cigarette butts dropped by German and then Ami soldiers were plentiful. He collected the discarded butts, emptied them of any remaining tobacco, and rolled "new" cigarettes. Like so many things he taught himself, this was yet another source of pride.

Mitka talks about how it made him feel important that he would give cigarettes he'd made to Gustav. When he and Oma arrived at the destination to visit Gustav after the war, Mitka was not permitted to see him. However, Oma assured him she would tell her son that the cigarettes were a gift from Mitka. From an upper-story window, Gustav waved to Mitka.

When Mitka talks about Gustav, his speech is flavored with both vinegar and honey, as when he explains that Gustav had been tried and convicted of war crimes.

In Kassel, at district court, Gustav faced a reckoning with the law. For his role in Rotenburg events of 1938, which preceded Kristallnacht, he was tried on criminal charges. The judgment was recorded on May 26, 1948. Gustav Dörr was found guilty of charges against him, but he never served time in jail. The court dismissed punishment for unrecorded medical reasons.

As the investigation of Mitka continued, authorities slowly and persistently accumulated additional information from various unidentified sources. A document from the spring of 1948 summarizes information authorities had gathered up to that point in time. The document reads:

Information Obtained from Tracing Bureau checked with child.

Child was living in a Kinderheim at Bialacevkiew or Bialacevka near Kiev. He does not remember anything about his parents, can only recall living in this Kinderheim. He remembers the care as being good, went to school. Approximately 4–5 years ago, he ran away and joined a transport of slave-laborers to Germany where so many people were sent, to have a look there himself. He stayed for some time with grown-up Russians in several camps, the names of which he does not remember. The original group he left with was now scattered around. In the middle of 1942, he arrived in a camp at Hersfeld where he was registered by the Labour-Office. Dec. 1942 he was employed by the family Dorr, at Rottenburg a/F for work on the land they own and in their business of old iron and clothes. He was then approximately 10 years of age. He is still doing the same job, getting as a reward food, poor clothing, and a small amount of money to go to the movies. He has not been sent to school by the family, does not write and does not remember the Russian language any more. The family wants to get rid of him as he is growing up and going to be a more expensive worker. Therefore returning to his country is applauded by them under the pretext that it is better for his future. The boy himself is not very definite in his wishes but is inclined to prefer staying with the family. However he is not really objecting to going back to Russia as he has no fear for it. According to the family, he is a good worker, usually easy to handle, having now and then a mutinous day, announcing that he will "quit." The boy is badly clothed, which is logical as the family is living a low standard–life as far as housekeeping and ability for education of children is concerned. It is definitely best for the child if he leaves this family to be repatriated after a period of adjustment in a Children's Center (Aglasterhausen) to get some school and language training. Clearance with the Liaison Officer prior to a request for removal to M. G. [Military Government] seems desirable. It is difficult to get a clear picture of the character of the boy as he is more or less overwhelmed by the family. He is shy but seems to respond to friendliness and is probably still young enough to react properly to good and understanding guidance. This case is not known to any German authority except the ration bureau and formerly the labour office, which personnel has changed after the war.

The report goes on to list a number of actions that had been taken in Mitka's case.

Several points are worthy of note. A memorandum on December 23, 1947, lists "KALINSKI, Mitka" along with the names of seven other children and certifies that these children "have been accepted as nationals of the USSR, eligible for repatriation." The memo further requests that the "children be transferred to one of our Assembly centers as soon as possible for repatriation" to Russia. A month later, an official letter was submitted to the Official Military Government, or OMG, requesting removal of all seven children for return to the USSR. Almost exactly a month later, on February 19, 1948, a memo from Jean L. Bailly, acting field representative of the International Relief Organization, reported that, in Mitka's case, the request had been denied. Two reasons were given for the denial. The first was that the child, who was mistakenly listed as a fourteen-year-old girl, "prefers to stay with present family," and the second was that his "background is unknown, [and his] nationality not definitely determined."

For reasons that are not entirely clear, one Jan Madurowicz, a tracing and child search officer with the IRO, was not content to accept the refusal of the OMG to transfer Mitka from the Dörrs. On April 13, 1948, Mr. Madurowicz wrote a memo to a senior tracing officer in the International Tracing Service (ITS), making a case for the removal of Mitka from Badegasse 14. His memo included the following points:

This case does not concern a girl (as mentioned in the OMG statement) but the boy. Although there were no documents regarding the child's nationality found, the question of his nationality is quite clear according to his own statement. Nevertheless, he refused to be repatriated and would like to stay with present family.

1. Anyhow, after the discussion with the child about his future and education, I made the suggestion to the child to transfer him to the IRO-Children Centre for further care and education. The boy answered: "*Mir is egal.*" It means that makes no difference for him.

2. The foster parents, both over 50 years of age, do not want to keep him any longer.

I would suggest to transfer the boy to the IRO Centre as soon as possible.

With this memo, Mitka's case took a decisive turn.

On September 27, 1948, ITS issued an official "Transfer Slip," signed by Area Director Phyllis Harvey, Senior Tracing Office Area no. 1, authorizing Mitka's transfer from the Dörrs per "I.T.S. Field Order No. 3."

Three days later, on September 30, a letter with the subject heading "Removal of United Nations Child from German Foster Home" was sent to Jean L. Bailly, IRO field representative, APO 633, US Army, authorizing the removal of Mitka from the Dörrs. This letter specifies that Mitka must, however, remain in "the Zone," meaning the US zone. It had not yet been decided where Mitka would be relocated. That decision would require additional investigation and authorization.

The decision conveyed in the September 30, 1948, letter to remove Mitka from the Dörrs would not be acted on for eighteen weeks. Then, beginning in mid-February 1949, the pace of events quickened. A letter from A. M. Jacobsen, a child-care officer in Fulda, was sent to an unnamed child-care officer in Frankfurt, stating that "the unnamed child"—Mitka—"will be transferred to Hanau Children's Center on Tuesday the 22nd of February."

On the day Mitka was to be taken from the Dörrs, however, an unexpected twist set things back. As Jacobsen related,

The boy could not be transferred Tuesday 22/2, 1949 as he had run away (not for the first time according to his foster mother) and could not be located through the German Police. It was arranged with *Jugendamt* in Rotenburg that if the boy turned up they would get hold of him, and we would transfer him Friday 25/2, 1949. Area Child Care Officer in Frankfurt informed 22/2, 1949 verbally about the case.

Mitka had not, in fact, run away. He was simply doing what he often did—working some distance from the home, as bidden by Anna. He returned that evening, unaware of what had transpired earlier.

Friday, February 25, was like any other day for Mitka. He woke that morning and set about his usual routine. He smelled manure, from which he didn't recoil. He smelled hay, sweet and familiar. He saw straw dust suspended in air before it drifted lazily to the dirt as he filled feed cribs for the horses and cows and goats. He ladled slop into his cupped palm and shared breakfast with the pigs. He milked Lotte and cleaned stalls. He loaded the manure wagon and harnessed and hitched Schimmel to the wagon to go to the fields to spread manure. As he rode he saw a lone man walking toward him. He drew closer and recognized the man. It was Gustav.

They spoke briefly. Gustav ended the conversation with three words: "Remember me, Martin." It meant nothing to him at the time.

Mitka continued on to the fields, completed his work, and returned to Badegasse 14. Back at the house, Tante Anna took him aside and told him to go to the *Rathaus* to deliver papers that he had previously pressed into cubes. He thought nothing of the request. It was an ordinary duty. He did as he was told.

When he arrived at his destination, he was stopped and then escorted to the same cell where he had been incarcerated after receiving the beating from members of the Hitler Youth. This time, he remembers, he was not handcuffed.

His mind raced with horror at the thought of being returned to Pfaffenwald. That the war was over, that Pfaffenwald no longer existed—these facts were not a part of his consciousness.

He doesn't remember the details exactly, but sometime that day or the next he was loaded into a Willys Jeep and taken—first to Fulda and then to Hanau. Jacobsen wrote one final report:

> Kalinski, Demitro (Mitka). The boy has been located and transferred to Hanau Children Center, Friday, 25th, 1949.

Mitka's enslavement with the Dörr family in Rotenburg an der Fulda had ended.

Reflecting on the moment, Mitka says, "Leaving the Nazi family didn't mean nothing. But I didn't get to go back for my accordion." There's a catch in his voice and a pause. When he speaks again, it's with a sadness. "I didn't say goodbye to my animals. I wish I'd said goodbye."

CHAPTER EIGHT

Bad Aibling

Bad Aibling, 1949–1950

The one-hundred-mile drive from Rotenburg to Hanau, with a brief stopover at the IRO Displaced Persons camp and office in Fulda, left Mitka in a state of shock and bewilderment. Sudden, abrupt, and unexpected, his removal by American GIs ignited old fears. Initially, he was terrified that he was being returned to Pfaffenwald. "I thought they were taking me back. It was what I thought when I was in the *Rathaus* the first time, and it was that again. I always thought if I was bad, they would take me back. By now, I didn't even remember the name 'Pfaffenwald.' It was just the *lager* [camp]. I was scared, so scared."

There were other fears, too, that confronted the boy. Whisked away from the *Rathaus* in a Willys Jeep, Mitka left behind a life that, by any civilized standard, could only be described as inhumane; nonetheless, it was a life he had come to navigate quite well. For approximately nine years, beginning at a *Kinderheim* in Bila Tserkva, he had been victimized by one of humanity's greatest evils. Yet it was not the horrors of Nazi cruelty that caused Mitka's greatest pain; it was his fundamental aloneness.

Ignoble, cruel, and dehumanizing though it was, his home with the Dörrs afforded him the stability of a constant place, a relative predictability in his days, and a life on the borders of a family. He imagined no life other than what he knew. UNRRA officials had apparently accepted the designation of Oma and Opa Dörr as his foster parents, and at some level, in fact, they were. Now, for him, that life was over. Of necessity, his departure was without warning, without his assent, and without the opportunity to say goodbye.

Mitka arrived in Hanau on Saturday, February 26, 1949, where he would stay for three weeks. Seventeen miles east of Frankfurt, Hanau was a city almost completely destroyed by Allied bombing during the war. Starting in April 1945, with the fall of Hanau's airfield to American forces, various US military and humanitarian relief organizations operated from the city. It was at this IRO facility for displaced persons that a prepubescent Mitka began a two-year period that had, in many ways, more chaos and upheaval than his time in Rotenburg. However, it would also be a time of dramatic and heartening growth.

Although he was only in Hanau for a few weeks, Mitka has keen memories of his time there. He recalls, "I got a handful of something given to me—like clothes—a shirt, socks, things I'm not familiar with." Among the unfamiliar things was his first pair of underwear. He laughs as he remembers, "They gave me underwear. I didn't know what they were." And for the first time in his life, he had "real" shoes, shoes "like the other people had."

Many new experiences at Hanau left Mitka wide-eyed. His face lights up. Ebullient, he recalls, "Oh yeah, they got showers, they got flush toilets. These things I never seen before." It was also here that he was given something that would become, for him, a kind of talisman. A soldier, an Ami, gave him a small, gold, US Army lapel pin. This pin represented, for Mitka, the one reality that, above all, left him euphoric: "In Hanau I was told something—that I was free—and crazy me, I started screaming and jumping around, 'I'm free! I'm free!' If a man in a white coat had been there, I would have been taken away. I'm screaming, 'I'm free!'"

Hanau was only a temporary placement for Mitka and others with him. On March 18, 1949, Mitka and four other "unaccompanied children and youth" were moved 275 miles to the IRO Children's Village in Bad Aibling. The five boys ranged in age from twelve to seventeen years old. Only one, Mitka, had no birthdate listed. His age was listed as fifteen, his nationality as Russian. Jean "Johnny" Daussy, one of these five boys, and Mitka struck up a friendship during their stopover at

Hanau. This friendship would carry forward to Bad Aibling and play prominently in Mitka's time there.

When Mitka arrived at the Children's Village on that Friday in March, he entered the gates of a former German military air base built by the Nazis in 1936 on the outskirts of the southern Bavarian town of Bad Aibling. Until the end of the war, its garrison buildings housed Nazi combat troops. American forces moved into Bad Aibling in early May 1945 and took over the air base without resistance from the remaining Germans. For the next fifteen months, US forces used the extensive grounds as a prisoner-of-war enclosure, through which passed tens of thousands of German POWs. Simple wooden barracks were built to house these inmates. From September 1946 until late 1948, the camp was repurposed to house some of the 4.5 million displaced persons roaming around the western zones of Germany after the war.

Sometime in the fall of 1948, the IRO, having already assumed administration of the camp, decided it would be a suitable facility in which to consolidate several camps of displaced children. On November 22, 1948, the Children's Village at Bad Aibling officially opened. Four months later, Mitka would enter the site, fumbling to understand his new life. Like him, the administration and staff were working hard to gain their own footing in forming an environment with lofty purposes for its young clientele.

When Mitka came in March 1949, he was one of 389 residents. All told, 2,300 children would pass through the Children's Village. Although circumstances gradually improved over its three-year existence, unrelenting challenges continued until the camp was closed. The IRO, as the lead agency, worked with others, including the American Friends Service Committee (AFSC), a Quaker organization; the Organization for Rehabilitation through Training (ORT); the Jewish Relief Unit (JRU); and the Young Men's Christian Association (YMCA). Each organization bore specific responsibilities for programs of education, vocational training, medical care, recreation, housing, and nutrition. On the fly, a self-sufficient community was built that employed nurses, supply officers, caseworkers, typists, messengers, janitors, electricians, locksmiths, carpenters, barbers, seamstresses, shoemakers, tailors, kitchen

staff, bakers, cooks, police, and especially teachers. The largest source
of labor was adult displaced persons. In this, the adult DPs gained em-
ployment and the camp had a ready supply of skilled labor. However,
these DPs rotated constantly out of the camp as they were resettled or
repatriated.

That the operation of the Children's Village was messy and disjointed is not surprising. Resources were scarce and conditions were
far less than ideal. Indeed, one of the relief workers described her first
impressions of the setting with these words:

> To this day, all the particulars of our arrival in B. A. remain a big
> black smudge, a chaotic collage made up of iron gates, barbed-wire
> fences, dun-coloured barracks buildings without heat—in most
> instances without plumbing, windows out, no electricity. Adults
> wringing their hands, children clinging to each other crying or wide-
> eyed staring, babies blue with cold.

The residents of Bad Aibling's Children's Village ranged in age from
newborns to teenagers, their health often compromised by malnourishment and illness. Most of them had experienced great trauma in their
young lives. Thus, there were behavior problems. The older children,
especially, presented enormous challenges to the Village staff, often ex-
hibiting inappropriate and even criminal behavior. On top of this were
the constant political tugs-of-war between nations and relief organizations that had to be managed.

In some of its physical characteristics, the Children's Village—with
its gates and guards, its crowded and often inadequate sleeping quarters,
its poor and scarce food, and fighting among the inhabitants—resem-
bled the camps that had once housed Mitka. A naïf when he walked
into the Children's Village, Mitka did not understand, at first, how this
camp was different. He quickly learned, though. Hastily put together
and woefully unprepared for its enormous task, the Children's Village
nevertheless possessed something that exceeded its lack of material
resources. Its leaders—to a person—were filled with compassion for
helpless, displaced children. Measuring the odds, no rational observer
would bet that these idealists would succeed in rebuilding and restoring

cast-off lives such as Mitka's, the detritus of Nazi ruin. Yet succeed they did—not entirely, of course, but in a measure that afforded many children with opportunities to live happy and productive lives.

Kathleen Regan was the first person to greet Mitka at the Reception House—the place where each of the children who entered the camp was isolated for one to two weeks to avoid the spread of disease. Kathleen was a member of the AFSC, the Philadelphia-based Quaker organization that was founded in 1917 to give conscientious objectors an alternative to military service. Since its founding, the organization had been involved in humanitarian efforts around the globe. Now five of its team members found themselves serving the children at Bad Aibling.

Years later, in a KFTY-50 Santa Rosa news broadcast, Kathleen recalled her impressions of Mitka:

> There was something about Mitka. He was one of the ones that you never forget. He was very shy and quite confused by everything that was so new to him. We gave him some things when he first arrived, and he had no idea what to do with them. I'll never forget that when we first gave him toothpaste, he thought it was candy, and he started squeezing the tube into his mouth. I think he ate the whole thing. We didn't understand all that he had been through—although we certainly could guess that it had been pretty terrible. He badly needed attention and affection. I hope he got those things from us.

One thing of inestimable value that Mitka got from the relief workers was a reclamation of his name, Mitka. Up to this point, documents had always identified him by some form of the name "Demitro Kalinski," with the earliest known record coming in 1946 from an investigation by the UNNRA. Going forward, his first name appeared in many variants on documents: Dymitro, Demtri, Demetri, Dimitro, Dimitris, Dimitri, Dmitry, Mitke, Mitro, Mitheka, and Mitka. His surname was written in more consistently, as Kalinsky or Kalinski. Perhaps a misspelling or a typographical error occurred when recording his name. Another real possibility is that these variants reflect the different nationalities of the authors of the forms or reports—or perhaps different assumptions about Mitka's country of origin. Dmytro is Ukrainian;

Dmitriy, Dima, and Mitya are Russian; Dymitr and Demetriusz are Polish; and Demetrius, Dmitriy, and Dima are variants that were commonly used by Jews. UNRRA and the IRO presumed Mitka's nationality to have been Ukrainian because his first memories were of Bila Tserkva. Ukraine might have been his country of origin, but so, too, might Poland or Russia.

Mitka, in the meantime, believed his name was Martin. Yet, from 1946 forward, and throughout his time at the Children's Village, relief workers knew him as and called him Demitro Kalinski. This name had a source, but what was it? Were there records that caused UNNRA to identify him so? The provenance was a mystery.

Gustav, decades later, implied that he had had records of the boy. If he ever possessed such records, they died with him. It is likely that he knew Mitka's real name when he took him from Pfaffenwald. Gustav did many things to erase Mitka's identity. Mitka feels that stealing his name was central to this effort and among the cruelest of Gustav's many attacks on the boy's humanity.

Sometime after his move into the Children's Village, Mitka heard an unforgettable sound, something strangely familiar. Someone called him by a name he recognized. He listened with a faint knowing he had heard it spoken in his past. In that instant he knew this was *his* name. Someone at the Children's Village called him Mitka.

The sensation Mitka felt confirmed for him what his intellect could not: that he did have a connected identity after all. He had answered to other names, but this name validated him as an individual. With just one word—*Mitka*—he owned himself. It was something no one could take from him. More than sixty years later, he remembers only one time at the Children's Village when he was called Mitka, but that was enough. In one ineradicable moment, he was someone. He had a name that belonged to him.

In his whimsical poem "The Naming of Cats," T. S. Eliot uses the phrase "his deep and inscrutable singular name." When Mitka, years later, talks of hearing his name, it is evident that it was, for him, something "deep," "inscrutable," and "singular." The name belonged to him and confirmed that his life did not begin with the Dörrs. He had a past. He did not know what it was, but he knew he had a story, a history. This discovery mattered. Years later, he hints at the importance of this moment with these simple words: "In 1949, Martin went away and Mitka came out."

The phrase "Mitka came out" reflects other steps that Mitka was taking. He had begun an uncertain journey to uncover his self. Often awkward, he lurched forward like teenagers do. The discovery and development of his personality, of his identity, would be incomplete when he left the Children's Village. Yet he had set a course that would someday enable him to introduce himself, saying with confidence, "My name is Mitka."

While Mitka stayed at Bad Aibling, reports, memoranda, and letters documented his life as never before. For example, a "Resettlement Registration Form for Unaccompanied Children," dated May 12, 1949, noted that he weighed 51 kilograms (113 pounds) and stood 155 centimeters (5'1") tall when he arrived at the Village. On this form, as in all others pertaining to him, most questions regarding his family are either unanswered or merely marked "unknown." An explanatory note amplifies these responses with the words "He doesn't remember anything about his identity."

Another report by Dr. Margaret Hasselmann, chief medical officer at the Village, provides additional details about Mitka's physical condition, noting that

THE BOY, KALINSKI, DIMITRO
BORN 14.12.32, UCRAINIAN ARRIVED HERE
ON MARCH 18, 49 IN A VERY NEGLECTED
AND UNDERNOURISHED CONDITION.

Although official documents include notations that Mitka's date of birth was December 14, 1932, the staff at the Children's Village clearly recognized that this assigned date was a fiction and that "there were no documents whatsoever available to prove his age." All who had direct contact with Mitka at the Children's Village, however, recorded that the child they saw and heard was at least three, maybe five, years younger than the documents he came with indicated. In their judgment, he was not sixteen; rather, he had likely been born sometime between 1935 and

1937. Perhaps more telling, he behaved as a child even much younger than twelve or thirteen years old. Natalie Kent, another Quaker working at the Children's Village, said, years after her time there, "I suspect he was twelve or thirteen when he first arrived . . . no facial hair, his voice hadn't even changed yet. . . . He acted a lot younger than I thought he was." And Lukie Wijsmuller, a social worker at the camp, recalled, "I remember that he was slave labor . . . and abused . . . perhaps a little older than twelve."

Because of his assigned birthdate, Mitka was frequently grouped with older children and was, in fact, moved from the Reception House into a dorm with teenage boys. This group of older teens presented special challenges for the Village. Natalie recalled that many of the boys "were often difficult because they had been wandering around for so long." She further noted that the barracks that housed these teens, the barracks into which Mitka moved, were—only half in jest—called "the gangster house." Senior staff lamented the slow development of education and recreation opportunities that left older boys and girls with idle time to fill. They worried that sexual promiscuity, drunkenness, loafing, and physical confrontations with staff threatened an already fragile balance of control. The self-appointed teen leaders of the Village residents were skilled in trading their meager rations for many things, especially cigarettes and alcohol. They had quickly organized a black market, often trading for goods with adult DPs who worked at Bad Aibling.

When Mitka arrived at the Village, a rebellion of sorts was underway, led by adolescent residents. The seeds of the rebellion had grown out of the near-impossible task the leadership and staff faced from the beginning. Housing, food procurement and preparation, security, medical services, transportation, laundry, sanitation, education, recreation, hiring staff and service workers, furnishing the camp, setting up policy protocols and communication systems—all this and more overwhelmed the modest, though tireless and idealistic, leadership.

The tipping point arrived when movie privileges and dances were curtailed. Many of the older youth stormed the administration offices, setting off sirens, blockading themselves in rooms, taking vehicles from the transportation pool, and driving out of the camp and into Bad Aibling, where some were arrested.

Mitka remembers the events well, as they occurred just after he arrived in the Village. "There was a strike. I didn't know what a strike was, but I remember it. There were some riots and some fights, and there was this big concrete pit where some kids had started a fire." He adds, "The Nazis had hidden some things before they left, and I found some bullets. I don't know why, but I threw them into that fire. And it was *ping, ping, ping* all over the place." The fireworks display he initiated, although surely of concern to the Village leadership, ultimately resulted in nothing more than a fond recollection of the mischievousness of one of the newest arrivals to the Children's Village. Mitka has no memory of being reprimanded, and he's not sure now that his involvement was even noted. "I remember there was this kid with a machine gun. He found a machine gun that the Nazis had left. And this kid got up on a building. Everyone was worried about that kid. I don't think they paid much attention to me."

The Village's deputy administrator and program director, Nora Ryan, and several of the Quaker staff were able to de-escalate the mayhem by listening to the demands of the older children and making some changes to address their concerns. For Mitka, the event was eye-opening. He didn't know what was going on, but he could see that the young people had some measure of power, that they had control and influence, that their voices mattered. He wasn't conscious of thinking through what all of this meant, but he knew that his life was changing and that he might have some say in the direction it took.

Sometime in May of 1949, Mitka was taken to a nearby hospital. Diagnosed with appendicitis, he was given an appendectomy that was followed by at least a week of recovery. Looking back, years later, Mitka says he doubts if he actually needed the surgery. "I kind of had this crush on a nurse, and I kind of think I played it up a little. I wanted to go to the hospital. I don't know that I really knew about this surgery thing. But I got to see her because I was there for a while."

While in the hospital, Mitka met Wasyl Palijczjuk from Czechoslovakia, an older teenager who was in the bed beside him. Mitka recalls that when Natalie and her husband, Oakie—two of the AFSC workers—visited him in the hospital, he asked if there might be room for Wasyl in the Children's Village. As a result, Wasyl joined the Village, and a lifelong friendship between the two began.

Wasyl was one of several friends who began to figure prominently in Mitka's world. Indeed, in less than three months, Mitka had gone from a circumscribed life surrounded by a handful of known people to a life that involved multiple moves and a continuous flow of strangers into his orbit. Shy and passive as he was, Mitka simply moved with the crowd in these early days. He latched onto one friend, Jean Daussy, a French teen whom he had met at Hanau. They had entered the Children's Village together. Older than Mitka, Johnny (as he was called) was one of the "GI mascots" who "smoked, drank, cussed like a GI, trying to imitate their benefactors, good or bad." Resourceful, shrewd, and hardened by circumstance, such teens disrupted the Village. They often upended efforts to establish a stable, family-like structure for the children. They broke Village rules, continued their black-market enterprises, and took unauthorized excursions into Bad Aibling, the adjoining town of eight thousand residents, where police detained them. Truants from school, they found ways to stay in trouble, so much so that Program Director Nora Ryan would later say that these boys were "not only difficult, but impossible to handle."

On the one hand, the friendship with Johnny anchored Mitka; on the other hand, Johnny, and other GI mascots at the Village, swayed him in ways that were deemed "unfortunate as the mascot [Johnny Daussy] had a definite negative influence on Kalinski and . . . brought him into many difficulties."

Continuing into the summer months, Mitka's house parents, especially Kathleen Regan, Lukie Wijsmuller, and other Quakers at the Village, tried, as best they could, to create for Mitka the security of a family-like structure. They recognized his fragile psychology with observations like "he's painfully self-conscious and supersensitive and puzzled emotionally," and when "he's hurt or someone does something extra for him he runs away . . . and cries and disappears for a while."

Coming as he did, with no schooling, Mitka inspired the staff. They wanted to educate Mitka and tried to engage him throughout that first summer. One memo noted, "He's sorely embarrassed when they play writing games . . . during school time." It continued by stressing that school was mandated, "but he cut classes most of the time." Special private lessons in reading and writing were tried; however, these were irregular, and "Kalinski lost interest." At one point, he was put with five-

and six-year-old children, as they, too, could not yet read. He remembers feeling ashamed to be classed with such young children and refused to continue. Teaching Mitka to read and write failed.

As was the case in Rotenburg, movies—lots of them—captured Mitka's attention more than any activity. Despite attempts by the staff to discipline Mitka, he found ways to circumvent rules—and then off to the cinema he went. A good thing occurred, nonetheless. American films became a teacher of sorts; through these he learned a few words that he spoke in halting, heavily accented English.

As the summer passed, Mitka attached himself even more to Johnny Daussy. On one level, he did so for friendship. On another, he used Johnny as a crutch. "Daussy had been around a great deal and learned all different tricks in life," Wijsmuller wrote. This was much to the consternation of the Quakers, who saw in Johnny omens of trouble.

On Sunday, September 18, their fears became real. "Demitro was reported to have been involved in a theft at the Quaker's warehouse the previous night." On the following Thursday, September 22, he was told "to work under supervision of the Camp-police, which he refused to do." What followed his refusal was an overnight stay locked in a camp prison cell at the motor pool with Johnny.

The next day, Friday, Mitka appeared before the Youth Court, which had been formed for older children to participate in disciplining their peers. In the interrogation, Mitka admitted that he had been at the Quaker House with Johnny and another boy. In a report about the incident, Wijsmuller commented that "there was no resentment on the boy's side, but rather an impression as if he felt himself to be important to be amongst the boys who had caused all this uproar in the camp." The punishment meted out for Mitka and Johnny was two months in the reformatory and six months probation. At this point they were taken back to the camp jail, which was promptly deemed "unfit for detention of youth." This led to both boys being given house arrest and "paroled to an older boy in the camp."

Again, in her report, Wijsmuller noted of Mitka, "He says it wasn't his fault that he broke into the Quaker Magazine, but that Johnny said he would hit him if he didn't come with him." The Quakers believed Mitka, and they wanted to find a remedy—other than punishment—for his behavior. When he was asked for his ideas about alternative solutions, he said he would like to return to the Reception House under the supervision of Kathleen Regan. This was granted, in part to buy time to figure out how to save this damaged child.

On September 29 Mitka moved back into the Reception House and into the care of Kathleen Regan.

Wijsmuller visited Mitka on Saturday, October 1, at the Reception House. His first question of her was whether he could stay there permanently. "D's own words are that he would never think of doing wrong things by himself, but he easily listens and gets influenced by the bad boys in whose company he is," she says.

Just over seven months earlier, Mitka—at the onset of puberty—had been taken from Rotenburg and thrust into a situation of first-time experiences. He floundered a bit as he encountered expectations for which he had no orientation. The understanding and compassion he received from the Quakers, while lavish, had limits due to their own overwhelming workload. In great measure, he was still on his own, trying his best to work out in short order what other children had accomplished over years. Mitka was lost.

Staying at the Reception House put Mitka back under the watchful eye of Kathleen Regan, and it took him away from the influence of Johnny Daussy. However, it was merely a stopgap intervention, not a solution. A decision was made to send him to Piusheim, a reformatory school run by Lutherans. Sometime in late October he traveled fewer than twenty miles northwest, toward Munich, to his new school.

A letter addressed to "Miss Wijsmuller," one dictated by Mitka with adult help, provides the only written record of his time at the reformatory. Dated November 1, 1949, it reads:

> I have been here for a few days already. I like it here now a little better than at the beginning. It will be alright after some time. I shall pull myself together and try to be a good boy. I still work in a field. I do not know how long I am supposed to stay here. If you want to send me something sometime you may do that. I need a pair of shoes very badly. I was given one by the institution but they were given to me only on loan. Please give my regards to all and everybody and accept also my very best greetings for you.

Sixty-eight years later, reflecting on the four months he spent at Pius-heim, Mitka remarks, "It was a good thing. I didn't know nothing, and they taught me there. They taught me things like how to stand in line and how to cooperate." He adds, "I had too much freedom before." He returned to Bad Aibling on March 8, 1950.

On many occasions during his time at the Village, Mitka talked of returning to Rotenburg to visit the Dörrs. His motives to do so were complicated. The simple explanation was that he had never had the chance to say goodbye. This lack of closure troubled him. Saying good-bye to the animals he loved was, he felt, particularly important.

However, other forces were at play too. Something in the boy needed to show the Dörrs, especially Gustav and Anna, that he had become his own man. Years later, when speaking of going back, a kind of triumphalism leaks into his conversation. He needed to assert a pride that he was, if not thriving, at least growing in independence quite apart from them.

But this was not the whole of it. He held mixed emotions about the family whose cruelty he had borne. It would be too strong to say he had affection for them; rather, he had an attachment that would seem to defy logic. Nevertheless, the bond was real.

Dr. Renate Sprengel, the resident psychiatrist, thought that a return to Badegasse 14 would be a good thing for Mitka. She seemed to intuit that the visit might be a catharsis. Through her own examinations of Mitka and the reports of Kathleen Regan and Natalie Kent, she knew that any interventions that might help him resolve his past ought to be tried. Also, the IRO and the Children's Village staff had the mandate to do one of three things: return him, an unattached child, to his German "family," if that's what he wanted; repatriate him to Ukraine, his supposed country of origin; or prepare him for resettlement. If the first two options failed, then resettlement would become the only choice available for Mitka. The visit to the Dörrs would be, in many ways, essential in determining if the first option was a viable one.

One day, late in the third week of April 1950, a nurse from the Children's Crèche at Hanau accompanied Mitka and another child on a journey to Rotenburg. He carried a suitcase packed with a few belongings. One item he took with him was a box camera. Before the trip, he had spoken to Kathleen Regan, telling her how much he wished he had pictures of the Dörrs and of his Rotenburg home. The longing implied in his hopes moved Kathleen; she lent him her Brownie camera.

The trip on a passenger train was not Mitka's first train ride. Boarding the railcar, he chose to sit on a bench with a back, one rather like a short pew, among many in a row. On this car, he moved about wherever he chose to, and he found a bathroom other than the floor. The air in the cabin was clean, its odors neutral. Around him, the temperature was constant and pleasant. He didn't squirm to peer through cracks between wooden slats, as he had once done. On this ride, he looked out windows at Bavaria and its forests. As the train sped north, he could move from one side of the train to the other to watch four hundred miles of German landscape pass by.

On Friday, April 20, Mitka arrived in Rotenburg an der Fulda. He stepped off the train onto a platform he had seen many times before. Tante Anna, whom he had not seen in over a year, met him at the train station. They departed for Badegasse 14—a house in which he had lived longer than any other in his brief life. What was anticipated to be a three-week stay with the Dörrs, the Village staff characterized as a holiday for Mitka. In a sense, it was a holiday, if for no other reason than it was a break from life at the Village.

Mitka offers only sketchy memories of the time. When asked, he cannot remember where or what he ate, but he says, "I do remember that I ate real food. I guess I ate with the family." He speculates, but cannot say for certain, that he slept "on a bed or something like it." One thing he knows for certain. During his visit he stayed in the same room he had occupied for almost seven years—but he spotted a change. "The bars were gone."

Carla Hansen, a child-care officer from the Field Office in Kassel, went to Badegasse 14 on April 28 to interview the Dörrs and Mitka. Her purpose was to determine if it was in Mitka's best interest to return to his so-called foster family.

After Hansen's visit, she typed a two-page, single-spaced report containing her observations.

"During his holiday," she wrote, "he has repaired the foster parents' clock, and the foster family stated that he is very adroit and able to make things with his hands."

She noted that "the foster father and foster mother," Opa and Oma, were "67 and 64 years old" and that Opa had suffered a stroke days before. "This boy must have been a great help to them, and now that the foster father had had a stroke [he] would be still a greater help."

She continued, "Demitro had that day been with them in the fields helping to plant potatoes. They praised him for his ability and said that he had not forgotten what he had learnt" and that "he had always been a very quick worker, and he knows how to do it without explanation."

In her interview, Hansen asked the Dörrs why they had spoken with the *Jugendamt* (youth welfare department) "in order to have him placed in an institution." About this she wrote, "The foster parents did not dare to take the responsibility of his upbringing. . . . As the boy was a foreigner, all the blame was always put on him, when anything wrong had been done."

The report went on to state that the family "seemed to be pleased with his visiting them, and they all wanted him to stay for the Whitsun," and that "the foster mother told me that they had written the day before to Mr. Troniak asking for permission for the boy to stay over Whitsun-tide, as they would then have a festival." Hansen added that she agreed to support this request.

In a formal memorandum, John Troniak, chief of the child-care division of the IRO office in Frankfurt, stated, "We join Miss Hansen and request your kind permission for the boy to stay with his former foster family until May 31, 1950. Do you think it would be possible to arrange?" The brief paragraph was sent to the director of the Children's Village on May 5, 1950. The request was granted. Emmy Lefson, casework supervisor of the Village, was copied on the memorandum. She would go on to become one of Mitka's champions.

Hansen's account of her day of interviews and observation did not address incongruities in the Dörrs' answers, which revealed their mixed attitudes toward Mitka. She was more definitive about Mitka's wishes. At the end of her report, she stated, "The boy declared that he did not want to return to his former foster parents and was not able to express the reason, it was my impression that . . . he—in spite of his liking his foster family—had felt he was a foreigner and therefore wanted to get out of Germany and start in a new country." In further conversation, when asked again the reason he did not want to stay with the Dörrs, Hansen wrote, "He answered that he did not know it himself."

Hansen's account is a narrative of a boy conflicted about what he was feeling and how he thought of the Dörr family. Her recommendation was that Mitka should be resettled in a country of his choosing.

When Mitka returned to the Children's Village at Bad Aibling on May 31, he had not resolved all the contradictions that swirled within him. Two matters, however, he could set to rest: (1) he did not want to return to Badegasse 14, and (2) he had said goodbye to his friends— Whitey, Lotte, and the other animals.

Years later, with anyone who might ask, he shares his best memory from this time with his former slaveholders. He sits forward, taps his chest with his fist, and says, "I wanted them to see the pin that I wore. It was the United States pin that the Amis gave me. I wanted them to know we won. I won."

CHAPTER NINE

Demitro

Bad Aibling, 1950–1951

When Mitka returned to Bad Aibling, he was different. His physical slavery had ended in 1949 when American GIs took him from Rotenburg. However, pernicious psychological slavery had a firmer hold. Its ending would take time. In May of 1950, Mitka began, albeit slowly, to loosen these inner bonds. In that month he had, once again, resided with the Dörrs. This time he was not a slave, but a sort of guest, however contrived the Dörrs' welcome of him may have been. When he left Rotenburg, Mitka had made a choice, something that, in itself, was a new learned behavior. He left behind the idea that he could ever again live at Badegasse 14. He no longer thought of himself as Martin. He didn't yet know who he was, but he knew who he was not. This much was complete. Other challenges lay ahead.

For all children who passed through the Children's Village, both resettlement and repatriation required of tracing officers the painstaking task of tracking down facts of a child's existence: Were relatives alive? What nationality was the child? Did any relative want him or her? This research meant navigating a bureaucratic maze that was more inefficient than usual because of the disruption of war and the complexities of peace that involved the four Allied powers and a host of smaller, previously occupied countries attempting to reach agreements about displaced persons. Sometimes the work was relatively easy; most of the time it was not. In Mitka's case, advertisements placed by the IRO in Ukrainian newspapers, soliciting information about Mitka, failed to yield a single response. The same was true of search requests sent to the Red Cross in Moscow.

Authorities repatriated displaced children when possible. Since Mitka could not be repatriated, resettlement was the only choice. As to where he would be sent, Mitka had some say. It was policy to consider "the wishes of the child."

Throughout the last half of 1950, Mitka often heard and sometimes participated in discussions with his peers about which country they would choose. Mostly he remembers Australia, Israel, and America being discussed. He recalls boys bragging, "I'm going to Israel to become a soldier" or "In Australia, I can be a pilot." He took it all in and passed through stages of favoring each one. Finally, he landed on a country. He wanted to immigrate to the United States of America. The reason was simple. "I saw these movies and someone told me they were made in America. That was it. I wanted to go to America, where they made movies." He pauses and laughs at himself and his logic. "What did I know about these things?"

For cases like Mitka's, getting authorization to resettle in the United States was not easy. The United States did, indeed, accept displaced persons from Germany, but approval to immigrate was not automatic. In her book *In the Children's Best Interests: Unaccompanied Children in American-Occupied Germany, 1946–1952*, Lynne Taylor explains factors that would come to influence Mitka's situation.

> Numerous national governments, especially the United States, Canada, Australia, and New Zealand, but others as well, were interested in the displaced persons, but they looked upon them as a potential source of labor for their recovering economies. . . . None were keen to take on displaced persons who could not support themselves.

And

> While a number of governments agreed to allocate a certain number of visas to unaccompanied children, the visas were in the dozens or hundreds at most, and the programs were very carefully constructed to ensure that the children posed as minimal a burden on the state as possible.

The leadership at the Village recognized that, with Mitka, getting approval to immigrate to America might prove challenging. There was little apparent concern about his role in the break-in at the Quaker House. All were convinced that Mitka had simply been an immature follower and that he was exceptionally remorseful about his behavior. There were, however, other aspects of the young boy's life and experience that were worrisome.

As had been the case throughout his time at the Village, teaching Mitka to read and write had proven difficult and represented the biggest challenge to his being granted a visa to relocate to the United States. All who worked with him agreed he possessed the intellect necessary to learn to do what was needed. What stymied his learning was twofold. The Village, despite the heroic efforts of its leadership and staff, could not provide continuous, consistent, and effective instruction. The other barrier was Mitka himself.

For Mitka, being placed with the youngest learners because he was at their level relative to reading would seem to have been a natural choice; in fact, it was a mistake. "They put me with these little kids. . . . They should have known this wouldn't work. . . . I was so ashamed." He never recovered from the setback of this experience.

Mitka attended class, but only in sporadic bursts. Some interruptions were not of his making. Circumstances such as his time at Piusheim and his return visit to Rotenburg, for instance, disrupted his schooling, as did regular changes in teachers. He also, though, became a master of truancy, followed by bouts of remorse, only to return to skipping school. In his own words, "I knew that there were all of these kids getting out of school for religious holidays. So every time a holiday came along, that's what [religion] I was. I was a Catholic, mostly, because they had the most holidays. Mr. Deane [the Village director] caught on and he called me in and he said, 'Kalinski.'" Here Mitka slams the table with his open palm. "'Make up your mind!' So I thought real quickly and I said, 'Catholic.' And that was it. I was Catholic—just like that." Given his history of being called a *Judenfresse*, and his fear of yellow stars, it's not surprising that Mitka avoided identifying with Judaism, something he would do for most of his adult life. For now, being Catholic served a pragmatic purpose—getting out of school. He had a knack, too, for finding excuses other than religion to cut class.

But Mitka was as well equipped to succeed at vocational training as he was poorly equipped to succeed with formal education. All along, he showed a capacity for manual labor. It was, after all, something he knew. Of his time with the Dörrs, he revealed unwitting insight into one of the many paradoxes of his slavery when he told a caseworker that, because the Dörrs had forced him to work hard and well, "they made me a *Mensch*."

On several occasions Mitka asked for chances to work on jobs with which he felt comfortable—namely, farming. For a while, staff at the Village attempted a garden. Older DP workers had found shovels and other farm implements for the teenage gardeners. Mitka was one who participated and enjoyed the work, but overall the effort lost momentum and the garden was abandoned.

More promising was the vocational instruction of the Organization for Rehabilitation through Training (ORT). ORT offered one program to train cobblers. For a boy who had not worn shoes, it turned out to be a poor fit. As Mitka said, "What was this thing with being a cobbler? I didn't understand hammering these little nails into shoes."

Another ORT track, masonry, suited him well. Bricklaying—"that I liked, and I was good at it. I was very good at it." Importantly, he acquired a marketable skill. Success with masonry also had the advantage of imparting confidence to Mitka, an attribute he needed to go forward and that would pay off later in life.

The staff at Bad Aibling recognized Mitka's need for confidence. When he arrived at the camp, he cried often; he got angry at slight provocations; he expressed a disproportionate amount of remorse when he behaved badly; he withdrew when he couldn't handle a situation; he seemed passive, overly shy, and unusually sensitive; and he didn't understand or know appropriate behavior in many social interactions. Having spent his childhood isolated and without caring role models, deprived of schooling and play with children, he simply did not have age-appropriate social skills. Staff remarked about his melancholy longing, upon hearing him often say, "If only I had an older brother."

The Village had been influenced by the work of Anna Freud in Britain and, as a result, was keen to offer psychiatric support to children who needed it. Perhaps the most direct psychological help for Mitka came through appointments with the staff psychiatrist, Dr. Renate Sprengel. These visits, at least, allowed for an assessment of his psychological needs, which helped staff adapt their efforts on his behalf.

Also, Natalie Kent, with her husband, Oakie, made concerted efforts to reach out to Mitka and to include him in a range of "family-like activities." Sometimes his behavior—or, more accurately, misbehavior—derailed their labors. One example of this came when the Village established a kind of token economy. Printed "money" provided Mitka and the other children with the opportunity to buy items at the commissary and to earn privileges.

Mitka remembers, "I usually wasn't able to go on field trips because I didn't earn it." Then his eyes twinkle. "I remember this picnic. I couldn't go because I hadn't earned it. But I figured out a way. You know those military carts with three-quarter cover? Well, I got under the bench on one of those and snuck into a picnic." He laughs with a mixture of smugness and chagrin. "They had just enough food for the kids, so I think I caused some problems by showing up." Softly, he adds, "I had my first marshmallow at that picnic."

Two activities fostered emotional well-being in Mitka. A natural athlete, he found a home on the softball team and received affirmation of his leadership ability by the team's choice of him as their captain in the summer of 1950. Once again, though, it was music that occupied the most prominent role in cultivating his self-assurance and assertiveness, traits he sorely lacked when he arrived at the Village. The staff found him a harmonica, which he taught himself to play, and an accordion. Kathleen Regan noticed he could make his way around the piano fairly well too, but it was the squeezebox, which he played for talent shows and dances, that gave him the most pleasure. From his years in a hayloft in Rotenburg learning military marches, he had developed his musical gift. More than any other activity, playing the accordion brought him joy and enabled him to shine.

Observing Mitka's talent, the staff asked an adult DP worker, Mr. Jakobsen, who had been the leader of a professional, traveling polka band, to evaluate his aptitude for a career in music performance. Mr. Jakobsen was impressed with the boy's talent, so much so that he indicated his willingness to continue to work with Mitka if they happened to be living near one another after both were resettled. Even if that did not occur, he recommended that Mitka continue with the accordion under the belief that he "would gain considerable satisfaction and recognition" from his music.

At Bad Aibling, Mitka also grew physically. On March 3, 1949, soon after he arrived at Hanau, his measured height was five feet, one inch; he weighed 113 pounds. Twenty months later, on November 2, 1950, he was measured again. He had added 30 pounds and at least six inches in height. The five-foot-seven, 143-pound man-child's shoulders had broadened, he held his head high, and he sported thick black hair combed in a style that foreshadowed images of Elvis in the mid-1950s.

Throughout Mitka's final few months in Germany, the Children's Village director, Douglas Deane, social worker Lukie Wijsmuller, AFSC workers Kathleen Regan and Natalie and Oakie Kent, psychiatrist Dr. Renate Sprengel, Dr. Margaret Hasselmann, and team organizer Emmy Lefson had mounted a coordinated effort to prepare Mitka for meeting the standards for resettlement. They did so with little assurance that it would pay off.

These doubts were not without foundation. On September 26, 1950, Theodora Allen, the European representative of the US Committee for the Care of European Children, wrote to Director Deane and Wijsmuller. In the text she commended the reported progress Mitka had made since her interview of him two months prior. Still, she seemed unconvinced that he was a good candidate for immigration to America and wrote her impressions of Mitka:

> At the time I saw him, I thought he was quite a disturbed boy, and, from his behavior, I wondered if it would be possible for an agency in the US to really reach him. I also have questions as to whether he would benefit by a complete change of environment in a country where competitive factors . . . play a greater part and can have either a positive or a detrimental effect on one's social and emotional security. At the time I saw Dimitri, he indicated very pronounced

infantile behavior and great difficulties in relating to strangers, such as myself. His inability to be communicative seemed to be symptomatic of interdisturbance, which might be very difficult to treat at his age.

Those around Mitka already knew these observations of him to be true. What followed in her letter was a series of questions.

> We would be very interested in knowing if Dr. Sprengel is continuing therapeutic interviews with Dimitri. . . . Is Dimitri able to express his feelings and to speak freely about his interests? Does Dr. Sprengel recommend that he have further therapeutic interviews? If so, what does she expect could be accomplished through them? According to the report, Dimitri is showing more interest in school. We would like to know what his present grade placement is and what vocational interests he has. Is he given any definite work responsibilities in the Children's Village? How does he respond to them? How does he respond to his house parents?

Theodora Allen then concluded her letter,

> We are sending Dr. Sprengel's report together with Miss Wijsmuller's social history to our New York Office. Although I have not withdrawn the assurance for which we have nominated Dimitri, it will be necessary for us to get formal approval from the Catholic Committee for Refugees before we can accept him for planning. Do you think it would be possible for a psychometric examination . . . to know more about his native intelligence?

At the bottom of the letter Emmy Lefson appended a handwritten note to Lukie Wijsmuller: "Miss W. Let's discuss this with Dr. Sprengel when she comes. E. S. L."

What conversation occurred within the team is not known, but the letter, from a powerful authority, had gotten their attention. Allen had made her points. It was clear that permission for Mitka's immigration had not yet—and might never be—granted. Further, it seemed that she was identifying certain conditions before he would be "accept[ed] for planning."

Actions and internal memos of the Village leadership suggest a strategy was adopted on Mitka's behalf. The plan that emerged had several elements: evade direct answers to Allen's explicit questions; communicate anything positive in Mitka's development; continue to make best-case arguments for him in broad, enthusiastic generalities; work furiously with realistic expectations to prepare him for resettlement; and hope and pray they could get him over the finishing line.

In his time at the Village, whether Mitka ever mastered "enough" reading and writing to meet a standard of acceptability is doubtful. More likely, the staff fudged—just a bit—his level of literacy. Lefson, for example, writing with the support of Deane, crafted a short memo that reported, "He has had a special tutor . . . [and] we are happy to report that this youth has responded very well and will be ready to be called in for processing in just six weeks." A second memo, again written by Miss Lefson, noted, "His teachers reported that he is not at all dull but definitely able to read and write." In the end, when time was running out and the few remaining children had to be placed, arguments made on Mitka's behalf shifted from literacy to his fundamentally good character, which exceeded his competence in school achievement. These arguments, it seems, worked.

Since four years of age, the orphaned Mitka lived subject to the caprices of others. He endured bombings, forests, near execution, cattle wagons and camps, enslavement and beatings, starvation and cold. Whether by sheer will or by grace, or some combination of the two, he survived it all, choosing life.

During his time at the Children's Village he was called Demitro. One time, when he first arrived, someone called him Mitka. When he tells this story, his back straightens, he grips the edge of the table with his muscular hands, and his voice, insistent and clear, rises: "Not Demitro—I don't know this Demitro. But *MITKA*—that name . . . somehow, I heard it and I just knew."

When he remembered his name at Bad Aibling, when he heard the sound of it and sensed it belonged to him, that it differentiated him as an individual, then he knew he had power to choose. An epiphany occurred. Mitka recognized "I am free!"

There would be more epiphanies. But for now, it was enough that he had selected America and that his choice had been affirmed by those who had the authority to grant him his longed-for beginning. The fantasy he saw so vividly in every American movie might, just might, come true.

Unlike those who had lovingly worked to help Mitka overcome the traumas and setbacks of his childhood, he had no inkling that he was ill equipped to be tossed into a new world on his own. Mitka left Bad Aibling for Munich on Wednesday, January 3, 1951. He believed he was ready.

Having flung Martin and the ignominy of an assigned name on the dirt of Germany, Mitka Kalinski boarded an airplane to fly.

Mitka playing his accordion in 1950 and in 2019

Mitka's first family:
Colonel Kalinski,
Colonel Kalinski's wife,
Lala, Barbara,
and Mitka

Colonel Wladyslaw Kalinski, 1933

Mitka (right) with two friends,
Bad Aibling, c. 1949

Mitka, Bad Aibling, c. 1949

Mitka during a visit to the Dörrs, Rotenburg an der Fulda, 1950

Jakob-Grimm-Schule, Rotenburg an der Fulda, c. 1950

June 16th, 1950

S T A T E M E N T

I, (Miss) Marie-Luise W I J S M U L L E R, Child Care Officer,
(Identity-card No. 0819) being conscious that making a false
statement will involve severe punishment according to the existing
legal provisions

declare in lieu of an oath

that:

According to our I.R.O. registration Demitro K A L I N S K I
was born in B I A L C E V K I E W near Kiew, Russia.

He was placed with a German farmer in 1942, at which time he was
about 10 years old. His exact birthdate is unknown, but is
supposedly 1932. The day on which the boy celebrates his birthday
is 14.December, which was the day on which he arrived at the German
farm.

In view of the above our records all indicate Demitro's birthdate
as 14.December 1932.

Marie Luise Wijsmuller
Child Care Officer

We certify as witnesses the fact mentioned above as true.

Kristina Eliasson   Bette R. Sprung
Child Care Officer   Child Care Officer

IRO HQs, Area 7
MUNICH
Legal Office

The above signatures of Miss Marie-Luise Wijsmuller, Child Care
Officer, and the signatures of the witnesses Miss Kristina Eliasson
Child Care Officer and Miss Bette R.Sprung, Child Care Officer, have
been made in my presence and are certified to be authentic.

Munich, Germany
June 19th 1950
Reg.No. 3578

Area
Legal Officer
Area 7 Munich (S. BRSCHOSOWSKI)
Area Legal Counsellor

Statement from Bad Aibling child-care officer about Mitka's origins, Bad Aibling, 1950

Mitka (right) with his friend Carl Kugler after being fitted for his first suit, the Bronx, 1951

*Mitka and Adrienne
at a dance—
she liked to jitterbug,
he liked to waltz;
North Tonawanda, 1953*

*Mitka and Adrienne listening
to Eartha Kitt, c. 1953*

Mitka with Bill Shane's son, Baltimore, 1952

The Kalinski family—Mitka, Adrienne, Michael, Jimmy, Donna, and Cheryl; Sparks, 1966

Adrienne and Mitka dressed up for Easter Sunday, Sparks, c. 1967

Mitka kissing the Florentine Gold Cadillac before selling it, Sparks, 1970

Mitka and Willi Deist laying a wreath at Pfaffenwald,
November 1984

Mitka, Adrienne, daughter Donna, grandson Michael, and Willi and Martha
Deist at Pfaffenwald; November 1984

Dimitri "Mitka" Kalinski, 53, emigrated from Germany in 1951

Dimitri Kalinski doesn't know his birth date, his nationality or where he was born.

He doesn't even know his real name. But he does know what freedom means.

"I can tell you by the seconds how the freedom began," says Kalinski, nervously folding and unfolding his hands on the kitchen table in his Sparks home.

Liberation began when he was handed tennis shoes, socks, underwear, toothpaste and a toothbrush in a United Nations refugee camp in Germany in 1949.

Freedom became an inalienable right in October 1984 when the Russian child-slave became a naturalized American citizen. "I wanted to be an American citizen so bad," Kalinski says, leaning forward. "I can tell the world what freedom really is. The bottom line there is nothing better than right here."

When 17-year-old Kalinski arrived at the refugee camp, it had been seven years since he owned a pair of shoes. He couldn't remember ever wearing underwear. And he promptly ate the toothpaste, not knowing what else he was supposed to do with it.

As an 8-year-old boy living in the Ukraine near Kiev, Kalinski became separated from his parents during a Nazi air attack. Grabbed by SS officers, he was shoved in a railroad cattle wagon crammed with other prisoners. As people tried to escape, they were machine-gunned down.

"I still see this with my eyes, open or closed. I can still see them lying by the railroad tracks," Kalinski says.

Taken to a concentration camp in Germany, called Pfaffenwald, Kalinski was shoved into line with women, stripped and sprayed with disinfectant. "To this day I'm still in the room with the women all naked," he says, looking down at his hands.

A husky, balding man who looks comfortable in a T-shirt and work pants, Kalinski becomes embarrassed

See KALINSKI, page 3E

Jean Dixon Aikin/Gazette-Journal

TASTE OF FREEDOM: Dimitri Kalinski of Sparks, a child slave of a German Nazi officer for seven years, holds his U.S. citizenship certificate. Pictured with Kalinski are his grandsons Steven, 8, left, and Michael, 11.

Article in the Reno Gazette-Journal *congratulating Mitka on his United States citizenship, Sparks, July 1985* (© *Reno Gazette-Journal* – USA TODAY NETWORK, used with permission)

Adrienne and Mitka with Gustav's widow, Lisa, with a portrait of Gustav on the wall at the Dörr home; Rotenburg an der Fulda, 1984

Mitka and Adrienne at Bodega Bay, 1995

Mitka with Peter, Kasia, and Barbara Holownia; London, 1997

*Mitka at the grave of Colonel Wladyslaw
Kalinski, London, 1997*

Mitka speaks with students at Adobe Middle School; Elko, Nevada, 2017
(Photograph courtesy *Elko Daily Free Press*)

Mitka, Adrienne, and their youngest great-grandchild, Aiden Mitka, in one of their favorite places—Texas Roadhouse; 2020

*"Team Mitka": (from left) Joel Lohr, Bob Lucchesi, Adrienne Kalinski,
Mitka Kalinski, Lynn Beck, and Steve Brallier; Sparks, 2016*

Secrets

CHAPTER TEN

America

The Bronx, February 1951–1952

The airplane sat on the tarmac before Mitka like a shining vision—a dream he would enter when he climbed the stairs into the hollow, winged silver tube. He had seen planes in the sky before; he had even seen one crash. But his only travel, before this day, had been by foot, by trucks, on trains, on horse-drawn wagons, and in a Willys Jeep. Now, for the first time, he was about to board a craft that seemed more magical than real.

Mitka was both excited and afraid. It was a small comfort that he knew others walking in line, including Mama and Papa Bonderowska, two of the house parents from the Children's Village at Bad Aibling. He dared not show fear, he thought, though his chest felt as if it might explode at any second. He came to the top stair and caught a glimpse of the ground below as he stepped through the door. Following others down the aisle, he chose a row and settled into a seat by a small window, not knowing if it was the right thing to do. He tried to get comfortable. The effort was futile.

When Mitka got on that airplane headed to New York City, he had no idea that what was novel to him was novel to most everyone. Transatlantic passenger flights were a relatively new phenomenon in the fast-advancing commercial airline business.

He tells of peering out the window and seeing nothing but darkness, except for one mesmerizing sight: beneath him appeared "a sheet of ice." The endless sweep of white dazzled him.

Mostly, when discussing flying for the first time, Mitka describes his apprehension. Dropping from the sky to land on earth seemed impossible . . . and terrifying. When the airplane descended, Mitka thought his worst fear—crashing—was about to come true. The turbulence seemed to confirm it. He had already experienced turbulence at various times during the flight. About this he says, "I threw up in a bag like everybody around me."

Mitka's fears were not confined to flying in an airplane. The unknown that awaited him loomed in his mind. Flying across the Atlantic to a country Mitka knew only through movies, American GIs, and the Quaker staff at Bad Aibling had been a symbol of leaving his former life behind. But as the landing gear lowered and then touched ground, the symbol became actual.

The boy of fifteen or so who got off the plane that cold January morning possessed unusual physical strength, striking handsomeness, impish humor, and charm. Lacking the one thing he so sorely needed—maturity—Mitka nevertheless believed, in a teenager sort of way, that he could figure the world out to his advantage. Unfazed, he walked off the plane to launch himself into the fray with abandon. For months prior he had imagined, in detail, a mythical America of "cowboys and Indians," John Wayne, and a freedom he'd never known. A wing and a prayer—those prayers of caring Quakers—carried him to his new land.

Had Mitka known that he was one among 160 million people in the United States of America, perhaps his eager, carefree attitude might have been undermined. But, at least for the moment, he was not overwhelmed. He was aware of his challenges but confident he could manage them just as he had at Bad Aibling. He had long forgotten the Ukrainian language, and his Yiddish fluency was diminishing by the day to a few unforgettable and useful phrases. He knew a few American expressions; otherwise he spoke no English. He spoke—if not fluently, at least passably—a Hessian dialect of German that was difficult even for other Germans to understand. It was not helpful that he spoke the language of America's hated enemy. His was not a popular language or accent. Still, that he could not speak English had one benefit. It bought him time to hide one of his greatest vulnerabilities: he could neither read nor write.

Besides Mitka's language difficulties, there was a host of small but significant things unfamiliar to him. Habits and cultural norms that had become unconscious behavior for even non-English speakers of his age were utterly foreign. Early childhood development scholars write of the process of socialization that happens over time. Beginning at birth and thereafter, it occurs quite naturally through relationships with parents, siblings, relatives, playmates, teachers, and interaction with the world around a child. To call Mitka's socialization inadequate hardly gets at the matter.

At Bad Aibling, caretakers and social workers had made every possible attempt, under difficult circumstances, to accelerate Mitka's maturation, but when he left them, they knew he was leaving far less prepared for what he faced than they would have liked. In the almost two years he was at the Children's Village, he did mature, but by the staff's own account he had come under their care and tutelage poorly socialized, rather more like an infant. For two tumultuous years he played catch-up, but his development did not match his age.

Because the only records available placed Mitka's birth on December 14, 1932, his documents said he was eighteen years old, which in itself brought expectations of some maturity denied him by circumstance. But he wasn't going to contradict this assumption. If he was accepted as eighteen, then by Jove, that was that. He not only assumed his assigned age; he embraced it. Quite intuitively, he understood the benefits that accrued to him because he was now eighteen—especially the benefit of answering to himself alone. It was this liberty that propelled him even if he lacked the tools to handle it.

A synagogue in the South Bronx neighborhood of Hunts Point was where Mitka spent his first morning in the United States. He remembers it was on Bryant Street.

Records show that there was in fact a synagogue at 718 Bryant Street, which until 1953 was called the Shield of David. The four-story stucco house had a hall on the first floor for the Orthodox congregation, which at one time had seven hundred members; its other floors consisted of dormitories and dining rooms for the Shield of David Home for Orphan Girls. Today the one time synagogue is a charter school. This particular synagogue was probably where Mitka was taken, though it cannot be confirmed. There were four synagogues on Bryant Street at the time, but one detail he distinctly recalls narrows the search. "From the synagogue you could see the water."

The morning he arrived at the synagogue—by bus, he believes—Mitka recalls going to work. "House work . . . you know . . . kitchen cleanup, peel potatoes, wash the director's car . . . that kind of stuff. I've got a picture of me washing the car." A slight sourness seems to precede his next words but dissolves into acquiescence to what—now with hindsight—seems unfair. "I worked for twelve hours before I got paid. Then it was ten cents an hour."

Earning his own money was, however, a source of pride for Mitka. It was on the streets of the Bronx that he bought his first Clark Bar. "I had some money—maybe about five dollars—and I gave it to the lady. And I guess I thought she'd give me something back, but she kept it! Boy, was I a schmuck—those bars cost about five cents back then, maybe ten. And that one cost me 'bout five dollars, but what did I know." Asked if the Clark Bar was good, he replies with a big smile and a twinkle, "Oh yeah." And then, "I got some back here"—he leaves for his kitchen and returns with an oversize box of Clark Bars. He pulls one out, unwraps it, and grins before biting off a third of the crispy, chocolate-coated confection.

Indifferent to the incidentals of where he slept or ate, he references a dormitory and a dining room at the synagogue. "They fed us, but you had to be there at certain times."

Mitka also mentions services at the synagogue on Shabbat—the seventh day of the Jewish week, a day of rest and abstention from work. At the center of Shabbat are two interrelated commandments: to remember (*zakhor*) and to observe (*shamor*).

Quite understandably, Mitka was trying to forget—not remember—the treatment of Jews that he had witnessed and experienced firsthand. In fact, he was beginning to conceal his past experiences and identity, if only by not volunteering information about himself. He was likely placed in a synagogue because he was Jewish, though he did not acknowledge this fact. In Germany he had learned well the lesson that survival depended on hiding who he was. However subconscious this habit might have been at the time, it would continue, and grow stronger.

In Deuteronomy 5:15 of the Bible, in the midst of Moses's recitation of the Ten Commandments, he exhorts the Israelites to "remember that you were a slave in the land of Egypt and the LORD your God freed you from there with a mighty hand and an outstretched arm; therefore the LORD your God has commanded you to observe the sabbath day." At those Saturday services, in a hall near where he slept, Mitka did not know that Shabbat was, in part, about remembering that his ancestors were brought out of slavery in Egypt and into freedom. Like the Israelites, he, too, had been brought out of bondage. By his own telling, when he heard the voice tell him, "In the end you will find your purpose," it was, for him, a sign of divine intervention in his life. It would be something he remembered, a sign that his days as a slave would not be the end of the story.

Another significant thing happened to Mitka at these Shabbat services that startled him. He heard hymns in Hebrew, hymns that seemed familiar to him. How could he know these songs? The melodies evoked faded pictures in his mind, and he recognized the words too, though he did not know their meaning. It would not be the last time that readings from the Torah and hymns would haunt him. His reaction might best be described as one of longing, but for what he did not know.

Meanwhile, outside the synagogue Mitka was embarking on new experiences around the city. The excitement of discovery in everything he encountered jumps from his face before words tumble from his lips. Field trips he had known at Bad Aibling didn't compare.

"We took a shuttle bus to the Statue of Liberty and to Radio City Music Hall, where we saw a show."

There were, indeed, many field trips that filled his three-or-so-month stay at the synagogue. The YMCA, with its swimming pool, brought back memories of dog-paddling in the Fulda River. Ice-skating at the outdoor Rockefeller Center rink triggered a memory of ice-skating in Rotenburg. "The Dörrs were junk collectors, and they had some of those old ice skates that you needed to connect to your shoes with a key. And I tried those—but keys don't work so great on those wooden shoes."

And then there were movies. American cinema had played a big part in firing Mitka's imagination of America. Now, in America, he discovered that there were movie theaters everywhere. And he could watch films for hours at a time.

Mitka recalls one film that made a special impression on him. Having saved his earnings, he paid twenty-five cents at a theater to see *The Red Shoes*. The 1948 British drama was the story of a ballerina who joined a ballet company and then became the lead in a production of the same name as the movie title. The plot is dramatic, full of passion and love both realized and thwarted. All of this, for Mitka, was of little interest. With this film, as with so many others, he heard music.

For Mitka, hearing music was always a gateway to learning—how to play it, how to dance to it. By listening to German soldiers marching in time with the thumping cadence of military tunes, he taught himself to play an accordion. And by observing dances at the synagogue hall, he "learned how to dance just like that . . . tango . . . waltz. I learned it from my mind. I could see it in a movie and learn it. I play the music in my mind; then I can do it."

Dancing hit all the right notes for Mitka. He could move to the beat in sync with his partner, and he could hold a girl close. This is the first time in telling his story that he gives expression to an unsurprising fact: his wide-awake libido. He describes another incident in which a picture had been taken of him and another young man sitting on a park bench. Each had his arm around a girl.

Other adventures awaited in New York's subway system. Unable to read, Mitka nevertheless made his way down the stairs—"Have you seen the stairs that go down under the city?" He managed to get on the first train to come to the platform. Early in the ride "I started to count every stop we came to. I thought that was how I would get back to where I started." He got off at the seventh stop, wandered a bit, and then boarded another train.

"One, two, three—I counted all the way to seven, but it seemed to be a longer distance between stops. I got to the end and I was only to five." Mitka pops his thighs with his hands and starts laughing. "I didn't know what an express train was!"

There was another time he had gone to a movie and then to a bar—an upstairs bar where there was dancing.

"And I met these guys. And I guess I was trying to seem like a big shot. And they said something to me. I'm not sure what—something about how they could make me a pilot. And dumb me—I got into a car with those guys. I was in the back seat. And we drove across the bridge and came to this dark spot where there was no one around. And when we got out"—Mitka runs one hand against the other with a quick upward brush—"I took off. And I bet I could have won the Olympics that day, I ran so fast. As I was running, I heard one of the guys say something like, 'Hey, why did you let him get away?'

"Finally, I saw a police station, and I ran to it. But I couldn't speak English, and the police couldn't speak German, so I couldn't really tell them anything. I had to spend the night at the police station. The next day, a policeman came who spoke German. And he said, 'Where are you living?,' but I couldn't tell him where because I didn't exactly know the place."

An idea popped into Mitka's head. "I remembered that I had been to the movies and I had a ticket stub in my pocket. So I showed the stub to the policeman. And he said, 'If I get you back there, can you get home?' And I said, 'Sure.'

"So they took me to the movie theater, and I went back to the synagogue. I got into trouble for that."

Pleased with himself, Mitka adds, "Once again, the movies saved my life."

Hunts Point is on the southern tip of the Bronx, a place from which Mitka, as he says, "could see the water." Then he casually drops that "one time I walked from Hunts Point to Yankee Stadium. And I heard a big cheer. They might have scored or something. I didn't know, but there was a big cheer."

He knew nothing of "America's sport." When asked if he ever went to a game, he replies, "No. What did I know of American baseball?" Like Mitka, baseball was on the verge of a significant year. It was Mickey Mantle's first season with the Yankees. Willie Mays began his Major League career in 1951. The Yankees would go on to beat the Giants in the World Series in what would be Joe DiMaggio's final game.

In an aside, Mitka offers his opinion of another peculiarly American sport. His hands form the shape of a football. The look in his eyes tells us that a punch line is coming: "And this football thing. I know *Fussball* back in Germany, but I never seen such a thing as this crazy, egg-shaped ball. I don't know how you Americans won the war!"

Being fitted for his very own suit was a signature moment for the handsome young man. Well dressed in a smart style confirmed in him a growing confidence, a sense that he could pull off being an American. "I looked pretty good," he says playfully. "Can you believe it?"

When Mitka arrived in New York City in January of 1951, the nation's mood was upbeat and positive. Even though the United States had joined the Korean War on June 27, 1950, the end of the Second World War had infused the country with optimism. The Baby Boom had begun in 1946. The GI Bill was passed into law, which sent an entire generation of young men to college. Young families were being established, houses were being purchased in suburbs, and the country's economy was growing. It was this America that influenced a narrative of the 1950s as a happy decade.

A darker theme runs through the story, however. Schools remained segregated, Jim Crow laws stood throughout the South, and African Americans' civil rights were virtually nonexistent. Americans feared a nuclear attack; communists within the country were viewed as a threat; and the Cold War dominated foreign policy. A cease-fire in the Korean War was signed in November 1953, but at the cost of 33,651 battle deaths and 3,262 other deaths.

Other events shaped the era. In 1951, the United Nations Headquarters opened in New York City. Israel's Knesset designated April 13 as Holocaust Day. Four months before, the "bitch of Buchenwald," Ilse Koch, was sentenced to life in prison. On October 6, Joseph Stalin told the world that the Soviet Union had atomic bombs. By the end of the year, the Draft Eisenhower movement was building momentum, pressuring future president Dwight D. Eisenhower to declare his party affiliation and run for office.

Television was the new technology that brought the *Arthur Godfrey and His Friends* variety show and the soap opera *Search for Tomorrow* into Americans' living rooms. But it was Lucille Ball who captivated the nation in the sitcom *I Love Lucy* when the show aired October 15, 1951. Mitka knew little of this, though. For him, radio was enough because it connected him to music. In 1951 Mitka, along with most of America, was listening and dancing to Nat King Cole, Debbie Reynolds, Bing Crosby, Tony Bennett, Doris Day, Mario Lanza, Patti Page, Louis

Armstrong, Rosemary Clooney, Frankie Lane, Perry Como, and Dinah Shore. For the most part, these were "'feel-good' tunes, which genuinely reflected the mood of post–World War II America."

The mood of the nation was, indeed, optimistic and, at times, high-spirited. In this, it matched Mitka's state of mind. After three or so months in the Bronx, he was feeling his oats and off to his next stop.

CHAPTER ELEVEN

Tim

Baltimore, 1952–1953

The move from New York to Baltimore was an uneventful one for Mitka. He was sent to a Catholic Charities home because, he believes, "the synagogue was pretty crowded, so I guess they reached out for help and they put me on a bus to Baltimore." Again, there was a new bed to sleep in and new acquaintances to make, but the upheaval didn't have an unsettling effect on Mitka. Within himself, he had located an optimistic elasticity to adapt to each new situation as more welcomed adventure. It can be felt when he recounts, "In Baltimore, at Mount Royal, I reconnected with Wasyl. I had not seen him since Bad Aibling."

Jim Libertini, the director of the Catholic Charities facility that took in displaced children and teens, holds a revered place in Mitka's memory. According to Mitka, Mr. Libertini was just the kind of father figure he needed at the time. One of the myriad tasks the older man took on was to usher his "children" into their new world by finding them a job as quickly as he could. "Mr. Libertini was the director who helped me get work. That was his job. He took me to a government office where I got my social security card."

Mitka's first job was doing "pick and shovel" work at Memorial Park on East Thirty-Third Street. As he tells it, "I hit my finger with a hammer and I learned to say words you don't want to hear." When his short time on the baseball field didn't work out, his next job was working at a butcher shop. "I was the cleanup guy—night work. I didn't like night work."

Job assignments weren't lasting long for young Mitka. He flashes a sheepish grin. After some evasion, more out of affable embarrassment than anything mendacious, he proffers an answer for why this was so. He simply did not understand basic requirements of work, such as showing up the next day. As Mitka tells it, "I would get paid, and then . . ."—he rubs his hands together as if in anticipation—"I was off to the movies."

Work rules that were implicit to most, Mitka hadn't been taught. The idea that he was an employee with a boss and the expectations that came with a job didn't yet fully register with him, and sometimes his growing freedom was just too tempting. He did, over time, learn that his newfound freedom had boundaries. Trial and error, and especially Mr. Libertini, became his on-the-fly teachers.

To get to his next job, Mitka took the bus from the Catholic Charities home, across town, to the west side of Baltimore. With, again, Mr. Libertini's help, a Venetian blind manufacturer on Eastern Avenue gave him work. "You want to know anything about Venetian blinds, I'm your man."

By now Mitka was starting to pick up on the rituals and norms of being an employee. On his first day, "I learned about smoke break. Everyone disappeared for break. The next day I showed up with cigarettes rolled in my sleeve." When he speaks of smoking he says, "I never inhaled. When I was at Bad Aibling, everybody smoked—Pall Mall, Chesterfield, Old Gold, Lucky Strike. It gave me a headache. But I wanted to be American, so I carried smokes around like the others." Mitka ditched this job too. "What did I know? I would earn some money and then just walk away."

At about this time, Mr. Libertini laid down the law. Mitka, in a stern voice, repeats the director's rebuke: "This is the last time I line up a job for you. I'll put the fear of God in you. You can't leave another job."

Mitka got the message. He slaps the table for emphasis. "He kind of put the fear of the devil *and* God in me. And that was it. I learned."

When Crown Cork and Seal Company (founded by William Painter, the Baltimore-based inventor of the bottle cap) hired Mitka, it was Jim Libertini's last shot at turning around his young, unruly charge.

"And there I met Bill Shane. He was my boss. He had a boss over him, but he was my boss." A conversation ensued.

"And he said to me 'What is your name?'"

"Demitri Kalinski."

"Shit, I can't call you that. I know somebody that looks like you. His name is Tim. Do you mind if I call you Tim?"

"OK," said Mitka.

He reflects back on that singular moment. "And that was it. It kind of put a cap on my life. No more people calling me Hymie, Commie, or Nazi. I had an American name. I was Tim."

More than anything else up to that point in Mitka's new life, his boss's words gave him a chance he intuitively understood: in America, he could reinvent himself. In an instant, when he heard, "Do you mind if I call you Tim?," he grabbed onto an identity. This very American name—Tim—erased his past. He had crossed a threshold into his future. Henceforth he would not just be known as Tim. He would actually become Tim, or so he thought at that moment.

Forgetting his past didn't happen all at once for Mitka. In one way, he couldn't speak of his past because he lacked the vocabulary to do so. But that doesn't get at the core of it. In part, he felt a percolating desire to become fully American. He was—like the nation in which he found himself—alive with all the courage and optimism of an adventurer conquering new territory with each step forward. But he was sensitive too, possessed as he was with antennae to sense any subtle shifts of approval. He quite naturally dissociated himself from the taunts of having a foreign accent and name. Tim would do nicely. No one could fault him for what they didn't know. It was time to move on, and no prodding was needed. No one asked; he didn't tell. America was before him. There were girls to dance with, movies to see, and adventures to be had. It was a genesis for "Tim"—a time of secrets to hide and a new self to hold.

Mitka continues to describe his life in Baltimore. "Bill asked me where I lived, and I said, 'Highland Street.' He said, 'There's this lady named Mrs. McGovern, and she has a room. Why don't you go talk to her?' And I did, and I lived right around the corner from Bill and Rose Shane," who lived at 2815 East Monument Street. Close by were Bill's mother and stepfather, Harry.

Mitka starts to laugh. "And so I moved to Mrs. McGovern's on *Stripper* Street." There is a Stricker Street in Baltimore, but for the non-English-speaking boy, Stripper was the name that stuck.

At Mrs. McGovern's rooming house, Mitka got meals and a sparsely furnished bedroom. What he really liked was having a separate entrance to his room at the top of a flight of stairs. He could come and go as he pleased, and the food was homemade, unlike the bland institutional food to which he'd become accustomed.

Tim Kalinski had a new job making bottle caps, a boss who took an interest in him, and a new room of his own.

"At Crown Cork, I went into work at four and worked till midnight. I kind of liked that because before I went into work, I could go to the movies."

Mitka worked at a station next to Bill, where he operated a machine that stamped the cork into bottle caps. Working the swing shift had advantages. "When I got off at twelve, sometimes I'd walk home, but sometimes I'd go with Bill and Rose Shane—she worked at Crown Cork too—to a bar. And we'd have a beer and some crab on a cracker. Have you ever had that? We'd put some crab between crackers." Other times when he got off work, "I go to the movies. There were all these movie theaters on Eastern Avenue, and I walked down that street to go to work. And it didn't matter if I'd seen the movie yesterday. I saw it again. I tell you, I could tell you the whole movie from beginning to end . . . the whole thing. Movies were a quarter back then—all day, a quarter. Ten dollars gets a lot of movies."

Of the movies that Mitka saw during his time in Baltimore, several stand out, but none more so than *The Quiet Man* starring John Wayne and Maureen O'Hara. The story of a retired American boxer returning to the Irish village of his birth and finding love resonated with Mitka like no other. The John Ford–directed film had all the elements of a great story—romance, tragedy, fighting, death, and humor—but for Mitka, something more was going on besides mere entertainment, though that, too, was a piece of it. When John Wayne comes up, Mitka admits a reverence for the actor, but the film's impact on him goes beyond his being a fan. He can't explain it, nor does he try. Yet when he speaks of it, he reveals a visceral bond with the story and with John Wayne. Listening beyond Mitka's words, a sense comes through that John Wayne gave him an identity he could grab on to, imitate, and use to succeed.

There were other films Mitka saw in Baltimore, and, like *The Quiet Man,* he saw each one innumerable times. *Samson and Delilah*, directed by Cecil B. DeMille with Hedy Lamarr, Victor Mature, and Angela Lansbury, was a favorite, as were *Showboat, Lullaby of Broadway, Stagecoach, Tarzan the Ape Man,* and *The Fighting Sullivans. Scaramouche* with Stewart Granger and Janet Leigh also rates highly with Mitka, as do any Errol Flynn films, like *Kym, Adventures of Don Juan,* and *The Adventures of Robin Hood.* By seeing movies, especially listening to spoken English, he began to mimic the actors, repeating to himself lines he heard. He dreamed of the day when he could be free of his leaden eastern European accent.

Many lessons about life Mitka attributes to Bill Shane. It was Bill who took him to get his draft card. "I took the physical. My draft card was 1-A [Eligible for Military Service]. How I passed the test I'll never know. I got a call or something from the Selective Service. And I went down and took a physical for the army. And there was this guy there with paper, and I took a test. And there were 120 questions. You had to get 50 percent of them. And I got 69 right."

Mitka laughs. "Can you believe that? Here I can't speak English. I can't read and write, and I pass the damn test." He continues, "And I got a card, and it said I was 1-A."

When asked why he wasn't called up to serve, he says, "How in the heck did that happen? I don't know. You'd have to ask those yahoos who were running Washington at the time."

Another act of kindness by Bill stood out for Mitka.

"Bill—he did me a big favor. He held my money and he helped me learn about money. After a while, he took me to the Western Auto Store on Eastern Avenue. And I wanted a radio, so he helped me set up a credit line to buy a Zenith clock radio. I didn't know what this credit was, but Bill helped me get it. And oh, that clock radio was beautiful. It had all these knobs. And when I would come home from work, I would put it on. The songs were beautiful then. Johnny Ray and Nat King Cole and Patti Page and Mario Lanza. And the radio was set to turn off when I went to sleep."

For its time, the radio Mitka bought was a technological marvel. "You could plug a coffee pot in the back—the timer on the clock turns the coffee and the music on." Though he never used the coffee pot plug-in, the pride of owning such a high-tech product shows on his face. "I could go up to my room and listen to my favorite station. I still have that Zenith radio."

Mitka starts humming "Walkin' My Baby Back Home," which became a hit for Nat King Cole in 1951 and then again for Johnny Ray in 1952. He likes both versions, but Johnny Ray's is his favorite. He talks of "Because of You" by Tony Bennett and "Too Young" by Nat King Cole. He mentions other singers he loved. "Howard Keele, Kathleen Grayson . . ." He continues, "It gave me strength when I heard music."

On days off, Mitka's time was his own. With Bill Shane overseeing his money, he found that there was plenty enough folding money in his pocket for movies and dancing and meals at the White Coffee Pot. In those days, if he was not eating Mrs. McGovern's or Rose Shane's cooking, he could be found at the White Coffee Pot or any of several food stands on the streets.

On his first halting visit to a vendor in the Bronx, he looked at all the choices and had no idea what to do; his inability to read was a problem. The food truck did, however, have Clark Bars. He pointed to a Clark Bar, and to pictures of a hot dog and a 7UP. Problem solved. Thereafter, whenever he went to a street merchant, his order was the same: a hot dog, a 7UP, and a Clark Bar.

He confronted the same barrier at the White Coffee Pot. With the help of a friendly waitress, he managed to land on a meal that, again, became his go-to order. While he ate, he listened to "I Went to Your Wedding" or "The Tennessee Waltz" by Patti Page on the jukebox at his booth.

Pretending to know what he didn't, Mitka risked getting caught in his fakery, but it had a salutary effect too. In his bravado to be an American, with each new foray into the unknown, he learned.

There were other ways to enjoy his time. "There was this boat, and it would go out once a week on Saturday—and there was music and dancing. And so I would walk down there and go out and dance. Broadway and Eastern Avenue intersect. I turned left on Broadway and went to the water. Whenever I hear the song 'Shrimp boats is a-coming . . . *dah*, dah, dah, *dah*, dah, dah." He hums the tune. "That song was a waltz tune. Whenever I think of it, I think of that boat and dancing."

He says this with feet and arms moving in perfect sync with the music. A self-knowing smile comes over his face, his eyes now spry in answer to each beat. Dancing was one thing he didn't have to fake, nor did it require a word of English.

"I would stay for about three hours, and then I would walk back and get a hamburger from someone on the street. That's how I ate back then. I would go to those people on the street and get a hamburger or a hot dog and 7UP . . . oh, and a Clark Bar.

"I was in love with the world in those years."

CHAPTER TWELVE

Adrienne

North Tonawanda, 1953

Mitka had boarded an airplane to America on Friday, January 5, 1951. Now, almost two years later, he was, in a sense, still flying. From his perspective, every day was an adventure. Unexplored frontiers beckoned him. Eager and intrepid, he was like a child who doesn't recognize or accept boundaries.

Learning a new language, navigating social situations, becoming responsible at work, understanding money, exploring romance, and encountering countless everyday obstacles brought failures, but none were disqualifying. Like a traveler, Mitka kept moving forward—though not with a particular destination in mind.

That Mitka was blessed with a cheerful, optimistic disposition probably encouraged those he encountered to want to help him find his way. At times, he displayed a devious streak, but it was more impish than troubling. When he acted inappropriately and suffered consequences, he responded well. He did not rebel or defy correction. Rather, he was eager to learn proper behavior.

It was his indeterminacy that put him on tenterhooks. He had no idea of who he was or of what the future held. He relied on measuring himself against the behavior of those closest to him to navigate his course. All the while, he was making it up as he went. Importantly, Tim was who he was becoming. Mitka was hidden deep within him. Tim was public; Mitka was secret. Managing his identity was a high-wire act, a precarious show that required balance.

Usually Mitka managed to present himself with confidence. He was an immigrant, to be sure, but one who was adjusting well to life in his adopted home. One incident, however, triggered him, sending him reeling back to his time as a slave.

While riding a bus one day he looked up to a banner advertisement just above the handrail. He couldn't read the text, but what he saw was a skull and crossbones, the universal symbol used to suggest caution, as when handling poison. When the image appeared before him, he was instantly reminded of his death-laced past. His newfound confidence dissolved. The bus suddenly felt claustrophobic. At the next stop, he bolted. Later, he said of the experience, "I felt like Germany was coming after me."

Mitka would continue to experience sporadic triggers. Nevertheless, he had a few relationships that anchored him. Bill and Rose Shane were especially important to him. An encounter with another immigrant also proved significant.

One day, buying a hamburger from a street vendor, "I met Joe Katzenberger and he had a car—a '47 Chevy. So we used to go around together to bars and dances."

For Mitka, who relied on buses and walking to get around Baltimore, the appeal of a friend with a car is easy to understand. "I didn't drive cars then. I watched Mr. Libertini drive, and I knew there were these two pedals on the floor, but I didn't drive."

Mitka, too, had something of value to offer his new friend. "Joe didn't have a job, so I talked to Bill Shane, and he got Joe on at Crown Cork. So it was Bill Shane and me and Joe—all there at Crown Cork."

Reminiscing about their time together, especially the after-work adventures, he continues, "And Joe and me were underage. And we would go places and I would always get in, but they'd always stop Joe. He had a look or something. And I'd be waiting inside.

"I learned that from the movies. I became . . . what do you call them . . . a quick—no, a fast—talker. I kind of charmed them, and before you know it, I'm in." Mitka claps his hands together. A satisfied look washes over his face.

The bond between Mitka and Joe developed quickly through the shared experiences of two young men without a care in the world. They had jobs, some money, movies to see, girls to dance with, and beer to drink. Mitka had found a pal in Joe and a friendship unlike any he'd known before. Life was good.

When he speaks of his youthful longing for a family, Mitka often says, "If only I had had a brother." In many ways Mitka's friendship with Joe gave him, at least for a while, the brother he longed for. It met a real need that he felt—a need for male companionship, for someone to learn from, for a buddy with whom he could take on the adventures before him. Other friendships he'd made, particularly at Bad Aibling, hadn't clicked like the camaraderie he had with Joe.

Mitka thinks aloud about those times and about what they meant to him. "Joe's family was from Czechoslovakia or Ukraine. I got to know all of them.

"They were the ones," speaking of Joe's family, "who decided to move to North Tonawanda. And Joe came to me and said, 'Hey, Tim, why don't you go with us?'

"I had never heard of North Tonawanda. And we had been to this movie, *Niagara* with Marilyn Monroe. And Joe said, 'You remember that movie, *Niagara*? Well, this is close to that place.'"

What attracted Mitka to North Tonawanda was a geographical fact: the town was approximately twelve miles east of Niagara Falls. For his love of movies and Hollywood stars, it would seem natural that Mitka would be excited to move to the location where the sexy Monroe shot *Niagara*. Closer to the truth, it was the power and wonder of the falls that held him in a spell. He wanted to see the falls.

"I loved those falls. It was them—more than Marilyn. So I said, 'Sure.' But I had to get permission to go. So I went to Catholic Charities and I asked for permission to move to New York, and they said yes and gave me a blessing."

Joe had also made the argument that jobs were plentiful there, which was true. North Tonawanda, situated as it was by commerce-laden waterways, was home to thriving manufacturing plants.

Over leaving his friends Bill and Rose Shane, Mitka confesses he felt guilt but was confident that, if he could explain his decision, Bill would understand. "And he did," Mitka adds. "Bill was a good man."

Sometime in late 1952, Mitka was again on the move.

After the drive from Baltimore to North Tonawanda, a distance of about four hundred miles, the Katzenbergers, with tagalong Mitka, settled into the upstairs of a large house. It didn't take long for Mitka to get sideways with the landlord, who lived downstairs.

"The landlord—he was drinking and he used some foul language. And I didn't like that much. And I said, 'Shut your clap up,' or something like that. I was a strong one in those years. And he didn't like that. And he went in and got a shotgun. And the word he used to the Katzenbergers was either I go or they have to move out. And I was gone."

At this point, Mitka had moved so often that it was hardly disruptive—in fact, it was a rather humdrum occurrence.

"So that's when I found a house on Ironton Street. There was this old man there named Joe Cross. And it was a pretty good place for me. He was living by himself and I had a room, but basically, I more or less had the whole house. He would let me get into the fridge and eat his food and everything. He was a good man."

In Mitka's first two years in America he had begun to speak English, albeit broken and heavily accented. As from the beginning, his principal teacher was movies, which he saw over and over again. Bill Shane, Joe Katzenberger, and their families—and everyday life—also taught him. About this process, he says, "I was holding back a lot because I didn't want to sound like a DP—you know what that is, a displaced person. I wouldn't say a word until I could pronounce it. I wanted to be an American. Oh how I wanted to be an American."

Mitka's first job in North Tonawanda was working the night shift at Durez Plastics. "I believe that this was the first plastic in the United States. You know that Zenith clock radio I had? They made the plastics in that place. I'm sure of it."

At Mitka's station in the factory, molten plastic was delivered in a large bin. "There is a resin liquid, like syrup—and they dump syrup on the ground, and it hardens, and you take a sledgehammer and smash it. That's my job. And you put the broken-up parts in a barrel and put it on a conveyor belt and take it down somewhere." The plastic that was taken "down somewhere" was then shredded, melted again, and injected into molds for various products.

"And Joe Katzenberger got a job there, and he ended up staying there thirty years. But it was not healthy. Something there gave him trouble with his lungs. We didn't know those things in those days, but I'm glad I got out of there."

Mitka was fired from Durez Plastics, though he's not quite sure why.

"Three things could have got me fired. I guess you could say 'fired'— not because I was not a good worker.

"One thing was, we could sleep on the job. Twelve midnight to eight in the morning—you could sleep some of the time, but you could not hide.

"And I slept on barrels and stuff. And one time I was asleep and a foreman woke me up and I kicked him right here." Mitka gestures with his fist to a place under his chin. "I kicked him. I did not mean it. I didn't know what I was doing. He just woke me up."

As to the second reason, Mitka explains, "I must have been a lover boy without realizing it." He smiles. "I was going with a secretary there at Durez. Her name was Susan Kraft, and she lived on Colvin Avenue in Buffalo."

He speculates about the third possibility. "When I got the job I didn't know no union. So I was doing this stuff with the sledgehammer, and there was another opening in another place in the building. According to the union, you stand in line to get the job. But me, I was such a hard worker and all that I got the job in that other place. The union didn't like it.

"And now—either me kicking the foreman in the chin or the girl or the union and that other job—they got me out of there.

"But I really believe that it was the union . . . because I was a good worker. No matter where I work, I was always loyal to the job."

Mitka's telling on himself for things he did when he was younger without knowing better is a character trait that manifests in conversation over and over. This unstudied innocence usually comes across with a large dose of laughter. The naiveté of his choices elicits some embarrassment in him, which he deflects in droll, self-deprecating ways.

So much of what Mitka was experiencing was for the first time. Misapprehension led to mistakes; mistakes led to consequences. Usually the outcome brought about nothing more than funny stories. Other than dealing with his illiteracy, self-doubt was not an issue. Mitka learned with each new experience and pressed on with a boyish zeal over his good fortune.

"What did I have at the Dörrs'? Nothing," Mitka says. "And here I was in America."

The day after he left Durez, he, again, set out to find a new job. At the time, jobs were plentiful, especially for unskilled, general labor. But reading and completing an application stood in his way.

Unable to read or write, Mitka reflects on how he was able to fill out a form in an especially memorable incident. It's evident he appreciated the irony of his solution.

He says, "I had a form to fill out, and I looked around and saw a swastika on the porch rail of a house nearby. And I just walked up to the door and knocked. And I talked in German and explained that I couldn't write in English. So . . . Nazis helped me fill out the application. Nazis helped me get a job. Can you believe it?"

Once again, Mitka's ingenuity won the day. "And the job I got was at American District Steam Company. That's why they called it ADSCO."

Mitka can't hide his excitement as he reminisces, "And these were good times for me. These were happy times."

The job at ADSCO began for Mitka in a way that typifies his life in America. He arrived for his first shift, "and my job was driving a forklift. So the guy asked me if I could drive a forklift. And I said, 'Sure.'"

Mitka's confidence was unfounded, but that wasn't about to stop him. "I didn't know nothing about no forklift, but I knew I could figure it out. First I had to figure out how to turn it on. Have you ever seen one of those things? You look around and there is no place to put the key in . . . but finally I figured out how to turn it on here—down on the side." He motions to a place just below his chair seat, as if he's sitting on the forklift.

"So I got on," he says as he mimics the purr of a motor, "and I was carrying these big rings on the forklift, and I was driving along, and then I was coming to a wall. How the heck was I supposed to stop?" Mitka makes a screeching sound.

"All of a sudden, all the rings bounced off. *Ping, ping, ping!* How the heck I didn't lose my job that day, I don't know. But I didn't. And we got the rings back on, and I figured out how to stop the damn forklift," he says with a boyish smile.

Mitka survived the debacle of his first day. He kept showing up on time and worked hard. One day followed another, and gradually, he settled into a measured rhythm of labor.

Outside work, Mitka continued as he had in Baltimore. He and Joe went to bars to dance and drink beer. He learned how to get around by bus and by walking. He frequented certain places to eat or listen to music. Habits and rituals gave him comfort.

For instance, he says, "I started going to the Cozy Corner, and it was on the corner of First and Oliver Street. There was a lady there named June. She was the owner. She knew what I wanted, so I didn't have to order." And Mitka arranged an additional service with June. "She packed a lunch for me when I went to ADSCO"—every day. "What a nice lady."

The most significant event for Mitka during this time didn't seem significant at the time. It was something so natural to a young man of his age as to be unremarkable, yet it would change the trajectory of his life.

"I seen this girl walking to work. And one day I was driving the forklift, and I looked up, and there she was in the window of this office up above the factory floor." Mitka extends his right leg in a braking motion accentuated by the screech of a sudden stop. "I backed up, and I kept driving back and forth, back and forth." He watched the alluring woman, and with her every step, his imagination of him and her together ballooned. Mitka was smitten.

By his own telling, he was experiencing passion of a piece with being a young man. Beginning in Bad Aibling, movies showed Mitka a picture of romance between a man and a woman. He took this in and began thinking of himself through the examples of John Wayne and Stewart Granger. "I learned that you have to be strong but gentle too."

When he left Germany as a five-foot, seven-inch boy, his eagerness didn't mask how awkward, unsure, and timid he was. Now he filled a six-foot, one-inch frame and was up to about 170 pounds. A shock of black hair accentuated his chiseled jaw and blue eyes.

From his first days in the Bronx and subsequently in Baltimore, the magnetic pull of female companionship held him in thrall. The idea of having a girlfriend was never far from his mind. It didn't hurt that many young women responded to his tentative advances enthusiastically. Confidence grew in him—the young man with the unusual accent, muscular physique, and handsome features. Certainly, some alchemy of popular music, movies, dancing, hormones, and longing was at work in him. And not just romantic longing. Mitka yearned to belong.

Each ensuing day, as Mitka drove the forklift, he made sure he looked for the woman on the office floor whom he so longed to meet. He only knew that she, too, worked at ADSCO. Over time—a short period that felt much longer than it was—"I sort of got up my nerve, and I asked her if I could walk her home."

His courage was rewarded. He wasn't rejected. A conversation began as they walked. "She asks me what I do, and I tell her I drive a forklift. And then—don't ask me why I say this—I tell her that I make $150 a week. I was trying to be a big man."

He continues, "I ask her what she does, and she says, 'I work in payroll.' I say, 'What does that mean?'"

Mitka voice drops to a whisper. "And she says, 'I put the money in the envelopes every week.'"

His eyes twinkle, his head falls back, and he guffaws, "So she caught me."

In today's dollars, $150 per week is equivalent to $1,400. Mitka's actual pay was closer to $10 per week—or, in today's dollars, $93.

The petite, comely woman's name was Adrienne. As she hears the story—one she remembers well—Adrienne looks directly at Mitka and speaks her mind like a New Yorker with a glint of affection in her eyes. "He was always trying to be a big shot."

Adrienne, no innocent about human nature, recognized harmless braggadocio from the start. She wasn't put off. It was love at first fib.

Mitka jumps back into the conversation, which is like a Ping-Pong game of volleyed commentary. "So we sort of started going together then."

Adrienne Harder was born Sunday, June 16, 1929. Her mother died nine days later.

Her birth occurred at the cusp of a new era in America. In the preceding decade the country was emerging from the First World War. Its mood was upbeat; its citizens, prosperous. In 1920 the Nineteenth Amendment had become law, giving women the right to vote. The Jazz Age of Duke Ellington and Louis Armstrong brought a relaxation of sexual mores and the rise of flappers. Consumerism rose, and the Ford Model T, accessible to ordinary citizens for $250, changed everyday life. Symbolized by gangster Al Capone's notorious flouting of the prohibition of alcohol, organized crime thrived. Also, arts flowered during the twenties in myriad ways. The Harlem Renaissance and authors Sinclair Lewis and F. Scott Fitzgerald, among others, characterized the times. In stark contrast, the decade that followed Adrienne's birth started with the stock market crash on October 29, 1929, which ushered in the Great Depression.

With her mother's death, Adrienne's first years began not only in economic crisis but in familial difficulty. She recounts that her father was not a good man. In her words, "He wasn't suited to be a parent."

Recognizing that she needed to be rescued, Adrienne's extended family took her out of her father's care without objection from him. Thereafter, her father's aunt and uncle raised Adrienne as one of their own. Quite naturally, she called Matilda and Louie Cook "Mom" and "Dad." They had two daughters: Verna and Hilda. Adrienne fondly speaks of them as "my sisters" and says, "My sister Hilda was there. Her mom and dad raised me. She and I were very close. She's ten years older than me."

The neighborhood in which Adrienne lived was typical of northeastern cities of the time. Italian, Irish, and German immigrants clustered together in adjoining blocks. Catholics, Lutherans, and Jews could be found bunched together too. Family life was supported by structures of ethnicity and faith.

Everyone knew the dividing lines between ethnic groups, but in Adrienne's memories, they rarely interfered with children playing together. Ethnicity created something akin to cultural communes, but it was not, it seems, a source of tension. Adrienne also recalls roaming neighborhoods freely without fear.

Extended families tended to live in close proximity and leaned on each other. Though Adrienne did not live with her father, he was nevertheless someone she knew and interacted with throughout her childhood.

Like Mitka in some ways, Adrienne grew up without a mother and, in most regards, without a father. Yet she seems absent of bitterness, accepting of the facts, and grateful for family that stepped into the breach.

Bookended by the onset of the Great Depression at one end and the end of World War II at the other, Adrienne's childhood years were happy ones, surrounded by an extended, loving family. Like others raised during the thirties, she learned lessons of frugality, stoicism, and pragmatism, which would become an integral part of her identity.

After Adrienne graduated from North Tonawanda High School in 1947, she went into a nurses' training program. It didn't last long. "I didn't like nurses' training," she says, "so I dropped out after nine months." Blunt and to the point, she says, "I wanted to go to work." She had decided a career in business and secretarial work was for her.

Two of Adrienne's extended family members, Aunt Nell and Uncle Harry, lived in a home at 47 Chipman Place in North Tonawanda. Often she would visit to check on them. Both were ill. Nell died December 27, 1947, of cancer, so quite naturally, eighteen-year-old Adrienne moved in with Uncle Harry to care for him.

Sometime in early 1948, two neighbors, Ward Wooster and Henry Jago, helped Adrienne get a job working in the payroll department of ADSCO. She liked her work. Life was good, for the most part. She played on a bowling team, regularly went dancing, dated several suitors, and had many friends. Like most teenagers at the time, she smoked.

In 1953, when Mitka showed up, clearly taken with Adrienne, the family was not pleased. He wasn't what they had in mind for their Adrienne. "Her family never liked me. She was living with her Uncle Harry, and he never liked me. But I didn't give a damn if they liked me."

It turns out, Adrienne didn't give a damn either.

In their first encounter, Adrienne had busted Mitka, or "Tim."

In being found out, he experienced the vulnerability of being known yet not rejected. Adrienne had seen through his pretension and accepted him for who he was. Tim—the strong, tall man who barely spoke English—had found safety with Adrienne. In an instant, his love was anchored.

There were things, though, that were still unanchored for the young man.

"My mind was on so many different tracks. I had a lot of tracks of mind. How was I going to become a citizen? And I always thought about Germany. One track of mind was on 'What am I going to tell her?'"

As the identity of Tim was advancing, the secret past of Mitka was receding. Known only to him, his true name—Mitka—represented a life about which he would not speak.

"Secrets—maybe 'secrets' is the word. I was afraid to lose her. Maybe that's how my mind came up with making me something more than I am—like telling her I made 150 bucks a week."

Mitka's lack of fluency in English meant questions about his past, if they were asked at all, could be sidestepped.

"I didn't know how to talk about my past. Because if you would have listened, you wouldn't have wanted to be around me."

Emphatically, he says, "Because I'm nobody. Who wants nobody? This is in my mind. And I still say to her if she had found out in that particular year, her mind might have changed. Who wants you if you are nobody?—no family, nothing to give you something solid."

At this intersection in Mitka's life, he imagined that losing Adrienne was a real threat. His instincts told him to conceal what his experiences seemed to confirm: that he was nobody. The peril for him was genuine. He had to find a way out.

So each day, Tim set about reinventing himself, charging forward on little more than his brash charm, deft humor, and plucky spirit—the only resources available to him.

Adrienne felt passion just like Mitka did. But for her there was another bonding force at work too. Tim needed her. She intuitively perceived this and willingly became teacher and support to her new love.

So it was, that on a nondescript sidewalk in the northwestern corner of the state of New York, a remarkable love affair had begun.

As the romance budded, sometimes it was smooth sailing, but there were storms too.

With his landlord, Joe Cross, Mitka had found a stable living situation. He was paying rent, "five dollars a week," and he and Joe got along well. Joe was an older man and came to rely on Mitka for certain tasks. So Mitka wasn't surprised when Joe proposed a trip. "Joe—he had this 1952 or '53 DeSoto. And he said to me, 'Tim, I want you to drive me to Canton, Ohio.' He didn't know that I have no driver's license. So he asked me to drive him."

Mitka had often been a passenger. He had watched others drive a car, paying attention to every detail, but he had never actually been behind the wheel. Nevertheless, off they went for a 250-mile jaunt.

"Only thing I remember—I still don't understand it too much— centrifugal clutch. Have you heard of that? It's not automatic, but it's similar to automatic. You go, and then you have to wait, and then *click*, it slips into gear. Like I said, I was nothing, but somehow I could do things, like taking him to Ohio."

As Mitka continues to talk about his trip to Canton, the full story of his time there spills out. "He had family there, and I stayed with the family when we were there. And that's when she and I"—he extends his arm, pointing to Adrienne—"we were going together."

Mitka continues, "And there was some gal that fell in love with me when I was down in Ohio. And she wrote me a letter after I came back."

Once again, he points to Adrienne. "Dumb schmuck, me—I didn't know how to read it, so I gave the letter to her to read it to me." Mitka laughs. Adrienne doesn't move. Her expression confirms Mitka's words—dumb schmuck—as he repeats, "What did I know?"

Adrienne hardly remembers the event. While Mitka thought that he and Adrienne were an exclusive couple at that point, Adrienne wasn't ready to give up her independence. "It was early in the game for us. And we weren't going together or anything like that," she says.

Mitka continued on at ADSCO. "I drove the forklift first . . . and just like at Durez, they got me a new job with a little more money."

After Mitka's initiation, seasoned employees tried to teach Tim a few things, one of which is typical on any factory floor: don't stand out; conform to the norm. "I worked so fast that the workers came to me and asked me to slow down. I was not trying to hurt anybody. I was just working too fast."

It was at about this time that Mitka and William "Wee Willie" Davis became acquainted.

In the 1930s, Wee Willie had been a professional wrestler and then became a character actor in twenty-nine films from 1941 through 1955. His film career peaked in 1949 and 1950 with four credited roles, most notably playing Garmiskar in *Samson and Delilah*. Improbably, he was also an engineer of sorts at ADSCO, where he contributed to the invention of the Glowmeter, a device worn on a driver's head that projected a car's speed onto the windshield. It was one of ADSCO's short-lived products.

As Mitka tells it, "This Wee Willie—you must have heard of him—I think he could lift me up and throw me in a ditch.

"When they sold the building where they were making the Glowmeters, I was on a forklift, and I was moving a bunch of stuff out of the building. And Wee Willie was on the floor with a bunch of crap in my way. He had one of those goldarn snow-cone hats [the Glowmeter] on his head. And he just stood there. And I said, 'Move that!' And he says 'OK.'"

Mitka grins and adds, "Can you believe that? Here he was—this big guy—and I was bossing him around! I thought he might come after me, but he didn't. In those years, I didn't care how strong others was because I was pretty strong. He was big, but I didn't care. I would have took him on anyway."

Mitka likes to tell of incidents involving bravado and feats of strength. Through these episodes—occasionally confrontational but mostly just bluster and showmanship—he learned that he could command a certain kind of respect. Probably most significant for him, this unnatural physical power gave him an ace when he needed to pull a high card and thereby sidetrack attention from his weak hand—his illiteracy. It also got him his next job.

In late 1953, ADSCO was shutting down its plant in North Tonawanda and moving to Buffalo. Mitka was offered the chance to move with the company, but that wasn't an option. He didn't have a car to make the sixty-mile round-trip commute. He needed to find a new job.

"Jim Vona, he owned practically everything in town—cigarette machines, pinball machines. He was one of those . . . not mafia, but those types. He had pool tables and such. What do you call that kind of guy? Crooked? They are everywhere.

"So to get a job in construction, I was in his place. I spoke up because I needed a job, and he thought he could help me. He made a phone call to a guy named Elmer Nobilio, and he told me to see him. But first, he wanted to see how strong I was, so he began to wrestle with me. He had me in a headlock, and that's one of my favorite shots. And I lift him up and dropped him on my knee on his backside.

"We became friends later, and through him, I got into construction.

"Elmer was a concrete guy—sidewalks, driveways. We broke up sidewalks and stuff. That's where I learned concrete. I really liked outside work."

Now finished with the story, Mitka starts singing a Perry Como lyric. "'Find a wheel, and it goes round, round, round . . .' And that was playing when I worked construction."

Mitka found satisfaction, dignity, and confidence through work. From his perspective, it didn't matter that the work was menial. He felt no shame in being a manual laborer; on the contrary, work gave him independence, which he cherished.

Both on and off the job, Mitka was learning things at a breakneck pace. He had to. Each week brought encounters and situations he didn't understand. Often he felt like a pretender, because, at some level, he was.

As Mitka continued the process of enculturation, his English improved by the day; he used slang, sometimes to hilarious effect. And he plunged headlong—often impulsively—into new tasks. His mistakes were his greatest teacher.

Alongside all the positive developments, however, was the constant fear that someone would find him out. Instinctively, he knew his charisma, wit, and swagger masked a deep insecurity. He hoped it was enough.

Life and its lessons were coming at Mitka hard and fast. In a little less than a year, he found himself cramming to study and learn what it meant to be an adult, an employee, a friend, and a boyfriend. Things were about to take another significant turn, though he hardly comprehended any of it. He was bobbing and weaving as best he could. In matters of love, this bobbing and weaving led to results that were both disastrous and magical.

Mitka had a jealous, possessive streak. He wanted Adrienne, and he didn't want anyone else to have her. Unschooled in courting rituals, he simply followed his instincts. Unfortunately, his instincts led him to follow Adrienne whenever possible—just to be sure she wasn't, by chance, seeing another man. Here his path crossed Wee Willie's again.

"When we still worked in the factory, everybody went to lunch. I didn't go to Ziggy's, but she went to Ziggy's. So naturally, macho guy, I decided to go to Ziggy's, and I was following her. And that SOB Wee Willie Davis, he came and sat down, and that guy—he was wide as a table—took my view away. . . . I couldn't believe it. And I had to go back to work before she left, so all my trying to see who she was with didn't work. All because of that Wee Willie."

Adrienne jumps into the story. "I didn't know anything about this, but I wouldn't have liked it."

Shortly after his attempt to follow her to Ziggy's, things between Adrienne and Mitka "went south." It was Valentine's Day, 1953. The weather was cold but not unbearable, the temperature hovering right around 32 degrees.

Mitka describes the evening. "I'm not going to call it a date, but we got together at her house. And all of a sudden, I could feel it's not right. She said she had a headache or some damn thing—some excuse. So she got me out of the house."

Mitka continues, "I was clever—not smart, but clever. And I knew something's not right. So I went out there and I went behind the tree and I waited out for some time. And then, sure enough, here comes the car. And she comes out—no headache or nothing.

"So I was walking, and I try to follow the car. And I picked up a glove that she dropped. And I walked almost the whole North Tonawanda. And I kept missing them—being that you walked, it slowed you down. Missing them got me more mad."

The next day, Mitka returned the glove to Adrienne. She wasn't happy. "I didn't know he was following me. Like I said, it was early in the game. And we weren't committed. I had no idea how or why he felt like he did."

She told him off in no uncertain terms.

Mitka responds, "And that's the part right there, what started it— teaching me a little bit. Meeting somebody, going out, going together . . . I didn't know none of this.

"She told me, 'You don't own me.' I figured that she's with me, she's mine. I didn't know."

The breakup lasted a little over two weeks.

It was early March, and Adrienne had left ADSCO with friends. They were headed to Deluxe Lanes, the local bowling alley, for their regular bowling night. The team had scarcely had time to begin play when Mitka showed up.

Adrienne recounts what happened. "He walked in and looked at me. Then he headed straight to the jukebox. He pulled some coins out of his pocket and music began."

At this point, Mitka jumps in. "It was 'That's Amore.'" He begins to sing, "When the moon hits your eye like a big pizza pie, that's *amore*." Then he laughs, "Pretty good, that song was pretty good."

Adrienne picks up the thread. "He played that song over and over again. My friends were saying, 'He's crazy.' But I kind of liked it. I mean, he was good-looking and everything. He still wasn't going to tell me what to do, but I guess I loved him."

So Adrienne and Mitka were back on. Their romance quickly heated up. There were nights for playing cards and nights for dancing.

As always, when he danced, Mitka's insecurities vanished. "Every time I danced, my head danced along with me. I'm a different person when I dance."

He continues, "We danced on dates, but she had a different dance— the jitterbug—and I hated that one. Me, I'm from Europe—a nice tango, a nice waltz. But she loved that jitterbug." Mitka twitches all over.

Adrienne puts the coda on the conversation. "He was always a good dancer. And he was the sharpest dresser in those days."

Mitka still had much to learn. "Later she mentioned something about a ring, that a ring meant you were going together. So I went off to get a ring." And, just like that, Mitka and Adrienne were engaged.

Getting married was rather matter-of-fact, at least for couples in Mitka and Adrienne's circumstance and class.

They married in November 1953.

Mitka says, "Later I found out that it was at a justice of the peace—Niagara County justice of the peace—but then I did not know."

Adrienne, with the advantage of hindsight, adds, "Yes, he didn't know what he meant when he said 'I do.'"

CHAPTER THIRTEEN

Marriage

North Tonawanda and Lockport, 1953–1959

From the time Mitka arrived in New York as a teenager, his life was full of firsts. One of those firsts came Monday, December 14, 1953.

Because the actual year and day on which he was born are unknown, Mitka had no idea how old he was, and the day had no real significance for him. Nevertheless, on this, his supposed birthday, something happened that he would never forget: Adrienne gave him a birthday present. It was the first time someone had given him a present. She gave him a sweater.

According to Adrienne, he was embarrassed and responded with a goofy grin.

He wore the sweater. He even loved the sweater. But he didn't know how to react or what he should feel.

Only one month before, Mitka had married Adrienne. Even that hadn't been especially momentous. It was another event that occurred. He didn't have a true sense of what he had done.

Mr. and Mrs. Tim Kalinski were living at 47 Chipman Place then. The two-story, white frame house sat on a narrow lot, on either side of which were similar houses. Only driveways separated one house from the other. A set of concrete steps led up to the front porch, which was covered by a gabled roof. This was where Adrienne had moved to care for her Uncle Harry.

Unexceptional, like the other houses in the working-class neighborhood, it was nonetheless a spacious house. And it had particular meaning for Adrienne and, to a lesser degree, Mitka.

In this house, Tim and Adrienne began their union.

When Mitka reflects on his actions during this period, it's clear that he was following Adrienne's lead as best he could. He would gamely teeter forward with a dutiful sense of doing what he thought was expected. In his mind, though, he felt "lost."

"I was nobody, and I had nothing," Mitka says.

Pointing to Adrienne, he continues, "She had to teach me how to say 'our.' I always said 'your' because everything I had had been because of her. It was her house, her family. She would say it was 'ours.' That felt wrong to me because it was hers."

Mitka's sense that he was "a nobody" often intruded into his life. He longed to earn the right to say "ours" freely. Over time, the word did become comfortable enough for him to use it when he spoke, but self-doubt persisted. He hid this uncertainty in the same vault in which he held all his secrets.

In their second year of marriage, a significant life event happened to the couple.

Michael was born to Tim and Adrienne Kalinski on September 28, 1954. Mitka was a father and a young one—twenty-one on paper, but likely only nineteen. He speaks of becoming a father with characteristic candor. "I feel bad saying this, but it didn't mean nothing to me. I didn't feel nothing. 'Father'—what did I know of 'father'?"

Adrienne enters the conversation and defends her husband, insisting that "he was a good father." Then, for emphasis, she repeats, "He was a good father."

To underscore her words, Adrienne points out that Mitka did all kinds of things for his children. To this he replies, "I was just doing what I was supposed to do."

Late that year, Harry died. Adrienne, together with her "sisters" Verna and Hilda, inherited the house.

Adrienne recalls, "I always took Michael in to see Uncle Harry in the morning. That day, I checked on Uncle Harry and then took some time getting Michael dressed. When I went back in with the baby, Uncle Harry was gone. He would always sit at the window with his ear near a radio because he was deaf and that was the only way he could hear the radio. He was just sitting there. He died peacefully just like that.

"I called my cousin Cal and told him that Harry had died. I knew he would know what to do because he was a policeman."

Cousin Cal came to the rescue on another occasion for his relatives. Mitka tells another story.

"I bought a car before I could drive—a '47 Kaiser. Then I bought a '49 Ford. It was half-gone—muffler and all—but I put it back together again. This was all before I got a driver's license."

Mitka continues, "I was a big shot in those days. One day I was driving and I decided to park right in front of a fire hydrant—right where it said 'NO PARKING.'

"You know why I did that?" Here he laughs and slaps his leg as he often does when delighted with himself.

"I had seen those movies where guys were such big shots, and I learned from them. I figured that the cops would think that no one who didn't have a license would park right in front of a fire hydrant. So I thought I was safe."

He closes this memory with a familiar refrain. "Can you believe it? But back in those days, I thought I could get away with anything." In this case, Mitka did escape without a ticket.

Marriage to Adrienne helped him realize he was not as invulnerable as he had thought.

On one particular day, he said, "I was driving her sister Verna's car and, dumb me, I let it slip that I didn't have a license. Adrienne got so mad at me. I don't know how he knew, but the next day her cousin Cal showed up. He was a policeman and she said he'd take me to get my license.

"And so we went down to where they gave the driver's test. And this guy—what do you call him . . . an examiner—came out with this paper on a clipboard. It was the test that you are supposed to take."

As instructed, Mitka got into the driver's seat and left the door open. Cal stood outside the car over Mitka's shoulder. The examiner sat in the passenger seat.

"Every time the guy asked me a question, Cal would kind of lean over and point, and I would mark that answer. I got my driver's license that day."

Mitka quickly adds, "It's embarrassing how I got my license, but I honored it. I was so proud of it. From day one until today, I never had a wreck, never had a parking ticket, never had a speeding ticket—nothing."

After momentarily indulging his pride, Mitka becomes solemn.

"You know where that came from? I didn't want the law to get involved. So I was more than careful on where I parked, speeding, and all that stuff. I was not a citizen, and I did not want the law to get involved."

With a valid driver's license in hand, Mitka had gained a measure of self-respect. Like other first-time legal drivers, it was a big deal. But for him it was much more than the usual rite of passage.

Driving legally, holding a job, trying, as best he could, to be a good father—each of these achievements brought him a little closer to believing Adrienne when she would insist that he use the pronoun "ours."

Adrienne and Mitka recall happy times in their early marriage, but there were challenges too.

The jealousy Mitka had displayed during their courtship didn't end once they married.

"He was always jealous," Adrienne bluntly remarks. "He used to follow me if I went out. Even when I was walking Michael in the stroller, Mitka would walk along behind me on the other side of the street. It used to make me so mad. I mean, what did he think I was going to do? I'm walking with my three-month-old son down the street in broad daylight!"

"I don't know why I did that," Mitka says. "It made her mad."

Adrienne recalls speaking her mind to Mitka: "I may be married to you, but you don't own me."

Adrienne's independent nature came out full force in an episode early on in their marriage.

They had invited a couple over to their house for a night of card games. The foursome sat around a card table, drinks were served, and play began.

Suddenly, the fun came to a dramatic halt.

Adrienne tells it. "Mitka cheated. He just sat there smiling and hiding cards under the table."

Her reaction was swift and final. She stood up, grabbed the edge of the table, and flipped it upside down. Cards flew and drinks spilled. The card game was over.

Mitka chuckles at the memory. It's clearly a story he likes hearing. His smile widens. "That was the last time I ever played cards with her," he says.

Without missing a beat, Adrienne replies, "And that was the last time you ever cheated at cards."

Adrienne was a tough one, which turns out to have been exactly what Mitka needed. She didn't see anyone—even the man she loved—through rose-colored glasses. Her steely resolve and feisty personality belied another trait of hers—perceptive kindliness—that gave Mitka room to grow and left his dignity intact. In Adrienne, Mitka had stumbled upon a gold mine of mother wit, fierce determination, and love—firm love mostly, though sometimes sentimental too.

There was a yin and yang nature to Tim and Adrienne Kalinski. It found expression in their respective preferences. Mitka liked crooners singing romantic ballads backed by lush orchestral arrangements; Adrienne was drawn to rock and roll beats. He liked to waltz; she liked to swing. He liked shoot-'em-up westerns; she didn't. Altogether, it worked.

From 1954 to 1956, Mitka and Adrienne lived in Uncle Harry's house. This was a period of getting established. Mitka was working in construction. One toddler, Michael, filled Adrienne's days.

In late fall of 1955, Adrienne became pregnant for the second time.

Mitka recalls, "She got it in her head to move. I didn't want to. We were living in the house that Uncle Harry left her. And the way I figured, it was paid for. If we weren't paying rent, we had money for something else. I wanted to buy a Sunliner convertible. Have you seen one of those? Oh they are beautiful.

"But she"—pointing to Adrienne—"got it in her head that she wanted a house."

Mitka's convertible would have to wait.

Adrienne jumps in. "I used to take Michael for walks, and I would see houses. And sometimes I would go to open houses when they were for sale. I drew up plans for a house."

Uncle Harry and Aunt Nell were childless, so after Harry's death, the "sisters"—Verna, Hilda, and Adrienne, the respective daughters and great-niece of Mom and Dad Cook—inherited equal shares in the property. Because Adrienne and Mitka were living in the house, it was up to her to decide when and how they would realize gain from this inheritance. In the autumn of 1955, Adrienne instigated the sale of Uncle

Harry and Aunt Nell's home, splitting the profits with Verna and Hilda and using the rest for the next Kalinski undertaking.

With cash in hand for a down payment on a mortgage, Adrienne bought a lot on Beech Ridge Road on the western edge of the hamlet of Pendleton in Niagara County. She arranged construction financing, found a builder, and watched in anticipation as their house began to take shape.

"I don't remember what we put up as a down payment," Adrienne remarks, "but I know what we paid each month for the mortgage."

She pauses for dramatic effect and then says with pride, "It was eighty-seven dollars per month."

Bordered by the Erie Canal to the east and Tonawanda Creek to the south, Pendleton fit with Adrienne's dream to live in the country yet still be close to her relatives in the city. An agricultural community of around 2,500 people, it was only nine miles northwest of North Tonawanda.

Six months after construction began, Mr. and Mrs. Kalinski moved into their new house on Beech Ridge Road in late spring of 1956.

Jimmy, their second child, arrived July 13.

Continuing their banter about the project, Mitka says, "It was a nice house."

Adrienne jumps to a favorite memory: "Tell them about the doghouse."

Candy was Adrienne's beloved pet. Ever the animal lover, Mitka took quickly to Candy, as she did to him. Thus his enthusiasm was only natural when he set about to build a doghouse.

Mitka begins. "I built this beautiful doghouse in the basement for Candy" and, upon completion, "went to take it out to the yard."

Mitka slaps his forehead and begins laughing. "No matter how I turned it, I couldn't get it through the door. Finally I had to take the roof off to get it out. I ended up keeping the roof on with bricks after that."

Mitka looks over at Adrienne, satisfaction beaming from his face. He points to her as he says, "She fixed the basement up really nice. You know how they pour concrete basements? They frame it with these metal presses. When they take them down, it looks like there are blocks. Well, she painted each block."

Adrienne continues, "I found all of the cans of paint that they used when they built the house, and I painted each block a different color.

One was green, and the next was yellow, and the next was blue, and so on. It was very festive."

"Oh that basement," Mitka says. "We had some great parties down there. It was a big basement. At one end there was the hot-water heater and the washer and dryer, but that left the rest of the basement for parties."

From the beginning of their marriage, Adrienne took charge of paying the bills, managing the home, and tending to their growing family. Mitka, on the other hand, readily acknowledges that he was trying to learn how to be a husband and a father.

He encountered some bumps in the road.

"I used to go to Harold's Club on Oliver Street on Saturday night to play the harmonica. She," Adrienne, "had to talk to me and say, 'Tim, you're a father now. You can't be at bars on Saturday night.' And she was right. I learned."

Without a hint of resentment, Mitka says, "What did I know? I didn't know what it meant to be a father. But I didn't go anymore."

Sometimes, though, tempers flared. Adrienne laughs when she recalls one example.

"Jimmy and Mike were little—maybe two and four. One of the little neighbors was over with them. I was giving the boys a bath and was using baby shampoo in one of those spray bottles. They were playing and squealing like kids do. They weren't crying or fighting, but there was a lot of noise.

"Mitka never could stand it when kids were crying, and I guess their squeals sounded like that. Before I knew it, he had stormed in, pushed open the door, and grabbed the shampoo bottle out of my hand.

"Well, I wasn't going to have that, so I marched out and grabbed it back and closed and locked the bathroom door.

"That made him really mad, and he stormed in, pushing the door open, breaking the lock. I was up against the bathroom wall with the nozzle of the baby shampoo bottle aimed at him like I was going to squirt him.

"All of a sudden we just looked at each other, and we both started laughing. That was how it was with us. We'd get mad, but we'd get over it just as quickly."

Adrienne had plenty of nerve. She wasn't one to back down, which was exactly what Mitka needed, and he responded well. When she took charge, he was relieved. His love for her grew and deepened. And he was maturing with each passing day.

There was, however, a part of his life he couldn't share with Adrienne, at least not in a direct way. Some days, anxiety about his hidden past built up in him to the point of panic. Mitka was afraid he would be discovered for who he was and for who he was not. He was terrified that if Adrienne knew the man beneath the facade, she might leave him and that he would, once again, be alone.

One grace, however, never forsook Mitka. Since childhood, music had been his refuge, and it gave him a feeling of liberation.

Indeed, music provided him with a way to make sense of his feelings for Adrienne. "I fell in love with her through music."

As he tells it, "I had a song for her. It was 'Domino.'"

The song was recorded in 1951 by several popular singers of the day, but it was the Tony Martin hit that Mitka liked best. He learned the melody, and he loved to waltz along to the rise and fall articulated by the full orchestra.

But more than the music, it was the lyrics of "Domino," written in French by Jacques Plante and translated into English by Don Raye, that gave voice to Mitka's emotions. The songwriter had found the words that he could not—words that captured his fears and his longings, words he longed to tell his bride. "Domino, Domino, you're an angel that heaven has sent me," the song opens. "My whole world fills with music when I'm lost in your embrace." The speaker expresses how this woman is his everything, but he fears losing her to someone else, and being left alone. "Domino, Domino, won't you tell me you'll never desert me?"

With marriage and fatherhood, Mitka experienced yet more change. He didn't know how to be a father, but he did know how to work.

Construction was a natural fit for Mitka. He liked the work and took easily to its demands. As a general laborer on construction sites, he only needed to follow orders. Importantly, he didn't need to read.

He traces his construction roots to his time at Birkenau. There he helped make bricks, bricks he worries were used for ovens of mass human incineration.

Later, at Bad Aibling, he learned how to lay bricks. As fate would have it, his early training in masonry would be a skill on which he would rely later.

Working under Elmer Nobilio in New York was going well for Mitka. But after getting married and having two children, the stakes around work went up. He was no longer a carefree bachelor, working to earn money for movies and dances. He now had a family to support.

Before long, an opportunity presented itself to move into a new job that seemed to offer the potential for more earnings.

"While I was working with Elmer, we were using these steel beams. And this guy said, 'I bet you can't move those beams by yourself.'"

"So . . ." Mitka smiles, rubs his hands together, and says, "Just watch me.

"I first picked up one end and set it on some blocks, and then I picked up the other end and moved it. Then I took the end off the blocks and moved it over.

"And there was this guy watching me. And he said, 'I'll pay you fifteen cents more per hour if you come work with me.' So I started in masonry, working for Dick and Al Hoefer. Can you believe it? I took this new job for fifteen cents per hour more."

Once again, work fulfilled Mitka. It gave him purpose and a chance to prove his competence. The money, while not great, was enough for the young family. Things changed, though, when the company's business opportunities expanded in a way that brought Mitka's always-present fear to the surface.

"Dick and Al Hoefer got some contracts to work across the river in Canada. And to get there I would have had to go across the bridge.

"And I didn't want to do that because you had to go through guards, and they would say, 'Where were you born?'

"What was I supposed to say to that? I didn't even know the answer to that question. What if they found out I wasn't a citizen and sent me back? What would happen then?"

Fortunately for Mitka, another position opened up. This one was with Union Concrete, a company based in West Seneca, New York, that, in Mitka's words, "poured basements." It was another job that he enjoyed.

"And I was a good worker for them. But I worked so fast that the workers came to me and asked me to slow down. I was not trying to hurt anybody. I was just working too fast.

"And these guys told me . . . I was making them look bad, so I tried to slow down some. But that didn't make much sense to me. I was there to work."

He continues. "These same guys invited Adrienne and me to a picnic at Hamburg on Lake Erie. They had a cottage over there. And they had a wiener roast. And I ate seventeen hot dogs!"

Mitka thrusts his chest forward and adds, "I was a big eater, and Joe and Phil—that was their names—those guys told me, 'The next time, bring your own damn hot dogs.'"

When Mitka thinks about food, he remembers hunger. In Europe his every waking moment had been governed by his empty belly. The script flipped once he arrived in America. What had been constant hunger pangs became an insatiable appetite. He ravenously ate everything put in front of him. A late adolescent's high caloric needs and supercharged metabolism didn't seem to account for how much food he could consume. Those around Mitka watched in amazement.

Adrienne became accustomed to preparing extra helpings for him. "I used to make seven sandwiches for him to take to work every day."

And that wasn't all, as Mitka added with some bragging and a grin. "She made me seven sandwiches and some pickles and some hard-boiled eggs and half a watermelon."

"He was big but he wasn't fat—just big and strong," Adrienne clarifies, citing his height as six feet, two inches, his weight as just less than two hundred pounds of "muscle and bone."

One hundred twenty-four inches of snow hit Buffalo in the winter of 1957/58. In February alone, more than fifty-four inches were recorded. This had disastrous consequences on Mitka's work.

Adrienne remembers, "I never minded the snow, but in 1958 it fell so hard and so often that Mitka could only work five months. When he didn't work, he didn't get paid."

With two rambunctious toddlers to care for, Adrienne had her hands full. But it wasn't just Michael and Jimmy anymore. The brothers' sister Cheryl was born September 19, 1958. A new baby—and a little girl at that—was welcomed with joy, but an infant in the Kalinski household added to the strain. Adrienne now had three young ones to manage, and Mitka felt the pressure of yet another mouth to feed. When work was impossible because of weather, his stress grew.

Help came from a family member who had often rescued Adrienne and Mitka. In Adrienne's words, "My cousin Cal had moved out to Reno. One of his boys had a lot of asthma, and the doctor thought the climate would be good for him. And he said, 'Why don't you come out? There's year-round work here.'"

The discussion between Mitka and Adrienne was short. "We sold everything and packed our car and moved," Adrienne says.

The Beech Ridge house that Adrienne had designed, and that they both loved, had to go. All their furniture and most of their possessions were unloaded too. When all had been sold, they packed their '57 brown Ford station wagon with a few essentials.

"Mitka piled a mattress in the back, and the kids would play and sleep back there."

Michael was four and a half; Jimmy was two and a half; Cheryl was five months old. It was a Sunday morning, February 22, 1959, when the Kalinski family left Pendleton, New York, and headed west.

CHAPTER FOURTEEN

Heading West

Reno and Sparks, 1959–1963

On that cold Sunday morning—February 22, 1959—the Kalinski family, along with their dog, Candy, drove away from Pendleton, New York, loaded into a "minivan" of the day: a 1952 Ford Ranch Wagon. With two doors, a V6 engine, and a "three-on-the-tree" standard transmission, it was not Mitka's dream ride. Nevertheless, like other cars he had owned, it represented where he was in life, and he was proud of it.

Mitka was in control when in a car. He could go to or away from any place. A quintessential American symbol of independence, a car was a tangible reminder of his liberation from the Nazis.

Tim—the only name Mitka's family knew him by—was the American name he embraced. It gave him separation from his past and a fixed connection to everything his new world represented. The process of eliminating vestiges of his life in Poland, Ukraine, and Germany continued day by day.

Mitka was especially proud of the progress he had made in learning English. Though he thought he had discarded more of his eastern European accent than was true, its remaining traces didn't affect his confidence.

Only eight years removed from his landing in America, Mitka was a large and physically powerful man. In other ways, though, he remained a small, timid seven-year-old boy, haunted by his slavery. His gregariousness became a way to hide his past from others, especially from those he loved most.

Mitka's stays in the Bronx, Baltimore, North Tonawanda, and Pendleton had provided a necessary buffer, allowing him a delayed opportunity to pass from boyhood to manhood. As he drove beyond the western edge of New York, through Pennsylvania, and into Ohio, Tim Kalinski, husband and father, worker and responsible adult, believed that Martin, the cowering, needy child, was safely concealed.

Wending west, Mitka's imagination was filled with boyish excitement. He was going to the land of John Wayne and cowboys, the very backdrop of the stories he loved best, the ones that had formed his teenage fantasies and taught him English. Notions of the Wild West animated the journey from the outset. In many respects it was the American West, at least the romanticized version of it presented in the movies, that taught him how to be a man. Now he could see and experience the actual West. It hardly mattered that no house or job awaited his arrival in Nevada.

Adrienne had a very different attitude about the adventure on which they had embarked. Ever practical, she saw the move as a necessity. In making such a momentous decision, her hope rested on her cousin Cal's insistence that Reno was a place of opportunity. Leaving her extended family was the hardest choice she'd ever made, but the family's finances were exhausted, and she knew Mitka needed steady work. She believed this was the right choice for her family.

The trip itself was unlike a modern-day cross-country drive. In 1956 President Dwight D. Eisenhower, impressed by the German autobahn he had driven on during World War II, had signed into law the Federal Aid Highway Act. This was, essentially, a national plan for building an interstate highway system that, when finished, would form a strategic system of superhighways in America.

The two-lane roads on which the Kalinskis traveled were anything but super. Rest stops and convenience stores didn't exist. Motels could be found, but they were few and far between.

The family began the trip in the heart of winter. There were no weather forecasts, no seat belts, no AAA roadside service, certainly no GPSes or smartphones.

Adrienne, the family financial manager, kept meticulous records of the trip. For example, her ledger shows that on the first day, the family drove 380.6 miles and spent $0.52 on food (she had packed meals for day one), $6.50 for a motel room, $7.12 for gas, and $1.20 on tolls and miscellany, totaling $15.84.

Traveling about ten hours each day, they spent nights in Mount Victory, Ohio; St. Louis, Missouri; Junction City, Kansas; Cheyenne Wells and Steamboat Springs, Colorado; and Wendover, Utah. Mitka had never driven in mountains, but he learned quickly. "I figured out I could let some air out of the tires and get better traction." Throughout the trip Mitka did his own minor car repairs and added oil daily to an engine that was burning it at an alarming rate.

On the last night, in Wendover at the Utah-Nevada state line, there was one unplanned (and unrecorded) outlay . . . which yielded an even more unexpected windfall. Talking about that Friday night, February 27, Mitka gets excited. A grin spreads across his face as he rubs his hands together in anticipation of a fondly remembered story. He describes leaving the motel to cross the state line into Nevada.

"So I spotted this casino. I couldn't wait to drop her"—Mitka points to Adrienne with a conspiratorial smile—"at a motel and get over there to it. I didn't know nothin' 'bout nothin', but I walked in like a big shot.

"I saw what those others was doing, and I just put my money down on the line. Then I just stood there."

Here he folds his arms and looks around, whistling casually, imitating someone just hanging around.

"Pretty soon the guy says, 'That's your money.'"

Delighted surprise registers in Mitka's expression as he tells this part of the story.

"So I gathered up the money and went back to the motel. And back then it was silver dollars. So I gave them to Adrienne and she counted them. At first she thought it was half-dollars. She started to write down '$39.00.' Then she realized it was *dollars*—seventy-eight dollars! Can you believe it?"

Mitka had stepped into Nevada for the first time. It was an auspicious beginning. For him it marked the start of a lifelong ease with casinos.

On Saturday, the next morning, the Kalinskis began the 403-mile drive across the windswept Nevada desert headed to Reno. It was the final leg of their six-night, seven-day, 2,863.8-mile trip.

When they arrived, Adrienne's ledger of costs added up to a grand total of $193.79. Mitka's winnings of seventy-eight dollars at the craps table accounted for more than one-third of an already overstretched travel budget.

Together, Mitka and Adrienne had seen the vast American continent for the first time. They saw cities and towns and rolling Kansas prairies and snow-capped Rocky Mountain peaks and bleak Nevada desert. Their hopes of a new life grew with each panorama, and a love affair with the open road had begun.

For the boy who had first encountered a friendly American GI some thirteen years before in Rotenburg an der Fulda, for the young teen who had learned about English and life via John Wayne and westerns, the sights of America more than measured up to his dreams.

When they arrived for their first night in Reno, Tim, Adrienne, Mike, Jimmy, and Cheryl, with Candy in tow, checked into the Sandman Motel on Fourth Street, a half-mile east of downtown. Their first task was to figure out where to live. Cal had settled in Sparks, the town next door to Reno. It made sense to Adrienne to begin in the blue-collar town where the only person they knew lived. Plus, it was affordable.

Mitka's immediate concern was getting a Nevada driver's license. He had gotten his New York license with the help of Cal, but Cal was not in a position to arrange any favors as he had done in North Tonawanda. Mitka was on his own and anxious.

He went downtown and asked to talk to the sheriff, whose name was Bud Young. "And I just told him. I showed him my New York driver's license, and I said, 'I have this New York license, but I can't read to take the test here.'" His illiteracy was an admission he would make to no one, including Adrienne, but with the sheriff, as he saw it, he had no choice.

Mitka pauses with a characteristic self-satisfied grin. "And Bud says, 'You go to this place.' And I did. A man was waiting there with my license.

"I worship that license," Mitka says. "I've never had a ticket or nothing. I bet no one can say that. But I'm so careful. Every five years you have to renew it. And I watch for that and do it early so no one can ever take the license away from me."

With his driver's license in hand, Mitka set about to find work. It took only a couple of days. A man named Garth Ross hired him as a "hod carrier" of concrete. It seemed that Nevada was living up to its promise. Things were going well for Mitka and his family. That was soon to change, though.

After only a few months, Ross's workload slacked and he was forced to lay off Mitka. Ross lent him $200 to tide the family over with the promise that when work picked up he would hire Mitka back.

But "I couldn't wait on him getting work," Mitka recalls. "I had a family to feed." So he took a job with Jim Brussa, a masonry contractor.

When they came to Nevada in February of 1959, Mitka and Adrienne never imagined they would move four times in ten months. After staying in the motel for a week, they decided it wasn't a safe place for them. But even though Mitka had found work, the family had not accumulated enough for rent. At Cal's urging, they moved in with him and his family. Cal's thirty-foot car trailer was barely sufficient for his wife and three sons. The addition of the five Kalinskis, plus Candy, was, needless to say, a strain on everyone.

After two weeks Adrienne found a trailer to buy for $400 at the Wagon Wheel Mobile Home Park, a few miles south of Reno on Kietzke Street. It had been a quick decision and, as it turned out, not a particularly good one, as "it was way too small for us," Adrienne confesses. Very quickly, the Kalinskis found a small home to rent on Ninth Street, and Adrienne sold the trailer for $250.

The Ninth Street house was the Kalinskis' fourth dwelling place in Nevada.

Although it might seem as if now, in a house, the family was settled, that was not the case. As Thanksgiving and Christmas approached, Adrienne experienced a homesickness that overwhelmed her. It was devastating. Once again, she and Mitka loaded the station wagon with the kids and the dog and began the trip back to Lockport, New York. Since winter was approaching, this time they went south to Route 66.

They left Sunday, November 8, and drove to Las Vegas, then to Winslow, Arizona, to Tucumcari, New Mexico, to Chandler, Oklahoma, to Pocahontas, Illinois, and, finally, to Lockport, arriving Friday night. Adrienne did not drive then and still does not to this day, but Mitka was happy to take the wheel. He often drove into the night so they could fill their days exploring the sights of America with the kids. Now-faded, square, black-and-white photographs, snapped with a Brownie camera, reveal stops at various "Old West" attractions in Arizona, a visit to the reconstruction of an American Indian village in Tucumcari, and more. Simple roadside attractions provided the family with abundant opportunities to stretch their legs.

Many musical artists have recorded the song "Route 66" since its debut in 1946. It is the Nat King Cole version that Mitka remembers best. Like millions of other Americans who set out to "get [their] kicks on Route 66," the Kalinski family now shared in this iconic American experience.

Adrienne's need to go back "home" had been a relentless tug since their arrival in Nevada. "But once I got back to Lockport," she says, "we had Thanksgiving dinner with my family. I remember it rained the whole time. And that was that. I was ready to come back to Reno. After that I never looked back."

After two weeks and six thousand miles, the Kalinskis' future was settled: Sparks, Nevada, would be their permanent home. Mitka returned to work with Jim Brussa, and Adrienne found another house to rent, again on Ninth Street.

Then in late 1960 the family made yet another move, this time to a tiny three-room house that butted up against an alley. One more move still lay ahead on the merry-go-round of temporary stopovers.

Despite their poverty, their adjustments to a new community, and the challenges of so many moves, Mitka and Adrienne look back on this time as joyful. They were where they wanted to be and were busy making the best of the situation.

One day, late in 1961, Adrienne and Mitka picked Michael up from Robert Mitchell Elementary School on the corner of Twelfth and Prater. They noticed a For Rent sign on a little house not a hundred yards from the school's front door. Mitka recalls saying, "Hey, I kind of like that house."

The move to that house on Twelfth Street would be the Kalinskis' last move.

When Mitka and Adrienne rented the house on Twelfth Street—
one bedroom, one bath, and less than one thousand square feet of living space—it was smaller than the houses they had lived in in New
York. This was not, for them, a problem. They were ready to be settled, to put down roots. Mitka had steady work, and they established
comfortable routines. Money was tight, but that was nothing new and
certainly didn't alter their determination to keep moving forward into
each new day. They felt grateful for a roof over their heads and food on
the table.

In 1963 the landlord told Mitka and Adrienne she wanted to sell
the house and asked if they would consider buying it on a rent-to-own
contract.

When they asked her price, she told them $14,500.

Mitka tells the story. "So a little time went by while we decided.
And I asked her again, how much she wanted. This time, she said,
'$14,000.' Then *she*"—here Mitka points to Adrienne with his eyes
twinkling—"she said, 'No, it was $14,500.' So I always say she owes me
$500."

The deal was struck, and the Kalinskis added $35 each month to
their rent payment to count toward a down payment. Soon thereafter,
Mitka began the first of what would become many additions to their
new house. He chose to build a second story with three rooms.

When Mitka decided to add to their home, he faced an obstacle with
no obvious solution: he didn't have enough money to buy construction
supplies. Despite this, he formulated a plan. At various construction
sites, one thing had always perturbed Mitka: perfectly usable lumber,
bricks, concrete, drywall, nails, screws, and more were regularly hauled
away to the dump.

Mitka began scouting for construction materials he could use. Ever
loyal to his employers, he never took things surreptitiously. He always
asked for permission to take the scrap materials home. With consent
granted, he filled his backyard with all manner of stuff. Usually, it cost
him nothing. Occasionally, when salvageable goods had some value, he
struck deals to buy them for pennies on the dollar.

Once he had all the materials in hand, Mitka had another challenge.
He knew about masonry and concrete, but he had never built a home

with plumbing and electricity and a host of "code" issues to attend to. He approached this challenge like he had so many others. "I didn't know nothing about things like framing and Sheetrock and plumbing and electricity back then, but I would watch and I would ask questions—all the time, questions. You'd be surprised at how much people can tell you. That's how I learned."

Throughout the 1960s Mitka would add on to the house many times. When the upstairs was finished, he built out from the back wall of the house, doubling the square footage. He constructed a patio with concrete blocks that had been intended for use in Stewart Prison in Carson, only to be rejected by inspectors. He created a fifteen-by-thirty-foot family room with a fireplace. He added a storage room of similar size. He remodeled the front room, designing a fireplace he knew would please Adrienne. "Back in North Tonawanda, she saw a fireplace that had what you call a split face. I built that fireplace just for her because she liked it."

When all his construction was completed, their house on Twelfth Street had six bedrooms, a family room, a front porch and entry steps, a playhouse, two sheds, a workshop, and a garage. The lot was full. Mitka shows visitors around his home, bragging about how little he spent in its creation and pointing with pride to details of the home that he had built. Every wall is square and level; the brickwork is perfect.

Mitka says his house is "like that car in that Johnny Cash song, 'One Piece at a Time.'" The comparison is an apt one. Like the builder of the car in Cash's song, Mitka obtained construction material "one piece at a time," and all the parts that, together, went into his home very nearly "didn't cost him a dime."

Twenty years earlier Mitka had been brutalized in the camps and at the hands of the Dörr family. His name and past stolen from him, he had simply hung on. Somehow his hopes and dreams, such as they were, survived all these privations. Music and visits to the movies once the war was over were his shelter. Now Mitka, who for years had no family or home, had both. And, despite the fact that he could neither read nor write—a reality that tormented him—he was succeeding in a country he loved.

Two photographs in a family album provide a glimpse into the spirit that suffused the Kalinski family in the early 1960s. The first is a simple black-and-white photo of a small, square home. There is little in the way of landscaping. Only a 1940s-style car, sitting on a gravel driveway beside it, gives a clue that it is inhabited. The caption, handwritten by Adrienne, reads:

> *Beach Ridge Rd.*
> *July 1956–February 1959*
> *Lockport, N. Y.*

The second photo is of the Kalinskis' small home on Twelfth Street in Sparks. Scarcely an inch of their small yard has escaped a lighted Christmas decoration. Above the gate is a large "Merry Christmas" with tinsel garlands trailing below. To the left is an enormous teddy bear with a Santa hat—seated, it is more than four feet tall. Behind the bear are a snowwoman and snowman, and to the right is a team of prancing reindeer, led by the bulbous-nosed Rudolf. Above this photograph, again in Adrienne's handwriting, are the words:

> *Our Sparks, Nevada Home*
> *1959–"Forever"*

These pictures reveal more than merely where the Kalinskis lived. They suggest how the family's life had changed. The newly constructed Beach Ridge house in the first picture was, like the family who lived there, in the process of forming, of becoming. The house was solid and fully adequate for life in upstate New York in the 1950s, but it had no landscaping or other features that revealed its occupants' personalities. The house on Twelfth Street in Sparks was, clearly, not a just a place to live. It was "Our Home," a place full of light and joy and celebration. Adrienne believed that such a home would be theirs "forever." Sometimes Mitka believed that too, but for him, there was always a niggling fear.

CHAPTER FIFTEEN

The Sixties

Sparks, 1963–1969

Mitka's first experience at a casino, during their cross-country move, had sparked his curiosity. When he could find a little spare time, he would wander into one of the many casinos on the edge of the neighborhood where the family lived. He would stand apart from the action and observe, mentally taking notes on how the games were played.

He had a chance to test his gambling acumen in 1963 when, in a freak accident, Mitka's left leg was crushed by a cement mixer he had been pulling. Stubborn and stoic, he had tried to work with the injury, but the foreman who saw Mitka's leg bound in a work boot and swollen beyond all recognition pulled him off the job. Forced to take time off and to rely on disability, he thought it might be time to see if gambling could provide another source of income.

Blackjack was the game Mitka liked best and believed he best understood. Indeed, he reveals his recognition of how the house usually wins through his offhand comment "I call it 'Twenty-Two.'"

As he contemplated how he might beat the odds and do what most do not, Mitka crafted a strategy to make some money at the casino. His ironclad rules were simple and conservative:

- No drinking. You wouldn't drink at work. Treat this like work.
- Never take a hit card if "12" is showing on the table.
- Quit if you lose ten hands in a row.
- Gamble for a set period of time or until you win fifteen dollars.
- Don't get greedy. Go home once you've won.

Mitka arrived at these rules through a process he had used so often to great effect: he patiently watched others' actions, mimicked what he thought successful, noted what didn't work, and absorbed the lessons of each outcome, good or bad.

Without being conscious of it, Mitka created a plan that took emotion out of the game, thus adopting the discipline of a professional gambler.

At about this time, Adrienne's half brother Don Harder showed up in Reno with his own dreams. Mitka and Don started hanging out together, and Mitka got him a job with Jim Brussa's masonry company.

With his strategy for winning at blackjack established, Mitka convinced his brother-in-law to be his gambling partner. Mitka offered to split the ante and the winnings fifty-fifty. Their verbal agreement included Mitka's rules.

When the first night was done, they cashed in their chips and pocketed their profits.

Brimming with pride, Mitka recounts that he never lost his original stake. Clapping his hands together, he says, "I played with the same $100 over and over again." So the gambling was profitable. Sometimes the pair came home with only a few dollars; other times he and Don hit big. He always, though, ended the week with more money in his pocket than when he started.

But in his next sentence, Mitka turns sad. "Don broke the rules we agreed to." He goes on to relate how Don began drinking, betting aggressively, and taking more of the profits than his share. "When that happened, I was out of there."

Though disappointed that his brother-in-law's disregard for their rules halted their gambling success, Mitka can't hide his satisfaction that he boosted his income for the year he was off work. "I brought in at least fifteen dollars a day every day. I think it came to over four hundred each month. Back then, that was something."

As the family settled into life in Sparks, a middle-class dream was taking shape. There were hard times, to be sure, but there was nothing that couldn't be managed. The setbacks didn't detract from the overall progress the Kalinskis were experiencing.

One difficult time came in 1962 when eight-year-old Mike became sick with rheumatic fever. "I took him to the doctor, and I heard him say, 'Test him for leukemia,'" Adrienne recalls. "That was a terrible time for us. He missed school that year. He would just lie on the couch and ask me to sit beside him. But he recovered." And there was Mitka's broken leg, a circumstance that could have been much worse had Mitka not supplemented their income with casino winnings. There was also joy, especially when baby Donna arrived on October 6, 1964. Michael was ten, Jimmy was eight, and Cheryl was seven. It would be Adrienne's last pregnancy.

Around this time, Mitka and Adrienne began taking the family across Donner Pass into California for vacations.

"*The Birds* came out in '63 and we wanted to go see Bodega Bay where Hitchcock filmed it. But for a long time, we couldn't find the bay.... We would stay in Santa Rosa at a big Holiday Inn. And we swam there in the pool.... We finally found this road where you had to go five miles one way, and it took us there."

A campground at Bodega Bay became a magical place for the whole family, one they would return to year after year.

Other day trips filled the family's weekends. There were Saturday picnics at Pyramid Lake for swimming and sunning. A twenty-minute drive put them on its shore.

Some years, they saved enough to take longer excursions throughout California and other western states.

Adrienne documented each trip with her to-the-penny expense logs and had begun keeping a scrapbook for each year beginning with the move to Sparks in 1959. Today, bookshelves tightly packed with scrapbooks fill two walls of their living room.

Adrienne relates details of one of the kids' favorite stops at the Nut Tree in Vacaville, California, a popular tourist spot right off the highway, consisting of restaurants, gifts shops, and a mini-railroad.

"The kids loved to ride the railroad train there, and they never charged us a penny for those things."

Keeping the gas tank full, camping at state and national parks, sometimes staying in a motel or splurging for a restaurant meal, and always finding ways to be tourists of the West on the cheap—this was how Mitka and Adrienne built a habit of family fun into their lives.

Of these trips Mitka says, "I loved to see America. If I could, I would have shaken the hand of every American and said, 'Thank you for saving me from those Nazis.'"

The extravagance of these trips was, simply, time spent together. There was no money for anything else. Today each adult Kalinski child looks back and remarks how spoiled they felt and how joyful their family was.

Mitka worked hard to provide for his family. Jim Brussa, the contractor who hired him when work with Garth Ross dried up, was his most constant employer, but he also worked with others. Jim Gregg was another contractor who admired Mitka's work and often hired him for masonry projects and for special work at his home.

Mitka recalls one evening when he was working after hours at Jim Gregg's home.

"So he asked me to stay for dinner because it was getting kind of late. I says sure, and we sat down to eat.

"The family was having spaghetti. I think there were three kids, and they were all there. And they put this plate—one of those oval things—down. Well, it was in front of me, so I ate it. I ate the whole damn thing.

"And those kids were just sitting there. Can you believe it? I thought it was all for me! What did I know in those days?"

Adrienne sits stolidly as he tells this oft-repeated tale. Dryly, she inserts, "I'm glad I wasn't there. I would have died of embarrassment." It's clear that she, indeed, might have been embarrassed. But she also saw the humor in the event. Adrienne expresses her appreciation for all the extra work Mitka took on in those early days in Sparks. "Mitka couldn't stand the idea that his kids might want something and couldn't have it. He used to take on extra work to be able to get things for them."

She adds, "We didn't have a lot, but we always made it. I was a good shopper and would often walk to nearby stores and shop in the bargain basement. I was never ashamed to shop in a thrift store—and I'm still not. They always had good clothes, but they might have been used clothes. But shoes . . . I always made sure my family had good shoes. I never bought used shoes. I bought new, good shoes at Guys and Dolls Shoe Store."

When purchases went over the family budget, Mitka helped out. Together they would go to junkyards, where they rummaged for toys and other things of interest. Broken toys that could be rebuilt, painted, and restored occupied Mitka for endless hours in his shop.

Adrienne says, "We got bikes for all the kids there. Tim would find them and take them home and fix them up. He would take two or three bikes and take parts off them and then clean them up. He would always find a way. Our kids wanted for nothing."

Mitka would find other things—small appliances and clocks, mostly—at thrift shops or at the junkyard. He would repair and clean them, taking special pleasure in restoring intricate timepieces to workable condition. On Saturdays he'd pile children into his truck and drive over the Sierra Nevada range into California, where he could sell his renovated treasures to tourists visiting Rocklin or Roseville or Auburn or any one of dozens of small towns in the foothills of the mountains.

At home, Mitka was a hero to his children. He was the dad who would do whatever was required to provide for them. He could fix anything. He was funny and strong. And he had a knack for making life fun.

Today each of his children speaks, frequently, about their happy childhood and about what a loving, funny, and ingenious father they had.

Mitka wanted to be such a dad. But as each child entered school—and throughout his or her education—Mitka, almost daily, fought an inner battle. On the one hand, he wanted a good education for them; on the other hand, he believed he was an obstacle to his fondest wish.

Whenever they turned to him for help with homework, he was at a loss. He couldn't read, and he was too ashamed for them to know this. Thus, he handled these episodes in the only way he knew how. Gruff to the point of rudeness—even angrily at times—he told them to "go ask your mother."

"I never told the kids I couldn't read or write. I used anger to push them away because I was so ashamed."

His secret was intact; but his self-regard, once again, was shattered. Years later, Mitka speaks of how he "pushed his kids toward their mother." He pauses, touches his chest, and says, "I have to live with this every day, and it hurts me in here."

After a pause, Adrienne acknowledges that in this, Mitka did let the family down. "He hurt and confused the kids. They didn't understand, and I didn't either. I tried to help them, but sometimes I resented it." Then she adds a sentence that she often utters: "I understand now, but I didn't then. I didn't know anything about what he'd been through." She continues, "It used to make me mad. I understand it now, but I didn't then."

There were other things about Mitka that Adrienne did not try to understand. From time to time, he spoke of Uncle Gustav, Tante Anna, Oma and Opa, his "relatives in Germany." He also talked about Natalie and Oakie Kent and Kathleen Regan, his Quaker social workers from the Children's Home at Bad Aibling. Adrienne listened to him and even wrote letters to different individuals from Mitka's past, but she was otherwise incurious.

When asked what she understood about the Dörrs, the Kents, and Kathleen, Adrienne remarks, "I didn't ask questions about these people. I knew that he knew them in Germany. I just believed what he told me. He didn't exactly lie, but he didn't tell the whole truth either. He told me he had family in Germany—Uncle Gustav and Oma and Opa. That was all he said, and that made sense to me."

In sharing brief hints about his time in Germany, Mitka was constructing a past that he believed made him acceptable—a past about which he omitted certain hard truths. But even as he judiciously selected what to disclose, he could never forget.

As the months and years passed, Tim Kalinski became a familiar sight around Sparks. From the beginning he found ways to introduce himself to the mayor, to police officers, to the sheriff, to casino owners, and especially to waitresses. He describes his method. "I can't explain it, but when I watched someone like John Wayne, I took him inside me. I would make out like I was someone—you know, talking big even if I didn't know what I was talking about." He continues, "And Bob Hope—I learned a lot from him. I could be really funny, and that would catch people off guard." Through trial and error, Mitka fashioned rhetorical devices to disarm those he met and engage them in conversation.

The effect of these repeated encounters around town was that Tim Kalinski had a stature that set him apart. He intuitively recognized that relationships with important people gave him a measure of influence. Often he could be found at city council meetings lobbying for some issue that affected his neighborhood.

Mitka's efforts were occasionally rewarded. In front of his house there was no sidewalk. Every day, schoolchildren walked down the street to Mitchell Elementary School, only a few steps from his house. He saw how distracted youngsters could be and watched cars come dangerously close to some of them. For Mitka, this was unacceptable; he wanted to protect the kids. Today when he walks out of his front gate, he steps onto a sidewalk. He's quick to tell anyone how he had prevailed with the authorities to get a sidewalk poured. "I got all of the neighbors to sign a petition, and then I took it to the city. They were slow, and I kind of had to knock some heads together, but I did it."

In the meantime, the Kalinski children were growing fast.

It was 1966. Mike had begun junior high, and like his father, he took an interest in music.

Two years later, at fourteen, Mike had saved enough money to buy a starter electric guitar at the Western Auto Store. Mimicking popular guitarists became his preoccupation. At sixteen he got a birthday present from Mitka: two "real" guitars. Mike still has those guitars today. They are among his treasured possessions, in part because, in his words, "They were a gift from my dad."

Jimmy, an especially happy boy, still had all the wide-eyed innocence and curiosity of a fifth-grader. He shadowed Mitka, constantly asking questions of his dad while working alongside him.

Nine-year-old Cheryl liked playing big sister to two-year-old Donna.

Quite unexpectedly, things changed for the Kalinski family in August 1966. Teenage twins, Mike and Mitch Lovegrove, the children of Cal and Elaine, Adrienne's relatives, showed up on their doorstep.

"Two kids stood right here," Mitka says as he points to the front door.

"We were gone to Oregon, and when we got back, they were sitting on the front porch. Cal died a few months earlier, and their mom was alive but they couldn't be with her. She was an alcoholic, and she couldn't take care of them. They just showed up at our house."

Sorrow fills Mitka's voice, though only momentarily. "So what could we do?"

His mood shifts and he cheerfully adds, "Of course, we took them in."

Briefly, Mitka seems remote, as if he were traveling back to a time when he stood, like Cal's boys, on a doorstep with nowhere to go. He was determined to give the twins what he never got: a loving home and family.

Six kids filled every corner of the Kalinski house. It was tight, but the family managed, and, by all accounts, quite joyfully.

"The attic had been the first thing I built. I wanted each kid to have his own room. When Cal's boys came to live with us, we kind of had to double up, but it worked OK. The upstairs came in handy. We had one room with bunk beds for the boys, and it was perfect."

Adrienne adds, "Mike and Mitch were good boys. They lived with us until they graduated from high school."

Soon after the twins moved in, Mitka bought a car with money he'd received in a settlement from his broken leg. It was a purchase unlike any he'd ever made.

Mitka's eyes light up. He describes buying his first new car: a 1966 Cadillac convertible. The color, according to Mitka, who pronounces each syllable with great deliberation, was "Florentine Gold."

"I drove it out of Scott Motors—right out of the dealership. I think it was the only Florentine Gold convertible in Reno.

"Oh I was so happy, so happy," he adds.

The settlement windfall took pressure off the household budget and enabled the family to take a cross-country trip. The highlight of the vacation was seeing the national monuments in Washington, DC.

"We took that Cadillac to New York. We could pile all of the kids into it. We had Cal's twins with us then. The four boys would sit in the back. Cheryl would sit up front between Adrienne and me. And Donna would sit in Adrienne's lap."

Owning a new Cadillac, especially a top-of-the-line gold convertible, symbolized important things for Mitka. He drove around town
and noticed the stares of admirers. He could pull up to a casino and feel
like a high roller. It didn't matter that his modest house didn't match
his car. If anything, his blue-collar status magnified his pleasure. To his
mind, *nobody* had become *somebody*.

"That was such a good car. We took some good trips in that car."

In 1967 Mitka experienced a setback that, in the ensuing four years,
he would labor valiantly to overcome. He had been helping to build
condominiums at Incline Village in Lake Tahoe, a fast-growing enclave
with stunning mountain views, when, on an otherwise ordinary day at
work, he fell.

"We were building a balcony on one of those condominiums. I built
a scaffold up there, and it was a good scaffold. We were working on this
deck, and the scaffold went about thirty feet in the air. That's how we
got up there to work."

Mitka pauses and reaches for pencils to illustrate the shape of the
scaffold with its four legs.

"And guys would grab one of the legs and swing around it as they
passed by under the scaffold. A couple of guys did this, and it shook
the scaffold. I fell, and then the whole scaffold fell on top of me. I fell
thirty-seven feet."

The Occupational Safety and Health Administration, an agency
of the United States Department of Labor, wasn't yet established. It
would be three years before Congress passed the legislation, which
was then signed into law by President Richard Nixon on December
29, 1970. It could have prevented Mitka's accident. It would take many
more years for small contractors like Dick May, Mitka's employer at
the time, to adopt safety measures in accordance with the new national
regulations.

"When I hit, I was ready to jump up. I was mad at those guys. And
someone put a hundred-pound sack of concrete on me to keep me from
getting up." Plus, several coworkers joined in holding him down until
help arrived, restraining his impulse to react physically against those
responsible.

"They called an ambulance to take me back to Reno, and it turned out to be a station wagon. Can you believe that? My feet stuck out the back."

With a hint of humor in her voice, Adrienne adds, "It's a wonder that he didn't slide out."

Mitka continues the tale. "They took me to Washoe Med, but they were supposed to take me to Saint Mary's. That's where Adrienne was waiting.

"Nothing was broken, but I was black and blue—every color—all over my body. I was in a hospital for a long time—maybe three weeks. They did some surgery on me and took some cartilage out of my knee."

Mitka rises from his chair and says, "I went back to work, and I worked on building bridges all over Reno."

Now Mitka leans forward, bending at the waist. "But when I went to work, I was more and more bent over—every day I got worse until I was totally bent over.

"And the crane operator—he was a drinking buddy of the boss—saw me. And they said, 'Hey you need to get to a doctor.'

"I saw this doctor and he said that he could help me but that I had to do what he said. For a year I had to rest—not do anything. He said I was like a battery and I needed to recharge. And so he disabled me. He said if I went back to work I might not be able to walk at all. It was hard, but we made it."

What had once been the bedrock of Mitka's existence—his strength and resiliency—was damaged by the accident and by the doctor's order. The self-reliant conqueror of all previous trials was forced to acknowledge physical decline that he could not simply push through. More than the betrayal of his body, the blow to his self-made manhood hurt.

Adrienne took a part-time job at Saint Mary's Hospital while Mitka was recuperating. Disability income helped but was not nearly enough to meet the family's needs. Her modest paycheck filled the gaping hole left by Mitka's accident. Once again, Adrienne tightened the family budget and found ways to conserve.

A decade had passed since the Kalinskis moved out west—a decade of building a life together. Tim proudly watched his children grow, and his love for and dependence on Adrienne deepened. Though it played out in fits and starts, his work in construction had provided an adequate living, and when injury prevented him from working for a time, Adrienne took on work outside the home. To make a happy life was the most important thing to Tim. In most regards, he had done it.

The tumultuous 1960s didn't affect Tim and Adrienne much. They were aware of cultural and political touchstones, such as the assassinations of President John F. Kennedy, Robert Kennedy, and Martin Luther King Jr., the Vietnam War, the arrival of the Beatles, and the Apollo 11 spaceflight that landed Neil Armstrong and Buzz Aldrin on the moon; however, the world outside was mostly of little concern to them. Family came first, and they were living the good life.

But under the surface, secrets gnawed at Mitka. Ever conscious that he was illiterate, he hid but could not overcome the shame he suffered. And, in spite of the life he had created, he still struggled with feelings of self-worth.

"I didn't have no family, but nobody knew that. They all thought I was this big shot. What if they had known? I bet nobody—not even Adrienne—would have wanted me."

Keeping the past buried seemed to Mitka to be the only way to maintain his present life. He was determined to do that, but it wasn't easy. When he talks of the secrets he kept, he says, "They was like this knife in my side. Sometimes it twisted. Sometimes I barely felt it. But it was a wound I lived with every day."

For the Kalinski family, the sixties had been consumed with hard work and struggle and sacrifice but were nevertheless full of halcyon days. Greater trials lay ahead.

CHAPTER SIXTEEN

The Seventies

Sparks, 1970–1981

From a distance, Mitka and Adrienne view the 1960s as an idyllic time, and in many ways it was. As the new decade dawned, their expectations of life were optimistic. The long economic expansion of the 1960s had not yet given way to the rampant inflation and high unemployment of the 1970s. The family's income, helped by disability payments, felt relatively secure. At the beginning of 1970 the children ranged in age from five-year-old Donna to fifteen-year-old Mike. Adrienne especially, but also Mitka, was busy trying to manage activities for the younger ones while she kept an eye on a teen who was enthralled with his band, the Reverend Graves, and the converted hearse that carted instruments to gigs. The car parked in Mitka's driveway was a Cadillac. Everything seemed to be going well.

At the birth of his children Mitka had felt little, if any, emotion. Over time, though, something changed. Mitka's concern for his kids, although different from Adrienne's motherly attention, became a driving force for him. He was determined to provide for, protect, and, especially, indulge his children.

Celebrating each child's birthday with a party was important to both Mitka and Adrienne. At the Dörrs, Mitka had delivered a birthday cake for Rosemarie to Tante Anna's apartment, but he had not joined in. He had never even celebrated birthdays until he did so with Adrienne in North Tonawanda. Adrienne's birthdays were recognized, but with little fanfare. Both she and Mitka were determined that their children's birthdays would be different.

The Kalinskis' preteen Cheryl had become fixated on having a horse, a phase common to so many girls her age. Mitka was determined to make it happen.

"I didn't have the money, so I decided to see if I could trade for it."

Mitka continues. "My boss, Jim Gregg, wanted to have a basement dug in his house. So I did that in exchange for a horse he had.

"Every day after work, I would go to his house and dig that basement. At first I couldn't stand up, but eventually I dug enough that I could. I would throw the dirt out of a little window."

On Saturday, September 19, 1970, a group of girls gathered at the Kalinskis' home for Cheryl's twelfth birthday party.

Adrienne remembers it well. "I got this call from Mitka, and he says, 'Keep everyone there. I'm bringing a horse for Cheryl.' I thought it was a stuffed horse. Before the party ended, Mitka walks down the street with a real horse."

No one forgot that day.

Cheryl's smile is wide as she recalls, "That was the best birthday ever. I was so excited, and all my friends got to see that horse."

Cheryl named the horse Star. They boarded her in a local field.

"There was this lady and she had some land," Mitka says. "It was fenced in and not far from us, so it was easy to get there."

Star had a home with the happiest little girl in Sparks.

In 1972, though, another accident struck the Kalinski household. This time it was Cheryl. Adrienne begins the story.

"I was working at Saint Mary's then. Before I left for work, I told Tim, 'Don't let Cheryl ride that horse.'"

Mitka picks up the thread: "Cheryl always wanted to go see her horse. I told her she could but that she couldn't ride unless I was there with her."

Adrienne says, "She's always been determined. It didn't matter what Dad said. She saddled Star and rode her anyway."

Back and forth they talk. Mitka says, "I don't know exactly what happened, but somehow that horse got spooked. It didn't throw her; it fell."

Adrienne: "I felt bad for her, but I was also mad at her. She knew she wasn't supposed to ride, but she did it anyway.

"It was a terrible break. First, there was the hard ground, then the stirrup, then Cheryl, then more stirrup, then the horse.

"Her leg was completely crushed. She was in a cast from her hip to her toe."

The accident happened just when Mitka was nearly healed from his 1967 fall. His former ramrod-straight posture was evident again. And, although he had been forbidden to work construction, he could be found tinkering with clocks and toys. Yard work and building projects filled his days. He especially enjoyed driving his beloved Florentine Gold Cadillac.

At this point, without a hint of bitterness, he says, "Cheryl couldn't sit in the Cadillac because of the cast. So I had to sell it."

The next words he speaks in slow, melancholy measures. "I sold my beautiful car. Before I sold it, I kissed that car."

He seems to draw consolation as he adds, "We have a picture of that somewhere."

Upended again, Mitka drew on his innate optimism, just as he had for his entire life. With cash from the sale of the Cadillac, "we bought a motor home because we could put Cheryl in it and go places. So we bought the motor home for Cheryl, and it was a good thing. We loved that motor home. We could camp at Bodega Bay with it, and we went lots of other places too."

When asked what happened to Star, Mitka says, "We kept her for a while. I don't remember what we did with her. I think we must have sold her, but I can't remember."

Mitka, Adrienne, and everyone in the family remember what happened soon after.

In April 1974, Jimmy was almost eighteen and would soon graduate from Sparks High School. As a preteen Jimmy had taken an interest in law enforcement. The interest grew into a passion, and he read everything he could get his hands on about the profession that occupied his dreams day and night. One day he would become a policeman or a sheriff's deputy. It was what Jimmy lived for.

Adrienne tells the story of the fateful day in the spring of Jimmy's senior year.

"Jimmy was in the Washoe County Sheriff's Cadets. He was coming home from one of those meetings. A truck rear-ended him and slammed him into a light pole. It was on the corner of Fourth Street and Valley Road.

"A car coming in the opposite direction almost hit him too, but they missed."

When Mitka and Adrienne arrived at the scene of the accident, Jimmy appeared uninjured.

Adrienne says, "He didn't seem to be bad, but he was. He hit the back of his head so hard that it shattered the back window, but he seemed OK.

"We took him to the hospital. Mitka insisted that he be checked out even though he seemed OK. And they said he had a concussion."

Mitka and Adrienne took Jimmy home with the doctor's instructions that he would need rest for the concussion to heal. They breathed a sigh of relief that Jimmy was alive. But it was Adrienne's instinct that all was not well. Shortly after, her fears were confirmed.

"All of a sudden, he couldn't get up. He'd be sitting there talking to us and would just fall asleep. And we couldn't wake him up. It was almost like he was passed out."

She continues, "And there were times, he couldn't walk straight. Once he was walking home from school, and the police picked him up. They thought he was drunk because he was staggering so much. He couldn't walk, and he didn't even realize it."

The Kalinskis, again, took Jimmy to the hospital, where he remained for observation. They, too, observed their son, while feeling the ever-growing ache of helplessness. On one occasion, when Mitka and Adrienne were with him, the machines recording Jimmy's vital signs suddenly went flat.

"We were there in the room," Adrienne recalls, "and all of a sudden, Dad says, 'Hey, what's happening? Nothing's moving.' There was a nurse in there—and a doctor too, I think—and they pushed a button. Boy, people came running. They jumped into action and brought him back."

She continues, strain evident on her face: "That was the first time he received the last rites."

It was clear that something was seriously amiss with Jimmy. However, there was nothing the doctors could determine other than that he had a severe concussion.

In the midst of all the uncertainty, Adrienne did find some things for which she was thankful. "Jimmy was a good kid—always laughing. That didn't change." Also, "He was graduating from high school, and they gave him his diploma in the hospital."

Still, she wrestled with despair and fear. Mitka, anxious and fidgety, couldn't suppress an urgent need to act. There was, however, seemingly nothing he could do, and what was—for him—an unnatural sense of powerlessness overwhelmed him.

Searching, as they were, for answers to questions that at the time were little understood, Adrienne found hope in an unlikely place. As was her weekly habit, she read tabloid magazines.

"I had just read in the *Enquirer* about the 'CAT machine.'"

It was a thin reed on which to place her hopes, but this was her son. A single-minded determination, which had seen her through so much of her life, kicked into high gear.

Her son Jimmy had suffered a traumatic brain injury, though she wouldn't have called it by the name that is now commonplace. At the time, she saw her son suffering in ways she didn't understand; actually, neither did the medical professionals. She only knew Jimmy was acting and reacting in abnormal ways, and she rightly attributed this to his having his head slammed against his truck's rear window. She intended to go to any length to get help.

When she read the *Enquirer* article about a CT scanner, which had just been invented in 1972, she set about to see if she could find one. "There was nothing out there, nothing in California, but there was one in Buffalo." Buffalo, New York, happened to be the town next to all her relatives. So she directed her energy toward one objective: get Jimmy to Buffalo.

She and Mitka recruited Reno officials to help.

"The sheriff's department flew us to San Francisco. Then I had to buy six first-class seats for his stretcher to fit on the plane."

The cost of flying Jimmy broke the family budget. It didn't matter, nor did they give it a second thought.

"I borrowed from my family to buy those seats," Adrienne says. "We paid them back—every penny. It took some time, and we got an insurance settlement that helped. But I would have done anything at that point to get help.

"Jimmy was in Buffalo General. I never left the hospital, even though my family was there. I called everyone and asked them to pray for him, but I never left him. I slept in a chair in his room."

Jimmy stayed in the hospital for thirty-eight days. On two more occasions he received last rites.

Mitka remained in Sparks while Adrienne and Jimmy were in Buffalo. Donna, who was nine, and Cheryl, who was sixteen, needed him. And even if they hadn't, the cost of flying him to Buffalo would have been prohibitive. He has difficulty today talking about those dark days.

Adrienne remembers that they talked infrequently because of the complexities and costs of making long-distance calls from the hospital. She says, "I know it was hard for Dad. He had no idea what was happening. He just knew that things were bad."

Adrienne returned to Nevada with Jimmy but without a satisfactory diagnosis or a medical plan for Jimmy's care.

"He couldn't walk when he first came home," Adrienne says. "He got better, but he was never the same."

During the terrible days surrounding Jimmy's accident, the passage of time blurred for the Kalinskis. They struggled to maintain normalcy in their daily lives, without much success. Parenting Donna and Cheryl overwhelmed them in the throes of providing round-the-clock care for Jimmy.

When it seemed as if nothing else could go wrong, Cheryl got pregnant. When her son Michael arrived, she was not in a position to care for him. It was 1975, and she was only seventeen. Adrienne and Mitka assumed responsibility for their grandson and, in effect, became parents to a newborn.

A tumultuous decade was winding down. But the family had survived. Toddler Michael was a source of joy for all, and some balance had returned to the household. Trips to Bodega Bay in the motor home eventually resumed. Jimmy volunteered with the Sheriff's Department, though the effects of his brain injury limited his activities. He continued to experience symptoms like those associated with multiple sclerosis and, in fact, was later diagnosed with this disease. Teenage Donna stayed busy with school and household chores. Mitka remained on disability, but he did find ways to stay occupied with projects. He stifled his despondency.

Events, circumstances, and apprehension about his and his family's future had put Mitka in a vise. Beginning with his fall at Incline Village, followed by forced disability, then Cheryl's accident, then Jimmy's devastating brain injury, then Cheryl's unplanned pregnancy—each event squeezed the vise tighter and tighter. Even as he sought to cope with rapidly increasing stress, a new threat loomed.

What had triggered fear in Mitka came about because of his habit of watching television news.

As the seventies drew to a close, Ronald Reagan's presidential campaign was in full swing. Addressing and correcting the country's economic woes had been a core message of his campaign.

Part of Reagan's plan to revive the economy was a set of proposals to reduce government spending. Reagan described "billions of dollars of waste, extravagance, fraud, and abuse." In the sights of both the president and Congress were tens of thousands of disabled individuals receiving benefits under the Social Security Disability Act of 1956 and various amendments to this act.

Mitka had listened to news reports that legislation was pending that could jeopardize the benefits he had received as a result of his 1967 fall. These benefits; Adrienne's small income from occasional part-time work, babysitting and the like; small amounts of cash that Mitka picked up for doing occasional handyman jobs; and the rental income they received from a property next door that they had purchased at a low cost after a neighbor's death were, in total, the sole income for the family. The loss of Mitka's benefits would be catastrophic.

When President Reagan gave a televised speech on February 18, 1981, and another on September 24 in the same year, Mitka listened with his family's interest at stake. It was personal. In his speeches the president committed to reducing government spending by, among other things, reviewing and eliminating federal social support programs where "real need cannot be demonstrated." Mitka had heard rumors of what this presidential commitment meant, stories of reductions and even elimination of social security benefits. Alarm at what might happen to his family without his disability check dominated his thoughts. He was terrified.

As it happened, Mitka agonized over much more than his imminent loss of income. He relived the pain and suffering and fear and loss that he had kept hidden, at times even from himself, for thirty years.

His eyes fill with years of unshed tears as he says, "First Hitler took everything from me. Now Reagan is taking everything from me. All of a sudden, I am back in Germany. I am that boy."

In his heart and mind, Mitka had traveled back to Germany into its cattle cars and camps. He felt the beatings, the icy nights, the unrelenting hunger, and he saw Moly's flayed skin, a product of Gustav's vindictiveness. He remembered utter aloneness.

Then one day in December 1981, Mitka received notice that his was one of more than one hundred thousand cases that had been identified for review by the Social Security Administration. It was then that, quite out of the blue—or so it seemed to every family member—Mitka changed.

For two weeks, screams and clatter would erupt from inside Tim's bedroom at odd hours of the night. The kids would wake to crashing sounds, and Adrienne would rush to her husband's side. Then Tim would jolt awake with sweat dripping from his forehead and chin, his pajamas soaked, blankets cast across the room, and his bedside table knocked to the ground.

Adrienne, bewildered, would try to comfort him, but for agonizing minutes, he could not be comforted. Then the frenzy would subside, only to come back another night.

At the start of each new day, Adrienne questioned Tim. He would not talk. His silence increased Adrienne's burden of dread, which she bore in stoic calm. She felt angry too, and guilty for it.

Donna and grandson Michael could not tell what was happening to their hero, the loving father they thought they knew. Both children, anxious and confused, tried to pretend everything was OK. It was not.

Not much rattled Adrienne. This did.

Adrienne recalls, "He was falling apart. Sometimes we would hear him thrashing around at night. The next morning I would find the sheets all knotted up. And his clothes and sheets would be soaked with sweat."

In twenty-eight years of marriage, Adrienne had never seen her husband like this. She searched her mind and found no answers; nothing could explain what was happening. Their home and all she knew of her life felt threatened.

Nightmares were not new to Mitka; however, he had been able to deflect attention away from his occasional nightmares in various ways. To reveal what his nightmares had been about would undermine the secrets he had kept for so long.

On the day after Christmas 1981, a high wind made the temperature seem colder to Mitka than it actually was. The town of Sparks still glistened with Christmas lights, bows, and garlands. Casinos overflowed with confident gamblers fat with feasting.

In the Kalinski house, family pictures and bric-a-brac—things that once represented their happy home—felt alien. Adrienne was enveloped in fear regarding Tim's nighttime outbursts. "What was to become of us?" she thought.

But Mitka recognized something new. He had an epiphany.

Tim Kalinski is not alone. Tim has a family and, perhaps most important, a wife who loves him with a ferocity unlike anything he has ever known.

Just when it seemed like Tim's panicky, unnerved nights would not end, Mitka Kalinski broke.

It was on that Saturday morning, December 26, in his house on Twelfth Street, that Mitka spoke. He stood at his dining room table, the table of family life and shared bread, staring at his wife. His blue eyes looked vacant and leaden to the woman he loved, the woman he feared he might lose. It didn't matter. He knew it all had to stop.

In that moment, Mitka uttered nine words that would change his life.

"Adrienne, sit down. I have something to tell you."

Redemption

CHAPTER SEVENTEEN

The Phone Call

Sparks, 1981–1982

In 1951, upon coming to America, Mitka started building a dam. It was, of course, not physical but psychological—a barrier to block the river of memory behind it.

In the first two years of Mitka's American life, building the dam was easy—too easy, actually. He couldn't communicate in English, and, really, no one he encountered wanted to know about his past. At his first stop in the Bronx, and then in Baltimore, the individuals he encountered were focused on helping Mitka integrate into his new life. Because they were overwhelmed with responsibilities for a parade of refugees, Mitka's childhood, other than in its broad generalities, was not something about which they could be curious, even if under different circumstances they may have been so. He was simply one more immigrant among so many. This suited Mitka's inclinations. His focus was exclusive: stride into the future, move beyond the past.

Thus, laying the foundation of a dam happened quite without intention. When the confluence of natural circumstances caused the dam to grow, Mitka allowed it, whether deliberately or not, though likely not. It was instinctual for him; it was safety.

Only with the passage of time did his reservoir of memories become secrets. To reveal them would endanger his newfound identity as Tim— or so he supposed. To his mind, disclosure would undo everything he was building: his status with employers, his relationships, and especially his budding love affair with Adrienne.

Block by block, the dam was built, growing high and impenetrable. For nearly thirty years it held. At times, the barrier strained against the weight and pressure of the memories, but it did not break.

Sometimes a wave of Mitka's past would crest the dam, but he would offer a plausible explanation, such as, "Oh, I have some family still in Germany—you know, Uncle Gustav and Aunt Anna."

It was a near-perfect structure that Mitka could not and would not demolish, even if it had been sensible to do so. Its one flaw, though, was that it had no spillway. There was no mechanism to release the pressure of accumulated memory.

Then hairline fractures started forming in the dam. Mitka fell at Incline Village. Star, Cheryl's beloved horse, fell on her and crushed her leg. Jimmy's car accident resulted in brain injury. Cheryl got pregnant and gave birth to Michael. When the prospect of Mitka losing his income hit, it caused a crack he could not repair. It was then the dam burst.

Adrienne recalls the day like it was yesterday. "I sat right there at the table, right where I always sit. And he started talking."

For someone who had tried so hard to forget, now all he could do was remember. For two hours, Mitka spilled his story. He stopped walling off his anguish.

He told of being left at the *Kinderheim*; of escaping to live in the woods, only to be caught by soldiers; of the executions; of moving from one concentration camp to another—four all told—and then, in the final camp, Pfaffenwald, of being "rescued" by Gustav, only to be enslaved. He told of being liberated by American GIs and of the Children's Village at Bad Aibling. He told of beatings, of atrocities he saw, of cold and hunger, and of aloneness. He told of never going to school. He told of Moly and the animals he loved.

Waves of emotion and relief and guilt and shame surged through Mitka. Thoughts and emotions of all sorts tumbled in Adrienne's head too.

Mitka, a man in his midforties, was in crisis.

Mitka's crisis undoubtedly had roots in what happened to him as a child. However, apart from the horrors of his experience, another factor was at work in him. From his first conscious memory until he married Adrienne, he had known no family. When he finally gained one, it was his most precious possession and the source of his identity, security, and self-respect.

Mitka now felt that his ability to provide for and hold his family together was in peril. He had kept secrets to thwart the danger he perceived. Revealing the truth of his early life jeopardized, he thought, the very family through which he had gained identity. He was losing the war that raged inside him. He was undone.

Adrienne remarks, "At first I thought he had lost his mind. I had never heard such things. I just started writing down everything he said. I didn't know what to do."

When the flood stopped, Adrienne acted. "I got out the phone book and looked up synagogues. That was all I could think of."

The modern word "crisis" comes from a Greek word meaning "to decide." As a noun, the word came to be associated with a "vitally important or decisive state of things," a "point at which change must come, for better or worse."

A crisis specialist would have applauded Adrienne for how she reacted.

First, Adrienne believed Mitka. Whatever incredulity she felt, she suppressed and, instead, led by swift action. Also, she didn't leave, which was the one thing Mitka feared most. She did not abandon him. When asked if she ever considered leaving him, she pauses for a moment with a quizzical look and replies, "No, that never entered my head."

Adrienne's response to the watershed moment was exactly what Mitka needed. She was present and working feverishly on his behalf. She gave him what he had always longed for. She stood by Mitka when he was utterly vulnerable. Now a surety replaced the one overarching fear he had—that he would be abandoned. It was a security he had never truly known. For a moment, his fears dissolved. He slumped in the chair, exhausted.

The synagogue Adrienne called was Temple Emanu-El in Reno, a Conservative Jewish synagogue that describes itself as "Nevada's oldest Jewish congregation." Adrienne gave no thought to the fact that she was calling on a Saturday. "I didn't even know that Saturday was the Jewish Sabbath. I didn't know that they were not supposed to talk on the phone. I just knew that Mitka was in trouble."

Adrienne was relieved when a Rabbi Irnie Nadler picked up the phone at the synagogue; "it was kind of a miracle." She was told to call back on Monday to make an appointment. "I thought, 'Monday'? Mitka needs help now!" But she did as she was told.

While acting to help her husband, something else was going on inside Adrienne. As she reviewed their life together, many things about Mitka's actions and reactions came into focus. She saw his life with a new perspective. A new narrative was forming. She was beginning to understand Mitka's gruffness when their children asked for help with homework. This had covered the fact that he could not read. His anger at hearing babies cry took on new meaning. His utter distress—panic, really—at losing his disability income made sense when she saw its dark roots.

When Mitka met Rabbi Nadler, he says, "I just kind of poured myself out on him. And he loaned us $200. That money really helped us when we had nothing coming in."

Before their initial meeting was over, they settled on a time when they would return for more talk.

When they returned on January 2, they were in for a big surprise.

"We walked in and Rabbi Nadler was sitting there. And in the middle of this long table was one of those telephones with a big round microphone," Adrienne says.

Mitka joins in. "And Rabbi Nadler says, 'We're going to call that Nazi.' And I—" Mitka covers his face with both hands as if to show fear or horror. "And I couldn't believe it. Me—talking to that Nazi. Who am I to talk to him after all these years?"

Sitting beside Rabbi Nadler was a person named Grant Leneaux. The rabbi had reached out to Leneaux, a professor of German at the University of Nevada–Reno, because he wanted a translator present.

Adrienne recalls what happened next. "Rabbi Nadler had a big phone set up on his desk with microphones and a tape recorder." She then repeats Mitka's words: "He said, 'We are going to call that Nazi!'"

Adrienne continues, "Mitka trembled and broke out in a cold sweat at the thought that he would dare to question Gustav Dörr."

Professor Leneaux, some years later, recalled, "Rabbi Nadler told me that a former student of mine, who was a member of his synagogue, had recommended me as a German interpreter."

The professor came to the meeting without being briefed as to the nature of the consultation. Upon arriving, the professor recalled, "I sensed immediately that they were a loving and devoted couple. He was obviously very nervous, and she held his hand and reassured him. It reassured me as well."

Rabbi Nadler proceeded to give Professor Leneaux "a crash course in Mitka's early history."

According to all present, Rabbi Nadler had no time for small talk. Before him sat a man who, he believed, needed to speak to his former captor; so, without hesitation, he contacted an operator to place the international call.

"It was about 9 p.m. German time," Professor Leneaux describes. "A woman answered, and I introduced myself in German and asked to speak to Herr Dörr. She immediately denied that he was there and hung up. She was obviously panicked by a call from a German professor in America."

An English translation of the January 2, 1982, call transcript confirms Grant's recollection: the tape begins with Professor Leneaux speaking in German: ". . . connect me with Mr. Dörr. Is Mr. Dörr there?"

The professor's question was met with a curt "No," and after a few more exchanges an abrupt "goodbye."

Mitka, who believed he recognized the speaker as Gustav's daughter, Anni, spoke next. "She is scared. I can tell."

Professor Leneaux recalled the shared disappointment that permeated the small room when the call was cut off. Mitka was the one to penetrate the gloom. He, who had at first been afraid to make the call, was now determined to see it through. He had come this far and wasn't to be deterred. "Can I suggest something? Those were very scary words you were asking. Maybe tell her Martin is here. Will you, please? And if that is Anni, that's his daughter; then maybe you can kind of . . . She got scared. I could tell.

I can understand German. You said it fine, but you got this . . . really, really, I felt it, like you . . . you know, you scared her; she hung up."

All agreed to Mitka's suggestion, and another call was placed. As before, Anni answered the phone. Surprising everyone in the room with the calm in his voice, Mitka spoke: "This is Martin from America. Is Uncle Gustav or Aunt Lisa there?"

Hearing the name "Martin" broke down whatever defenses Anni had raised. Mitka recalls that there was excitement in her voice as she replied, "No, they are both already asleep. Just a moment, I'll call them. Maybe they're still up, alright."

Soon a gruff voice came through the receiver, a voice that Mitka had last heard thirty-two years earlier on a farm road near Rotenburg.

The first interchanges were formal and polite. Mitka spoke clearly, but he was shaken.

After exchanging pleasantries, Mitka and Professor Leneaux got to the reason for the call.

"Herr Dörr," said Professor Leneaux, "Martin would like to ask you a question. You know that he is now in America, don't you? . . . And he is now having some problem with his citizenship. He would like to get certain information, you see . . . about his origins."

Gustav's reply was quick but a touch evasive. "Yes, I'll give him that; he has to send it here in writing. Then I'll write him everything. I can confirm it for him. . . . He must write about the citizenship, for what purpose he needs it. Then I'll say. I'll write that I brought him from Russia, alright? He is a Russian."

Professor Leneaux leaped on the opening. "Ah, he is a Russian? You brought him from Russia?"

Years later, Professor Leneaux, Adrienne, and Mitka agreed that, at this point, Gustav's tone began to change. When he first came on the line, the German had been warm, seemingly excited to hear about Mitka and eager to share details of his own life and family. Then he became cautious. "That is hard to prove, because he was still a boy," Gustav said.

When Professor Leneaux pressed, "But he was a Russian? Where was that in Russia?" Gustav backpedaled.

"Well, I didn't really . . . I didn't bring him directly from Russia. You see, the German troops brought him from Russia." He added, "He speaks Russian . . . certainly he is Russian."

What followed was a disjointed exchange with Gustav asserting that Mitka was quite young, "four or five years old," when he first met him and repeating that he needed "the whole case," written with specific requests for information on Mitka's origins, because "I have to know what he needs it for."

At Gustav's last remark, Professor Leneaux, again, patiently explained that "because he can't say with certainty where he comes from, he is having a hard time getting citizenship here. For that reason we would like to find out—"

Interrupting Professor Leneaux's explanation, Gustav changed the subject. Following the "script" that had been used by members of the Dörr family years earlier when UNRRA was investigating Mitka's presence with them, Gustav began to portray himself and his family as Mitka's saviors, as kind people who, at some sacrifice, rescued and cared for a poor child.

. . . the German troops loaded him in, took him back here. . . .

He was filthy. We cleaned him up here. . . . Otherwise we would have to deal with disease.

And after he had been with us a few years, he spoke German just as well as we speak German.

I protected him. They would have sent him away. Those were simply the . . . principles of my actions.

In the midst of these self-serving claims and in spite of his hesitancy to release information, Gustav did let slip several important details.

First, Gustav both confirmed that he had taken Mitka from a camp near Rotenburg and provided a name for this camp. When asked, "Where did you find him? Did you get him from the German troops?"

Gustav's reply was confident: "In the camp Frankenwald in Bad Hersfeld . . . in the east zone."

Gustav had actually said "Pfaffenwald," but his Hessian accent had
made the word hard to understand. It would be three years before Mitka
and Adrienne would be able to identify the actual camp.

Gustav also offered up the names of people who might be able to
provide information. One was that of Eduard Gruschka, "the Pole"
who served as "the interpreter" when he "lived with us on the farm."
Gruschka had been with Gustav when he took Mitka from the camp
in 1942. Gustav also confirmed that the "Deist family," a family Mitka
remembered well, was still in Rotenburg.

Finally, Gustav provided vital information. He confirmed that Mitka's surname was indeed Kalinski and revealed that they had known this
name during the time when the boy had simply been known as "Martin."
Additionally, he indicated "the boy" was "a Jew."

As the conversation wound down, additional polite banalities were
exchanged. Gustav never wavered from his position that "Martin could
write" to specify the information he was seeking. Then, and only then,
would Gustav "get busy and work it up."

Near the end of the call, Mitka invited Gustav and his wife and
daughter to visit him in the United States, to which the German replied,
"We'll do that when we have gotten his genealogy."

The conversation ended with warm wishes from all parties.

Three witnesses to the long-distance phone call to Gustav—Rabbi
Nadler, Professor Leneaux, and Adrienne—sat in silence, each absorbed
in private thoughts.

In that moment in Rabbi Nadler's office, seeing and hearing Mitka—
especially for Adrienne, but for the professor and rabbi too—was like
meeting an icon. Mitka was, in this moment, man, boy, and symbol of
the pain that could be inflicted on one human by another. His life, like
that of millions of others, had been twisted by crimes that the three of
them could not comprehend. A flesh-and-blood casualty of evil with a
particular story, Mitka was also a stand-in for every victim they could
not touch or see or hear.

Years later, Professor Leneaux described what he experienced as he
came to know Mitka during the phone call to Germany.

"Adrienne squeezed his hand and he took a deep breath and spoke to him [Gustav] with a perfect accent in the Hessian dialect of the Rotenburg area. 'Guten Abend, Onkel Gustav. Hier ist Martin. Wie geht es dir?' (Good evening, Uncle Gustav. This is Martin. How are you?)

"I was spellbound. I was listening to the voice of an abused child speaking cautiously to an abusive parent.

"This made Gustav relax, and he seemed happy to resume his former role. He even asked his former victim how he was doing in America. Mitka answered with the deference he had so brutally learned to use on the farm.

"As a professor of German, I thought I knew all about the Holocaust and the horrors of the Nazi regime. I had read all the books and seen the documentaries and movies. However, as this large and gentle man across the table began to bare his soul, . . . the interpreter and professor became the student. It was my turn to learn, and it was a powerful lesson, a lesson of human suffering, but also a lesson of a miraculous survival—a lesson in *Überleben* [survival], as the German puts it."

Adrienne, who had for two weeks felt the brunt of her husband's despair, was encouraged. "Now we had leads. This was our first tangible link to Mitka's past with Gustav Dörr and Anna Dörr Krause. It was positive proof of the accuracy of Mitka's memories."

A compassionate man, Rabbi Nadler ached for the sufferer who sat across from him. He was angry too—angry at the evil that had been unleashed on his people. And he longed for justice. "How long, O LORD, shall I cry out . . . ?"

As for Mitka, he was still depressed and broken, but he had taken a small step toward reclaiming his life. "When the call was completed," Professor Leneaux recalls, "Mitka was emotionally drained. He was still trembling at the realization that he, Mitka—the little *Stoppelrusse*—had actually dared not only to call Gustav, but to question him."

During the call to Germany, everyone present realized that the extraordinary stories coming from Mitka's mouth had a basis in reality. Gustav said that German soldiers had taken Mitka to several camps, and that he and Eduard Gruschka had taken Mitka from a nearby camp. He described Mitka as "filthy" when they took him.

Gustav had confirmed that Mitka had lived with him and his family. He said he had come as a small child, maybe four or five years old, that he believed he was a Jew, and that his last name was Kalinski.

These corroborations of his story were important for Mitka but even more for Adrienne, who had been shaken by her husband's revelations. In releasing his secrets and by calling Gustav, Mitka had started down a path to liberation. It had been a necessary and courageous choice. It had also been costly, as it dragged him back into a life he had been determined to forget.

Adrienne recalls the days following the call. "Mitka was in an almost continuous state of depression because, in his own mind, the Nazis had taken everything away from him when he was a child. They had disabled his mind and body. . . . He was on the verge of a complete nervous breakdown."

It fell to Rabbi Nadler and Adrienne to respond to what all perceived to be a crisis. Mitka remembers the time vividly. With warmth in his voice, he speaks of Rabbi Nadler's patience, of how he talked with the rabbi, and of listening to him. He remembers how, at times, the rabbi would have Mitka stretch out on the couch in his office. In these instances he would talk Mitka into a deep state of relaxation to help him recall details and to let go of things long hidden. All of this took place under the supervision of a psychiatrist, a doctor who worshiped at Temple Emanu-El.

The healing that everyone hoped would come from these sessions did not.

Adrienne tells what happened:

A Roman Catholic priest, a Jewish rabbi, a psychiatrist, family, and friends were all trying to help Mitka face this situation realistically, but he could not. . . . His periods of depression were more frequent and longer-lasting and much more severe. The trauma of remembering and reliving those horror-filled years was taking its toll not just on Mitka but on our entire family. The past was suddenly the present for Mitka. Nothing—absolutely nothing—was more important than to search for his true identity. The nightmares came more frequently. Periods of depression lasted longer. Tensions were higher.

Now, Mitka was not the only person involved. Our entire family was being subjected to reliving and remembering the inhuman treatment Mitka had endured. Our children and our grandchildren felt the brunt of this. . . . Would our home ever be the same again?

The storm that had struck the Kalinski family on the day after Christmas in 1981 didn't blow over. It lingered, lashing them over and over again throughout the following year. Despite this, Adrienne worked tirelessly and with extraordinary persistence to find the truth about Mitka's past. She began educating herself, through reading, on all things World War II, and especially all she could find about Hitler, the concentration camps, and the Third Reich. Following up on Gustav's demand that he receive in writing the information they sought, she composed a cordial letter, gathered photos, and attached a long list of questions. All of this she sent to the Dörr address of Badegasse 14, Rotenburg an der Fulda. Gustav did not respond.

Adrienne wrote another letter, to which Gustav replied with a brief, chatty note. His reply had no substantive content; nothing about it was helpful to Adrienne. Her next letter had a different tone. She wasn't rude. She didn't reveal her disgust with him. But she took a strong, direct approach. "We are determined to learn about Mitka's background. You and your family (Anna) have answers to many of the questions we ask. . . . If you do not care to answer this letter and our original questions, then you leave us no alternative but to publicly research this most important issue—Martin's true identity." To this, there was no reply.

The ad hoc team—Rabbi Nadler, Professor Leneaux, Adrienne, and others—pressed other ideas as fast as they could think of them. Telegrams to the International Tracing Service were sent, and general "To Whom It May Concern" appeals were directed to any and all public agencies they could find. The responses to their entreaties left Mitka and Adrienne disheartened. They found no information about Mitka beyond the basic documents that UNRRA had accumulated: records of Mitka between 1945 and 1951, when he was allowed to immigrate to America.

Mitka continued in a psychological state of instability. The pressure of concealing so many secrets for so long abated, but now he faced a new task, one that was in some ways more daunting. The boundaries of his life as Tim were shattered. He experienced paralyzing shame about what had happened to him, a not-unusual phenomenon. He felt he had burdened, betrayed even, the ones he loved. A constant sense of threat, both conscious and unconscious, loomed over his days. The only comfort for Mitka seemed to lie in talking.

CHAPTER EIGHTEEN

Citizenship

Sparks, 1982–1984

In the two years following Mitka's breakdown, many in his life, including Adrienne, continued to call him Tim. He didn't object. They did so mostly out of habit. It was the name he had used for thirty-two years. The man who answered to Tim, however, was now an altogether novel creature whose revelations prompted many questions. "Who are you, Tim?" "Why did you keep the secret?" "What does this mean?"

Those around Mitka spent a lot of time just listening. His obsessive repetition of his stories frayed nerves, but none dared express this. How could they? Professor Leneaux, and especially Adrienne, sensed that his telling and retelling was the only way for him to process what had happened to him. Fierce and determined, Adrienne committed, without complaint, to protecting and advocating for her husband, which included listening for the umpteenth time to one or another incident as if she was hearing it for the first time. In this, she displayed endless patience.

Apart from the irritation and dread that came with each reprise of Mitka's stories, the Kalinski family members adjusted to the new reality. The family would never return to the existence they had once known with "Tim." But over time, they established a new equilibrium.

The other challenge to the family was Mitka's canceled disability payments. Frustrated by not being able to get answers or direction about how to get back on the social security roll, they hired an attorney, one recommended to them by Rabbi Nadler, to look into the matter. It took a full year, but the situation got resolved. Mitka received his back pay, and, again, he received checks each month. The attorney's fees were significant, so much so that it became an ongoing source of further resentment toward the government and, in particular, President Reagan. Mitka laughs about this and a further ambiguity: "I voted for Reagan in 1984."

On a regular basis, Mitka and Professor Leneaux met, usually for an hour, during which time Mitka told the professor his story. For Mitka it was cathartic; for the professor it was a time that "I was a student, not the teacher."

When Adrienne could find spare moments, she found someone to whom she could write. She was asking for help for her husband, help in locating information that might aid in finding his origins and somehow resolve his great angst. Her anger grew with each letter, however. Often it was visceral and intense. As she observed her seven-year-old grandson Michael, all she could think about was Mitka's childhood. She felt every cruelty he had experienced. As a mother, she could not fathom how someone could inflict on a child what had been done to Mitka. With every story, her determination to find justice for him grew.

Mitka's hope that revealing his past might alleviate his torment was not realized. So he simply tried to carry on with the next task at hand. He fixed anything that was broken. He buried himself in work of maintaining the house and property and motor home. He found ways to help his grown children: Mike, Jimmy, and Cheryl. He especially focused on helping Adrienne with Donna and Michael, who were both in school and living at home. Despite his inner anguish, what others witnessed was a cheerful, loving man.

In the midst of it all, Mitka and Adrienne did find ways to celebrate birthdays and holidays. Trips in the motor home to Bodega Bay continued and were their greatest source of happiness.

Adrienne speaks of what a reprieve it was for each family member as they began the trek across Donner Pass and the descent into California. The tranquil bay, fishing, crabbing, nights around a campfire, getting to know other campers, and especially the vast Pacific Ocean stretching before them—these experiences enabled them to transcend, if only briefly, the urgency Adrienne felt in trying to get evidence of Mitka's life.

It was on a camping trip in the summer of 1983 that the first breakthrough in Adrienne's quest to find out something—anything—occurred.

According to Adrienne, Mitka was, as usual, "talking to everyone." He met no strangers. With a hearty welcome and his large right hand extended, he introduced himself. In keeping with his nature, he would initiate his conversations with a humorous quip. He was in his element. Among those he encountered were Charlie and Val Viney. In the course of sharing small talk, Charlie shared with Mitka that they were going on a trip to Germany. As soon as Charlie spoke the words, "immediately Mitka began to tell Charlie about his hidden and shameful past."

The conversation developed, and Charlie was hooked, with both the man and the riveting detail about a former child slave's life. Perhaps Mitka asked or Charlie volunteered, but either way, Mitka remembers that Charlie was going to "go knock on that Nazi's door." Mitka experienced a rush of excitement that someone would confront Gustav. For him, it was more than getting information about his past; it was that Charlie would face Gustav on his behalf.

For Adrienne, though, Charlie's mission had one objective, which had nothing to do with confronting Gustav. She wanted facts. More than facts, she wanted physical evidence, such as photographs or documents and "a map or some postcards from the Rotenburg area."

Adrienne describes what she had thus far been able to piece together from Mitka's recollections:

With Mitka's help, I had—months earlier—sketched a map as he had remembered the area. We were curious as to how accurate his memories really were. He had designated specific houses, the church where he had delivered milk cans, the *Schloss* where the Belgium soldiers had caught Gustav hiding, the mass grave sites, the different execution sites, and the Jacob Grimm School where the English and other flyers had been kept prisoners. [And there were] scattered properties that were owned by the Dörr family, the flak gun locations on the Dörr property, the train station, and various other prisoner barracks in and around Rotenburg.

Mitka and Adrienne said goodbye to Charlie and Val with hope. They gave Charlie a flyer and some old photos, addresses, and Adrienne's hand-drawn map. Mitka cautioned Charlie about Gustav and

Dörr family members. In 1983 he was still gripped with fears about his former captors.

Charlie and Val did travel to Germany. Once there, they kept their promise to Mitka and made special arrangements for a side trip to Rotenburg an der Fulda.

Charlie spoke no German, which didn't deter him. When he arrived in Rotenburg, he went to a Mercedes dealership to ask for directions. It turned out to be a good choice. After his initial inquiry, he determined he needed a translator and was able to enlist the help of a young man who was fluent in English and German.

In bold American fashion, Charlie then made his way to Badegasse 14 with Val and his translator and knocked on the door. He hoped and expected to meet the Dörrs, at least one of them. A white-haired woman greeted him. After some introductory remarks, Charlie gave her a photograph and a flyer about Mitka. Upon examining the items, her response was to direct Charlie to a different address: Burgasse 14.

Charlie proceeded to the new address and knocked on the door. Another elderly woman answered. She saw the flyer, drew it close to her breast, and repeated a German phrase over and over again.

The interpreter was able to help Charlie make sense of the two encounters. The first woman he met had been Anna Jakob, the same woman who had lived upstairs in one of the apartments when Mitka was enslaved at Badegasse 14. The second woman was Frau Deist, the mother of Willi Deist, the same Nazi Youth boy who had beaten up Mitka but would later become Mitka's only childhood friend from 1945 until Mitka's rescue in 1949.

Charlie had made significant progress, the magnitude of which he didn't recognize. Frau Deist was the woman to whom Mitka gave eggs from the hen he discovered in the hayloft. She had been sympathetic to Mitka, even fond of him, while he had been at the Dörrs'.

Through the translator, Frau Deist promised Charlie that she and her family were interested in learning about Mitka, and she promised to try to help find information about his early life.

Frau Deist called her daughter and son-in-law, Kathe Deist Reiprich and Franz Reiprich, who were glad to learn of Mitka's life in America. Franz, who spoke some English, insisted on driving Charlie to the home of Gustav and Lisa Dörr.

Adrienne describes what happened:

> Once there at Gustav's farm . . . Lisa opened the door and Franz
> began to explain about Charlie being from America and that he was
> there on behalf of Mitka to see Gustav. Lisa was very alert. (Charlie
> did not realize at the time that Anna Jakob had already alerted them
> to his visit.) Lisa said, "I know why you are here, and I know what
> you want!" She firmly refused to admit Franz and Charlie into her
> home . . . as Franz kept insisting that Charlie just wanted to talk
> to Gustav. She adamantly refused . . . to let them see or speak to
> Gustav . . .

After the disappointing interaction with Lisa, the Deists invited Charlie and Val back to their home for a meal, but they had to return to
their planned itinerary. Ultimately, the Vineys had kept their promise
to Mitka and visited Rotenburg.

Charlie did come away from Rotenburg with a positive outcome,
even if it was not the outcome Mitka and Adrienne had hoped for. He
had connected, if only in a small way, with Mitka's past. Prospects for
communication between the Kalinski and Deist families were real. It
was the Deists who had observed the unattached boy living at the Dörrs.
They saw the beatings, the lack of clothes, the malnourishment, and
the suffering of Martin. A correspondence began that affirmed many of
Mitka's memories. Willi's letters were especially helpful.

Willi and his sister and brother-in-law, Kathe and Franz Reiprich,
offered to help find documents that might enable Mitka to obtain US
citizenship. This prompted them to get in touch with Eduard Gruschka,
the translator who had accompanied Gustav when he picked up Mitka
from Pfaffenwald.

From Poland, Gruschka sent replies to Willi's and the Reiprichs'
letters. He began by describing his role at the Dörrs'. Gruschka called
himself Gustav's "prisoner of war" and said that "from the 10th of November 1939, I worked as a team driver and from 1940, as a truck driver."
He added, "From 1940 on, I first delivered milk to Bebra, and then,
from 1942 on when the English wrecked and deserted Kassel, the [now]
deceased county governor, Erich Braun, took me for work in digging
out bombs."

Gruschka mentioned a few minor details that matched neither Mitka's memories nor the UNRRA records. Nevertheless, the letter affirmed many of Mitka's memories. It wouldn't be the last time the Kalinskis would need to sift what Eduard told them in order to get at what were hard truths.

Gruschka wrote of time at the Dörrs:

I took the boy (child) with Gustav in 1942 from Asbach [the municipality where Pfaffenwald was located] for work with the mother of Gustav in the fields. Yes, you know yourself how we were treated at Gustav's, but it has been a long time. The little boy did well with the rag gatherer—Christian Dörr, but he also received beatings often from Gustav. The worst was Anna after her husband died in Russia of some kind of fever.

Then he added a tantalizing bit of information:

The child was not Russian. He was the child of a Polish officer who, after the 1st WW resettled in the Ukraine. . . . His father was murdered by the Nazis in a concentration camp, and his mother and two sisters were killed (burned alive) by the Ukrainian SS soldiers.

Professor Grant Leneaux, who had translated the letter, conferred with Adrienne after she read Gruschka's words about Mitka's family. They made the decision that Mitka was too fragile to hear them. Adrienne says, "I was afraid of what he might do if he heard that his mother and sisters had been burned alive." In an attempt to shield him from the details of the deaths, they chose only to tell him that his family had all died. Their plan to shield him, however, did not work.

Mitka tells the story. "I wasn't sleeping much and I got up in the night. The letter [in German] was sitting there on the table, and I just stared at it and stared at it. I couldn't read, but I could make out letters."

He pauses before continuing. "And I saw this word—*VERBRANDT*. I could read the letters, and I sounded them out. And I knew what it meant. It meant 'burned.' I could see it was beside the letters 'SS.' So the next day, I asked Adrienne about it. That's when she told me what Gruschka had said."

As it turned out, Gruschka's words did not distress Mitka as Adrienne and Professor Leneaux had feared. On the contrary, it fueled his desire to know more.

A month later, in a letter dated January 21, 1984, Gruschka wrote directly to Mitka, using an address he had gotten from Willi Deist. In the letter he made the same points that he stated in his letter to the Reiprich family. One new item stood out. To begin his letter, Gruschka wrote a simple statement with each letter capitalized.

YOUR NAME IS MIECZYSLAW KALINSKI

Gruschka followed this with a screed about Gustav. He was a "pig" and a "swine" who, after the war, had been "locked up—put in jail—as an active Nazi participant and because he was torturing the Jews."

Gruschka continued, stating that "der Eisen Gustav" had not joined the German army and had, in fact, been viewed as "a shirker or a draft dodger." He was, however, "in the SA as an active murderer on the Jewish Estate." These harsh words were meaningful to Mitka and Adrienne in that they confirmed what Mitka knew. The man and the family who had enslaved him were active collaborators in Hitler's malevolence. The stories told by Anna to UNRRA representatives after the war that they were fostering an abandoned child, and Gustav's words in the phone conversation two years earlier suggesting that he acted with courage and compassion to save a Jewish boy—these were lies.

Gruschka then turned his attention away from Gustav to Mitka. He wrote:

> The name Dimitri was given to you by the camp supervisor in Asbach because this was the desire of Gustav—to wipe out all traces of your origin. . . . Your real name is Mieczyslaw Kalinski from Czortkow, Polish Ukraine—Poland. Your family comes from a rich Polish family. Back in history your ancestors were ennobled by the great Polish head man Zokkiewski, for your father's ancestors took part in the battles with rebelling Cossacks.

Gruschka's words captivated Mitka. He wanted to believe him. But could he? It was the first time he had heard this story. He wondered—with some bitterness—why Gruschka never mentioned a word of this to him when he was at the Dörrs'. "I used to say if only I had a big brother. He could have been that for me. Every time I took milk to Bebra, he rode on the wagon with me. And we went to Kassel together. Why did he never tell me these things?"

Adrienne became suspicious, and then Mitka as well. They wondered whether Gruschka might have wanted money in return for information. For example, he requested that they send him "$150.00 for [a] trip to West Germany," during which he promised to seek more information that could help Mitka. It was the first of many times that he pleaded for the Kalinskis to send him money.

Gruschka's letter otherwise piqued the Kalinskis' interest. It gave them some leads to pursue. Adrienne and Mitka chose to downplay the new information until they could corroborate the report. After two years of writing agencies and individual authorities to no avail, they decided to take their search to a new level. They decided it was time to go to Germany.

Adrienne, more so than Mitka, felt an urgency to go back to the source of all that had fractured Mitka. She was done with patience. For two years she had watched her once strong, fearless husband fall apart. She was discouraged but not defeated. She was angry too. As Mitka said, Adrienne wanted to go to Germany to "knock some heads together." She describes her motives with slightly different words.

> I kept thinking about Michael [their grandson]. When Tim first told me about what had been done to him, Michael was seven—just about the same age as Tim when he went to the Dörrs'. I couldn't imagine how anyone could treat a child that way . . . especially Anna. She had a child of her own. I wanted to confront her and get her to tell me why.

Adrienne began to contemplate how they might pull off a trip to Germany. In the interim, Mitka, in spite of the face he presented to the world, battled stress and depression.

Fighting what felt like a "losing battle," Adrienne received a sudden, unexpected streak of inspiration one night. She recalls:

Unable to sleep one night, I got up, and in the darkness of one early morning I began to write. I wrote of Mitka's life and of the pain and suffering and frustrations he had endured as a child. By the time I had finished, I realized that I had written a poem of fifty-six lines. It was all there on paper. Somehow just reading it and knowing that it was something very special for someone very special to me made me feel good. I titled it "Mitka."

I said nothing to Mitka nor anyone else about that writing. I decided I would read it to him at an appropriate time.

[In the meantime] I read where a publisher was looking for "short poems" to be included in their new publication. "Mitka" was not a short poem, but I mailed it anyway. . . .

A short time later, I received notification that my poem had indeed been selected to be published. This was the "appropriate time." While Michael was in his karate lesson, I finally told Mitka what I had done. The look of disbelief on Mitka's face was indescribable. He could not believe that I had actually written this just for him.

Mitka had longed to be a US citizen from his earliest days in America. He decided, however, that it was a dream beyond his reach. To return to Germany, Mitka had to obtain his citizenship. This was the only way he could leave the country. He was highly motivated, as Adrienne was threatening to go to Germany without him. Indeed, she had purchased four tickets—for Mitka, herself, Donna, and Michael—to fly from San Francisco to Germany in November 1984. On the to-do list: get Mitka a passport.

"She made me get my butt out of the chair to try to get my citizenship," Mitka says. "We talked to this lawyer, and he found out that they could ask me questions so I didn't have to read them. So I paid fifty dollars and signed up to take the test."

Preparing for the test was a particular challenge for Mitka given his illiteracy. "I learned about government by movies and TV—especially the news. You'd be surprised what you can learn if you just pay attention."

The first time Mitka took the test, he said, "I thought I passed but I didn't. I think I just missed."

The next testing date was in mid-October 1984.

"So when I could take the test again, I didn't have to pay the fifty dollars. I just had to go take it. Oh, I was so nervous. A lady from our lawyer's office, Becky, went with me—not to help with the test, but for . . . what do you call it? Moral support.

"And the judge was asking questions, and I was doing pretty good, but then he asked me this question, 'How many judges are on the Supreme Court?' That was one I didn't know. I knew that Reagan had appointed Sandra Day O'Connor, but I didn't know the answer to the question. Was it six? Seven? Nine?

"Finally, I looked at him, and I said, 'Which Supreme Court? Nevada or the United States?' He smiled at me, and I had passed.

"Oh, I was so excited. I jumped over to give him a hug, and I knocked a chair over, and the guards came rushing in. I think they thought I was going to hurt him or something."

On Friday, October 19, 1984, Mitka was sworn in as a citizen of the United States of America. He stood with other newly minted citizens in the Reno Courthouse to pledge his allegiance to his beloved adopted country. What happened next moved him from excited celebration to poignant tears. All the other new citizens had chosen Mitka to receive the flag to which they had pledged their allegiance moments before. Mitka overflowed with joy and thankfulness as the flag was ceremoniously folded and presented to him. Mitka kissed the flag. For almost thirty-four years he had dreamed of this day, but without hope that his dream would come true. It did. He was a citizen of the United States of America.

On Monday, October 22, Mitka and Adrienne traveled to San Francisco to get Mitka a passport.

One circle had closed. Mitka was going back to Germany.

CHAPTER NINETEEN

Back to Germany

Rotenburg an der Fulda, Early November 1984

Once again Mitka was embarking on a journey. Since gaining his citizenship, which in itself was a necessary condition for international travel, he could think on little else. The last time he had flown—early in 1951—he left behind a cruel childhood that now he was confronting once again. This return to Germany was something he had to do.

The journey began in Reno on Thursday, November 1, 1984, when Mitka, Adrienne, sixteen-year-old Donna, and nine-year-old Michael boarded a plane to make the short hop to San Francisco. Adrienne was exhausted before the trip had even begun but, as was so often true, had her wits about her. Michael was about to make his first flight; Donna, her first international trip. Both were excited. Mitka, however, was, to put it charitably, a mess. Adrienne recalls:

> Poor Mitka was shaking. He was certain that the plane would never get off the ground one minute, and then the next minute, he was terrified that it would crash. Suddenly the gentleman next to Mitka said, "Your first flight?" He nervously began to respond, but not before we were well on our way. The stewardess was soon offering 7UP, and, as tense as he was, Mitka began to talk excitedly, spilling out the reason for our trip. He became so involved in talking that he lost all track of time or distance.... Then he started worrying all over again. "The runway is too short." "I hope the brakes work." "Do you think the pilot knows what he is doing?" And on and on and on.

Once airborne, Adrienne, Donna, and Michael fell asleep. Mitka sat by the window, gripping Adrienne's hand.

During the eleven-hour flight to Germany, Mitka never once rose from his seat, nor did he sleep. "I never moved," he says. Some bragging comes across when he adds, "Some bladder control, huh?"

Mitka's fright rose dramatically when the pilot came over the intercom and instructed passengers to fasten their seat belts in preparation for landing. Adrienne says his fear grew when the pilot added, "We are experiencing heavy fog conditions." As she remembers, "Immediately Mitka was on alert and tensed up even more. He sure hoped the pilot knew what he was doing. 'What if he couldn't see the runway?' 'What if the instruments weren't working?' 'What if . . . what if . . . what if . . . ?'"

When the plane landed safely, Mitka finally relaxed—after a quick trip to the restroom. He was now back on German soil.

After orienting themselves, the Kalinski family went about the business of typical tourists. They rented an Opel that could accommodate the four of them and Donna's enormous suitcase, which was an irritant to Adrienne from the start. They started the process of adjusting to the time change, and they visited a friend of Adrienne's who lived in the suburbs of Frankfurt.

On Sunday evening, November 4, they decided to let Willi Deist— Mitka's childhood adversary and subsequent friend—know that they were in country. They placed the call from their hotel, the Via Claudia in Augsburg.

Willi and his family had been quite helpful in locating Eduard Gruschka, and Willi seemed sincere in wanting to help Mitka in his quest. Something in Adrienne, however, did not trust Willi. He had, after all, been a member of the Hitler Youth and did participate in beating and kicking Mitka. It was Willi who had reported Mitka to authorities for asking, "What's so special about Hitler?" For this offense, Mitka had spent time in the *Rathaus*, subsisting on bread and water. To young Mitka, the most frightful part of this ordeal was the prospect of being returned to Pfaffenwald.

Adrienne could not forget these facts when she thought of Willi, nor could she forgive him. Yet she recognized that Willi could be useful in their search for information.

The first piece of information Willi shared with the Kalinskis in the call could hardly have been more jarring: Gustav had died just months earlier. Upon hearing this news, Mitka experienced an acute sense of loss. It was a strange reaction—that he would feel grief rather than *Schadenfreude* (malicious joy). The man had been his captor and tormentor. But Gustav had rescued Mitka from certain death in Lager Pfaffenwald. So Mitka felt a peculiar alchemy of emotions.

More so, though, the news crushed Mitka's hope that Gustav would be the crucial link to uncovering his identity. He remembered so well that Gustav, during the 1981 call, had intimated that he had information regarding Mitka's genealogy. If only they had arrived before he died, perhaps they could have gotten the papers that Gustav said he had. The thought devastated him.

The family next visited the Children's Village at Bad Aibling. It was there that Mitka's spirits lifted. It had been the place where he began to experience kindness and caring, where he began to imagine a life that had been thitherto unimaginable. Adrienne says the Children's Village gave him "a first glimpse of a human lifestyle."

The family went to Bad Aibling with the hope of touring the Children's Village. It was not to be. Adrienne recalls, "Where the big arched sign had once read 'Bad Aibling's Children's Village,' it now read 'Bad Aibling Station,' and there were guards at the gate now." They were not able to go into the camp, as it had been repurposed into a military station. Through the fencing that surrounded the base, they did get to see the barracks in which Mitka had stayed. From this sight they got a sense of where Mitka had spent two formative years as a young teenager.

Despite their disappointment, they made the best of their time in Bavaria, touring the quaint town of Bad Aibling and enjoying family time as tourists. Mitka found some solace in his mostly happy memories of his time at the Children's Village. The visit was a small but important step toward healing his damaged self.

And it ended on a happy note, as Adrienne describes:

Too soon it was time for us to leave this quaint little Bavarian town that was nestled there in the mountains. As we drove down a side street, Mitka spotted a music store. There, inside, was a beautiful four-row button accordion. He began to play "Lili Marlene," and such beautiful tones came forth as his big rough hands and fingers gently touched the buttons. He played with such feeling that the storekeeper came from the back room to see who was making such beautiful music. Then the man went and got another accordion, and together they played the "Snow Waltz." I cannot begin to describe the beautiful sounds that filled the little shop that day.

When the Kalinskis left Bad Aibling, they traveled north for eighty-two miles through picturesque Bavaria. What awaited them next was a preplanned stop at Dachau. There could be no preparation for such a stark contrast.

Mitka was initially stoic, tense, and silent. He walked around the grounds, observing everything, his hands buried deep in the pockets of his black leather coat. As he walked on, his body began to quiver, a physiological reaction he couldn't control.

Michael had not been able to comprehend his grandfather's story, though he had heard it often—so often that he grew tired of it. But when he took in Dachau—saw Mitka shaking, felt the soulless ground beneath his feet—for the first time, his grandfather's stories became real. On this day he saw his grandfather step into one of the scenes from those stories. He couldn't shake the experience.

Michael needed to acknowledge his newfound understanding. He chose to sign his own name in the guest book. With the script of a boy, he carefully wrote, "Michael Jason Biesel—nine-year-old grandson of Dimitri Kalinski, a survivor of Dachau."

From Dachau, the family headed toward Rotenburg. At Willi's insistence, they stayed in his and Martha's guesthouse just outside town—a generous offer that Adrienne accepted only reluctantly, as she still had misgivings about Willi.

The visit began with cordiality, and one significant fact emerged in the first conversation: the name of the camp from which Gustav had taken Mitka.

For the three years since the 1981 phone call to Gustav, Adrienne had searched in vain for any information about the camp. Mitka's memories of the camp had a profound effect on Adrienne. She heard of him witnessing pregnant women being cut open and what he thought were puppies being thrown against walls. She heard of the medical experiments on him—the tube up his nose, the materials he was forced to ingest, and the hot glasses on his back. And she knew there were other things about the camp he would not disclose, even to her.

For three years Adrienne had searched for the name of the camp. It came to nothing. She had a couple of clues. Mitka knew the name of the town where the train stopped—it was Asbach. Working with paper maps that lacked detail, Adrienne could not locate Asbach. In the phone call with Gustav, he had mentioned the camp as "Frankenwald"—or at least that is what everyone heard.

So, in that early conversation with Willi, Mitka told him that he hoped to learn about "Frankenwald," the camp located near Asbach. Martha overheard the exchange and came from the kitchen saying, "Ach du lieber Gott—Pfaffenwald."

Mitka understood. "Oh my god—Pfaffenwald."

As Adrienne recalls, he began to shake uncontrollably.

Mitka describes the moment. "The sound of this name hit me like a stroke. That was the name that had been buried, and no one had remembered."

Martha then said that she and her family had heard of a Lager Pfaffenwald. Willi said he had not and expressed his skepticism. Martha held firm. Her confidence that the camp was nearby and a real place gave Mitka and Adrienne corroboration of one of Mitka's stories. It also created in him a kind of imperative. He needed to return to this place of horror. He needed to confront his memories and, more importantly, honor those who had not survived.

The next day—Thursday, November 8—the Kalinskis went back to the Deists' for lunch.

That morning, Willi had gone to work. Despite his skepticism about the existence of Lager Pfaffenwald, he decided to investigate. Over lunch, Willi reported that he learned that Susanne Hohlmann, a graduate student at the University of Kassel, was engaging in research on Lager Pfaffenwald. Now he was eager to help Mitka find the camp.

Adrienne wondered about Willi's quick change of mind toward Pfaffenwald. With her, every action, every word of those with whom Mitka had interacted and was interacting with once again gave her pause. She examined each bit of evidence with skeptical eyes and ears. Given her protection of Mitka and her knowledge of his past, her general distrust was understandable. Yet she pushed forward out of practicality. She was not one to look a gift horse in the mouth. Thus, after lunch, Willi and the Kalinskis set out on a road trip to find Pfaffenwald.

Willi, at his insistence, drove. This irritated Adrienne further. Her sense was that Willi was trying to exert too much control over Mitka. Mitka also had suspicions. "He said there was no such thing [as Pfaffenwald], and now he's all ready to help us find it." Regardless, they put their feelings aside and headed off with Willi in the driver's seat.

"We started at Asbach. There was this dirt road that was headed toward Beiershausen. I don't remember how we ended up walking, but we did. We came to this place and Willi said, 'This is it,' but I didn't think it was."

What Mitka remembered were trees—*Buchecker* trees—underneath which he had collected beechnuts for his sick and starving companion inmates. The trees around Willi didn't look right to Mitka; they were too tall and too old—probably eighty years or so. The beechnut trees he scavenged under had been small and supple and young; they would not, then, have been eighty years old in 1984. On this day the search for Pfaffenwald ended in frustration.

Willi and the Kalinskis returned to Asbach and sought a bakery for warmth, coffee, and pastries. Mitka says, "There was this man there—Hohlmann. Willi says to him, 'We are looking for Lager Pfaffenwald.' He talked in German, but I could understand him."

Then Willi added, "We thought it was over there, but my friend says it can't be."

Mitka straightens up and beams as he recalls that Hohlmann immediately replied, "Your friend is right. Pfaffenwald is about two kilometers north of there." That Mitka knew more than Willi and had bested him was a significant marker for Mitka, an establishment of credibility. He was pleased—and relieved—that his memories were proving to be accurate.

Mitka continues, "Somehow this Hohlmann . . . he asks about why we are looking for Pfaffenwald. And Willi says, 'My friend here—he was a survivor.' Hohlmann became so happy, and he said, 'You must stay here while I call my daughter.'"

This was the same Susanne Hohlmann Willi had learned of earlier that morning, the graduate student whose thesis was on Pfaffenwald. When her father called, she drove straight to Asbach.

Mitka says, "I told her things she didn't know. She didn't know that anyone had survived."

The next day—Friday, November 9—Mitka, Adrienne, Donna, and Michael drove from Willi's guesthouse to the neighborhood in Rotenburg where Mitka had lived. The first stop was Willi's mother's house. Mrs. Deist was the woman that Mitka had given purloined eggs to so many years before. Mitka wanted to introduce his family to her and her daughter, Kathe Deist Reiprich. As Adrienne remembers, it was a happy reunion tinged with poignant memories for Mitka:

> Oma Deist embraced Mitka like a long-lost son! Guilt and sadness of the past mixed with tears, smiles, and excited chatter amongst everyone. . . . Willi's sister, Kathe, embraced Mitka like a long-lost brother. Finally, Michael was able to present Oma Deist with a big bouquet of flowers for this special occasion!
>
> There was so much to say, and everyone was trying to talk excitedly at once except for Donna, Michael, and me. Even though we were all made very welcome, and we were very much included in the special reunion, this moment really belonged to Mitka, Oma Deist, and Kathe. Willi actually said very little. That happiness was contagious, though, and we were all smiling, talking with hands, trying to explain, etc., with both German and English. Kathe had prepared a beautiful table that held several different cakes as well as coffee, tea, and soda (no ice) for our arrival.
>
> But just as when we first arrived, all the happiness and joy and smiles did not seem to erase the past memories that seemed ever present. Everyone kept their eyes on Mitka, almost like they couldn't believe that he was really there, sitting at their table, and actually eating with them.

The next stop would be more difficult for Mitka. For a long time he had anticipated this day. He was about to come face to face with the woman who had viciously beaten him time and again. His dread of the moment was visceral. Still, he knew he must confront his fears. Gustav was dead, and one of his only links to papers about his past was Anna.

Adrienne describes their arrival at the home of Anna Dörr Krause on Richard Wagner Strasse:

> Rosemarie led us to the entrance, and from an inner room, an elderly woman emerged. Her gray hair was pulled neatly back from her face. She walked with a cane and a slight limp. . . . Her piercing blue eyes seemed to glare at Mitka even though she kept a forced smile on her face. She kept repeating *"Nein, nein, nein* . . . This can't be Martin."

Anna seemed so tiny to Mitka that he was startled. As she continued to say, "Nein, nein, nein," he dropped to one knee so that he could look up into her eyes. He said, simply, "Do you remember me, Tante Anna?"

Anna had no reply.

Slowly and, at least to Adrienne's mind, reluctantly, Rosemarie and Anna led them into a sitting room.

Dread hung over Mitka like a cloud. He kept moving forward to the room with the thought that Anna might be persuaded to give him access to papers Gustav had indicated he had. It was a long shot, but if anyone knew of such papers, Mitka thought, it was surely Anna.

The conversation did not begin well. Mitka opened by talking about Gustav taking him from Pfaffenwald. Anna shot back in an instant. "*Nein*, it was my father. It was Georg—not Gustav. Georg took you." She said it over and over again. Rosemarie picked up the refrain, repeating the words her mother had uttered.

The falsehood of mother and daughter riled Mitka. To his own surprise, he turned to Rosemarie and said, "Rosemarie, ruhe. Sie wissen nichts darüber," meaning "Rosemarie, be quiet. You don't know anything about this." Rosemarie, seemingly equally surprised, fell silent.

Mitka turned his attention back to Anna and asked a direct question about the records Gustav had said he had. Adrienne remembers a shudder moving across Anna's face, followed by her curt reply: "Wenn Sie die Aufzeichnungen meines Bruders wollen, dann musst du meinen Bruder danach fragen" (If you want my brother's records, then you must ask my brother for them).

Mitka was visibly frustrated by Anna's refusal to assist him. He looked into her eyes and, again speaking German, asked, "Anna, do you remember that time you made me go with you on the road to Bebra?"

Adrienne did not understand German, but she did recognize "Bebra." She describes Anna's response. "Fear or perhaps shock showed briefly on her face, but she still remained silent. It was as if she was holding her breath."

Mitka persisted, this time in English. "You made me watch when those soldiers executed the prisoners. Then the soldier shot everyone in the head."

Upon hearing these words, Anna lifted both arms to her face "as if to shield herself from an oncoming blow."

Lowering her arms, Anna hissed, "This one—he has a good memory."

Her guilt was laid bare. Mitka was validated. It was a turning point. He breathed deeply. He was in command.

"Anna, I would like to have a drink with you."

The test of wills between Mitka and Anna was over. Mitka felt liberated, so much so that he offered the magnanimous gesture of sharing a drink with his longtime adversary. He had gotten from Anna what he needed: the tacit admission of her complicity in the cruelty he had been subjected to as a child.

Rosemarie's husband responded to Mitka's request by entering the room with poured drinks and a bottle on a tray. One glass, filled with an amber-colored drink, was handed to Mitka. Anna, Rosemarie, and her husband took the other glasses that held ruby-colored drinks. Mitka raised his glass, offered a toast, and returned his glass to the tray.

That Mitka was offered a different drink confirmed to Adrienne that Anna and her family still intended Mitka harm. She believed the drink was poison. There is no evidence that this was the case, and her suspicions were never tested because Mitka chose not to take a sip.

The next two days offered a respite from a deep dive into Mitka's memories. The Kalinskis shopped at the nearby *Marketplatz*. They had "tasty and delicious" meals in their own lodgings and with the Deists.

On Sunday, November 11, Willi drove the Kalinski family to a section of the Iron Curtain at Philippsthal and Heringen, two cities where the border between the East German "Russian zone" and West Germany was clearly evident. Seeing farms across the border gave Adrienne the chance to put her anger about how Mitka had suffered into a broader context. She realized that there were victims all over Europe, victims on both sides of the conflict. As she said, "They're human beings with families and feelings like us." The experience pressed home the reality that Mitka was but one of millions who suffered terribly because of war.

The next day, Monday, November 12, was Mitka and Adrienne's anniversary. It passed without fanfare. Their focus had returned to finding truth about Mitka's past.

Oma Deist, Willi's mother, had invited the Kalinskis to join Willi and his sister Kathe for cabbage soup, mashed potatoes, and sausages. After lunch, Mitka and Willi drove to the *Rathaus* in Bad Hersfeld to search for records that might provide clues to Mitka's origins. Michael played with a new friend, a young German boy, and Adrienne and Donna went shopping. The trip to the *Rathaus* yielded nothing of value.

Leaving the *Rathaus*, Mitka and Willi returned to the Deist home on Burgasse, which was close to Badegasse 14, the site of Mitka's long enslavement and his only childhood home. What happened next was of inestimable value to Mitka and his family.

At the time, Anna Jakob (not to be confused with Tante Anna) resided at Badegasse 14, a fact the Kalinskis had learned from Charlie Viney when he had visited Rotenburg on Mitka's behalf a year earlier. Mitka, as a child, had known Anna Jakob when she had rented an apartment from the Dörr family. When Charlie had knocked on the door of Badegasse 14 carrying a childhood picture of Mitka, Anna had turned him away.

This refusal by Anna made the Deists and the Kalinskis cautious about an approach. They devised a plan. Kathe Deist Reiprich—not

Mitka or Adrienne—would request that she meet Mitka. The reasoning was that Kathe, a former neighbor of Anna Jakob, would not elicit an immediate rebuff, whereas Mitka might.

Kathe knocked on the door. Mitka, Adrienne, and Donna—nervous but hopeful—walked around the house (which occupied a block) as Mitka pointed out various things he recalled. When Anna finally came to the door, she saw Mitka and called out to him, "Ich habe dein Bild erkannt" (I recognized your picture). A wall came down; the door was opened. The picture Charlie had shown her was the catalyst for her inviting them inside.

It all came back. Once again, Mitka was a little boy. Room by room he showed his family the scenes of his childhood. His stories came alive through the walls and staircases, the halls and haylofts. Then they entered the room he slept in. There was no straw and the bars were gone from the lone window, but the room was otherwise unchanged.

When the family came to the window where he had heard the voice, a hush came over them. In the silence, Mitka heard the words again: "In the end you will find your purpose." As others moved along, he answered the voice. "Hello, it's me. I live in Sparks, Nevada, in the United States." Recalling the incident later, Mitka wants to explain why he shared his address. Believing that the voice was that of God, "I wanted him to know where to find me."

The group had one more visit to make before nightfall. Would Gustav's widow, Lisa, consent to see them? After all, she, too, had refused Charlie Viney's attempted visit. When they knocked on the door of Gustav's country home on Martin Luther Strasse, Lisa answered. Adrienne remembers:

> My first impression of her was that here was a hardworking farm woman who was very straightforward. . . . She seemed very firm and very confident, very much in control, even though she was obviously very cautious.

Mitka had hoped that Lisa could and would offer him access to Gustav's papers—to documents that might hold clues as to who he was and whence he had come. Lisa, however, refused, saying she knew nothing about her husband's affairs.

Sitting in a cluttered office in the only chair in the room, Lisa raised her hand about four feet from the floor and said to Mitka, "You were this tall when Gustav got you at Pfaffenwald." Then she offered Mitka advice: "Forget the past. And be glad that you are alive. You'll be much healthier that way."

CHAPTER TWENTY

Fobianka

Rotenburg an der Fulda, Late November 1984

The Kalinskis' time in Germany was not over. On Wednesday, November 14, another event would bring memories to the fore. Martha Deist had learned that a man named Fobianka, who had been a commandant at Pfaffenwald, lived four houses away from them on Friedlosser Strasse. Without telling Fobianka about Mitka, Martha and Willi invited him to their home.

From the time Adrienne first planned the trip to Germany, she had wanted to maintain a diary of everything that happened. One way she did this was to carry a portable recorder with her to every meeting. Donna had the same idea. When Fobianka arrived at the Deist house, Donna slipped her hand into her purse and turned on the recorder. Sometime later, Adrienne was able to get a transcription and translation of Donna's tape. As a result, she has a record of the odd meeting.

Both Adrienne and Mitka recall the moment when Commandant Fobianka was introduced to Mitka. In Mitka's words, "We was just standing there, and then Willi said, 'This is Mitka. He was in Pfaffenwald when he was a little boy.'"

Mitka continues, "His head jerked up and he just stared at me. And he never took his eyes off of me the whole time. He just stared—like he couldn't believe it."

"I think he was afraid," Adrienne elaborates. "He knew what they did in there, and he was afraid Mitka would talk."

Indeed, the transcript of Fobianka's words suggests that the Kalinskis' impressions were correct. In 1984, Pfaffenwald was a hidden

211

part of German history. It seems likely that Commandant Fobianka was afraid that the full truth of Pfaffenwald would be revealed. In this meeting, Fobianka insisted that Lager Pfaffenwald was "a gathering camp for sick Russian civilians. They came to Pfaffenwald when sick. When they were well, they went back to Russia." He denied that a solitary, unattached child like Mitka was there. "I did not have a single child without anybody."

Willi challenged Commandant Fobianka. He declared that Gustav had gotten Mitka, "a single child," from Pfaffenwald. Fobianka responded by repeating his previous assertion: "I did not have a single child without anybody." He then went on to avow other things that are contrary to Mitka's memory. "Abortions were never performed," he said. And he claimed that he, working with physicians, "dispensed medications," that "nobody was permitted to be beaten," and that he "always tried to keep families together."

As Fobianka told stories to accentuate his good and responsible leadership of the camp, he took the opportunity to impugn Pfaffenwald detainees and also Susanne Hohlmann, who he knew had written a soon-to-be-published thesis about Pfaffenwald. It was her research that uncovered facts about the camp—murders, abortions, medical experimentation. Fobianka said he and others should sue Hohlmann for her scholarship.

Fobianka also remembered the camp's interpreter, possibly the woman who spoke to Mitka in Yiddish, as "Jewish and from Moscow . . . a music student." He continued, "She was short and fat."

At one point, Adrienne tried to question him. In the recording Fobianka derisively muttered that she was a *dumme Amerikanerin*— stupid American. It was perhaps fortunate that he said this under his breath and in German, because Adrienne did not understand him. It's not difficult to imagine a biting reply from Adrienne if she had heard the insult.

Fobianka chuckled cruelly as he described camp inhabitants. "Things were not always peaceful around there. People were sometimes running around naked, and then the whole camp was screaming."

Fobianka ended the conversation with self-congratulation. "I got along with the people very well."

During the next two days, Mitka and Willi sought records that might contain any more clues. It was a tedious and boring search not suited to Mitka's temperament. Frustration mounted, and nothing came of the search. Adrienne responded in anger that Willi dominated Mitka's time, which increased Mitka's stress.

Unbeknownst to them, word had spread of the Kalinskis' extended stay in the region. If they had realized that they had become objects of curiosity, that they were minor celebrities of a sort, Mitka and Adrienne might have tempered what they were feeling.

Late in the afternoon on November 15, a development occurred. Three writers—journalist Reinhard Renger from the prestigious *Stern* magazine, a reporter from the local Bad Hersfeld newspaper, and Susanne Hohlmann—wanted to interview Mitka. Willi Deist most likely contacted the two journalists. Susanne Hohlmann had been introduced to Mitka by her parents in the chance encounter at the bakery in Asbach. She wanted to learn about Mitka's experiences, as she believed Mitka to be one of few survivors of the camp.

News of Mitka's presence in Germany inspired one other event: local citizens planned a *Volkstrauertag*, or National Day of Mourning, ceremony. Captives at Pfaffenwald had buried some of their dead in a small, rundown cemetery at the camp. The idea was to have Mitka, as one of two known survivors of the camp, honor the Pfaffenwald dead there. If the site was an act of defiance by the inmates of the camp, it would now continue to serve that purpose.

Words from Adrienne's unpublished manuscript capture an early morning visit, done in preparation for the ceremony and the memorial that was held that afternoon.

> Sunday, November 18, was cold and dreary with a fine misty rain that seemed somehow connected to the fact that we were going to visit a very dismal place. I was confident that Mitka would be strong even though the emotional impact would undoubtedly have a definite traumatic effect on him. Even though I had brought his prescribed tranquilizers with us, he had not taken even one during our entire trip. He was determined to see, to hear, to feel with a "clear" mind—not a mind or body dulled by any medication of any

kind. . . . We rose early that morning and took Donna and Michael
to spend the next few hours with Martha. Then Willi, Mitka, and
I headed for Asbach. There we met Susanne and Reinhard. . . . We
were soon on a narrow little country road. There was no other traf-
fic, no homes, just country. There was absolutely nothing around.
The sky was dull and overcast. The only thing we could see in the
distance was the autobahn bridge in one direction and trees, trees,
trees in every other direction.

There were some barbed-wire fences still strung along what had
apparently been an unpaved road. Mitka stood there in silence,
gazing at the bridge far away. Then slowly, he turned to look off
into the rolling hills and deep forests and the complete emptiness
and silence.

His hands were buried deep in his coat pockets. He said nothing, just kept on nodding his head slowly as if saying, "Yes, this is
the place."

It was Lager Pfaffenwald, more than any other camp Mitka passed
through, that riveted him. He couldn't rid himself of the ghosts of that
place, of the experiences he had there, including incidents about which
he has never spoken.

Mitka and Adrienne had enough time to prepare for the ceremony.
One thing they did was purchase a wreath with a banner. The banner
was inscribed with the words:

> *Als zehnjähriger Junge habe ich mit dir vergeblich gelitten. Als Über-*
> *lebender grüße ich Sie in schmerzlicher Erinnerung.*

> As a ten-year-old boy, I suffered with you in vain. As a survivor,
> I give my regards to you in painful remembrance.

Donna, Michael, and Martha rejoined Adrienne, Mitka, and Willi,
and the memorial ceremony began at 2 p.m. on Sunday, November 18.
Adrienne wrote these words about the minutes preceding the event:

> We're all just standing around waiting for whoever would be there
> to mourn these poor souls. . . . Then quietly, very quietly, a group

of perhaps ten or twelve German citizens—men, women, and children—emerged from the depths of the forest. They did not come up the path that we had come from. Instead, they came from the opposite direction. They were neither hostile nor friendly, just very much present, very serious and very silent.

Some attending were not there to mourn. One man stepped forward to protest. He said this was not a memorial for Germans.

"Let no one here forget that there are no Germans buried here."

Susanne Hohlmann took in what the man said. Upon hearing the words, she turned and spat on the ground. Her contempt for the idea that only dead Germans were worthy of their honor on this Day of Mourning couldn't be contained. It was a disgust Adrienne shared, but her attention had shifted to Mitka.

Adrienne heard the music. She saw the small crowd gathered to mourn, and she saw her husband kneeling before the plaque that marked the place where so many had suffered and died. After a few quiet moments, Mitka rose in reverence. He held the wreath and banner that he and Adrienne had bought. There at the plaque, in the ruins of Pfaffenwald, he fixed his tribute to those who suffered and died.

Michael recalled, "It was the first time I saw my grandpa cry."

In the Kalinskis' remaining time in Germany, Mitka and Willi continued to search for records. The effort was futile.

After the ceremony, the *Stern* reporter, Reinhard Renger, went to speak to Anna Dörr Krause. He told Adrienne and Mitka that he wanted to report her side of the story. He reported back to them that, to his frustration, she had little to say other than that she barely remembered the "poor little orphan boy" helped by her family.

Then Renger went to the home of Lisa Dörr and, in his words, was "thrown out" by her with a stern warning to "print absolutely nothing about Gustav or her family."

Finally, Renger spoke with Fobianka. Renger reported to the Kalinskis that, rather than rebuffing him, Fobianka said, "Pfaffenwald was a good camp where we made people well and then sent them home with a paper, stating that they had served the German government well."

Undeterred, Renger used information garnered from Mitka, the Deists, and others and was unstinting in his descriptions of how "sick farm workers were murdered and disappeared from Germany." And he did not hesitate to offer details of Mitka's "torture on the Dörrs' property."

(Disappointed, journalist Renger wrote to the Kalinskis in May of 1985 that he was "regretful and ashamed" to report that the article he had written was not going to be published. For reasons that were not entirely clear, the "big boss" had decided that there was "no room" for it in *Stern*. He did, however, share what he had written with them.)

During the next few days of their November 1984 visit, Mitka showed his family more of Rotenburg an der Fulda. Together they toured the places that marked his childhood. His detailed memories, in their particulars, had been affirmed. All Mitka's early years passed through him, and so did profound gratitude for his loving family and for the country where he now lived.

One highlight of the time was an encounter with Father Reinhard Sheffer, a Catholic priest from Beiershausen who was present. Old and full of sorrow, he told of his regret that he had not spoken out sooner about Pfaffenwald. He could not rewrite the past, as he wished, but he did give the Kalinskis and Renger the names of two Russian doctors who had worked at the camp. Also, he told them that a baby born at Pfaffenwald had survived and that she lived nearby but had no memory of the place.

In a last gesture, Father Sheffer invited the Kalinskis to return to the Pfaffenwald cemetery on Wednesday, November 21. Adrienne could not ignore the irony:

> All these years—nobody even bothered to acknowledge there were more victims. And yet now, just because Mitka had returned like a ghost from the past, these people would suddenly have two memorial services in four days' time. But we all agreed . . . yes . . . we would be there.

Father Sheffer led the memorial, joined by twenty or so German citizens. The service seemed to be, in some ways, an afterthought, which Adrienne saw as an attempt to atone for wrongs that family and neighbors and friends had committed or were at least complicit in. Setting aside her initial, cynical response, Adrienne appreciated the effort. She saw in it a chance for these Germans to bring about some healing. The event was a fitting postscript to a meaningful trip.

After the service, the Kalinskis and Deists went to Asbach to visit the Hohlmanns' bakery. There they shared a formal tea with Susanne and her family. Hanging on the wall of the bakery was a charcoal drawing of a young boy. His thick, dark, overlong hair was tousled. His slender, handsome face was serious. He was not smiling. His eyes were full of longing—or perhaps sadness—as he rested his arms and hands on a windowsill. Willi commented on the strong resemblance between the boy in the drawing and a young Mitka. This prompted Susanne to take the drawing down off the wall. She removed it from its frame and rolled it up so that it would fit into a travel container for transport to the United States. Today this picture has a place of honor just to the left of the fireplace in the Kalinskis' living room.

The family returned to the Deists' for their final night in Germany. Packing, exchanging gifts, and saying goodbye were all that remained.

The journey had been a success in unexpected ways. The discovery of records about Mitka, however, would have to wait for another day.

The Kalinskis flew back to America on Thanksgiving Day.

CHAPTER TWENTY-ONE

"My Brother"

Sparks, 1997

The Kalinskis were on their way home. Everyone was ready to be back in his or her own bed. Donna and Michael had missed ice-cold drinks, American TV shows, their friends, and more. Adrienne was eager to return to the comfort of her routines and some tension-free hours. She was especially glad to leave behind her ambivalent relationship with the Deists.

Mitka's emotions were complicated. He was happy to be back in Sparks, where he could relax in familiar surroundings, putter with this or that project, and watch movies and the news. Also, a weight fell from his shoulders when he left Germany.

But another feeling also flooded Mitka: homesickness for Germany. It surprised him. He found it to be a little out of place and confusing, though not so perplexing that he needed to dismiss it or find an explanation. Taken all together, he was exhausted and struggling. What clamored the loudest amid his warring emotions and his churning thoughts was taciturn disappointment—he had not found evidence of his family.

Adrienne felt the disappointment too. She was, however, able to confirm the truth of Mitka's childhood. Consistent with her nature, she dismissed her discontent in short order. She was not about to be defeated.

On July 4, 1985, Adrienne wrote Anna. The letter was, on its surface, professional, but there was anger behind it. She asked Anna to release the paperwork held by the Dörrs that could provide answers. She lacked

proof of his country of origin, his parentage, and his religion and records of his persecution by the Nazis. She believed Anna knew more
than she was willing to reveal about Mitka's identity—facts that could
help him reconcile his past with his present but also facts that were
necessary to satisfy German government requirements for reparative
compensation.

Adrienne wrote Anna for one more reason. As a mother and a
grandmother, she couldn't grasp that Anna—also a mother—would
abuse a child as she had abused Mitka. She tried to comprehend it.
Her attempts to understand went further still. She asked Anna why,
and how, this could happen. It was a question that lingered from her
own childhood and her broken relationship with her abusive father. The
question didn't stop coming to her even though she knew that answers
weren't to be found.

Two months passed with no response from Anna. Adrienne set
about typing another letter. She took a different tone in this letter. Fi-
ery and direct, she recounted the facts of Mitka's history and demanded
answers. She threatened legal action, and in the letter's final paragraph
she wrote:

> Now, on behalf of Mitka and his family, we demand payment from
> you personally, as partial compensation for the years 1942–1949 that
> you, Anna Dorr Krause—personally controlled Mitka's very life.
> We challenge you—Anna Dorr Krause—to testify UNDER OATH
> about the specific years 1942–1949.

So far, pursuing answers through various agencies had proved un-
successful and frustrating. Nevertheless, Adrienne continued to devote
some of her time to the task almost every day. Dead end after dead end
put her on another, more personal approach: she decided to reach out
to German individuals and ask for help. Maybe someone had knowledge
or sources that could help her find duplicates of the records Gustav had
possessed or other records pertaining to Mitka.

With this new approach, Adrienne penned a letter to *Hersfelder
Zeitung*, a newspaper that published the article about Mitka when he
returned to Rotenburg in 1984. In it, she used a prospective book and

movie deal as a pretext for research about Mitka. She implored the
people of Rotenburg to come forward with any information they had
about Mitka. The newspaper published her notice in a five-paragraph
article.

When the article was published, Adrienne got a swift reply from
Anna. An attorney, Wolfgang Both, responded on Anna's behalf. He
addressed the Kalinskis and the author of the proposed book. In his
January 21, 1988, letter, he asserted four points:

1.   Dimitri Kalinski was called "Martin" while in the Dörrs' home, but
      he was *not* "Martin Dörr."
2.   Thus, he (referring to Mitka) must not "publish the book under the
      name Martin Dörr or refer to [himself as] Martin Dörr in the book."
3.   If Mitka were to represent himself as "Martin Dörr" or "mention in
      the book things that do not relate to fact or are untrue," Mrs. Krause
      would pursue legal action against the Kalinskis.
4.   On behalf of his client, Both had submitted a notice to the *Hers-
      felder Zeitung*, stating, unequivocally, "There is no such person as
      Martin Dörr." The notice acknowledged that the boy was called
      "Martin" and stated that the family "neither knew his name nor his
      whereabouts."

The heated rhetoric from Adrienne and from Anna's attorney subsided; no legal battle occurred, in part because no book was written
or published.

Adrienne, reflecting on the period after returning from Germany,
wrote privately,

> The years following our trip to Germany were filled with many
> happy occasions to celebrate as well as many disappointments. We
> continued to search for any information about Mitka's past with
> very few leads. It was beginning to look like we would never learn
> anything new. But during those eight years from 1985 to 1993, there
> was never a dull moment. Our grandsons Michael Jason and Steve
> Michael and granddaughter Julie Marie were soon welcoming new
> cousins. Nicholas James (Jimmy) and Joshua Jennings (Donna). Five

beautiful grandchildren helped fill the emptiness in Mitka's heart. Weddings and birthdays kept us all busy and our minds occupied. Still Mitka could never seem to stop searching, grasping for straws for even the slightest chance that somewhere, sometime, someplace, he would finally connect with someone who could help him.

As was true throughout their marriage, Mitka and Adrienne found a counterbalance to whatever outside pressure they felt by focusing their energies on family. At home in Sparks, but especially in Bodega Bay, they had purposefully chosen an alternative to the turmoil surrounding Mitka. No place gave the Kalinskis more joy than Bodega Bay. Since the family had discovered the bucolic village on California's northern coast in the early 1960s, it had become a refuge where they enjoyed countless days of camping and, subsequently, RV living. They latched on to everything it offered—fresh seafood, a paradise of fun activities for the children, nights around a campfire, new acquaintances made by a jovial Mitka, and tranquility—in short, a retreat from home and hot Nevada summers.

Adrienne puts it succinctly: "When we bought our motor home, . . . we traveled there as often as possible to camp as long as possible."

Therefore, it was an easy decision when, in 1993, Adrienne and Mitka were asked to be camp hosts. Yes, of course they accepted the offer. They couldn't have been happier.

Doran Beach became their base of operations during the camping season. From "headquarters" in their recreational vehicle, they reveled in the responsibilities of the job. Mitka and Adrienne developed an easy partnership. She handled the paperwork; Mitka made all feel welcome by his gregarious nature. She was the administrator; he was the maintenance troubleshooter and problem solver. It worked like magic.

Mitka, as was now his wont, told his story to anyone and everyone who would listen. And it received attention from visitors to the Bodega Bay campsite.

One such person came to Mitka for relief of sorts. He tells the story.

Ellen DeGeneres, who in 1993 had not yet starred in the eponymous sitcom that catapulted her to stardom, knocked on the RV door. She was in a hurry. She asked to use the bathroom. Mitka was happy to oblige.

Later that day he came across Ellen in the camp and began a conversation. As with everyone, he related his story about being a child slave in Germany. At the close of their chat, Mitka commented, "You know, the Germans didn't lose the war." After a pause, "They came in second." Ellen laughed. To this day, Mitka says that one day he will meet Ellen again and remind her of the time she needed to pee.

His story got the attention of the media as well. In 1995, when local media were running pieces about the fiftieth anniversary of the end of World War II, a number of reporters came to Mitka.

Out of this came a three-part series written and reported by anchor Michelle Franzen of KFTY in Santa Rosa, California. When the second episode begins, viewers hear Adrienne before they see her. She is reading a portion of her poem about Mitka.

> Yes, Mitka was robbed of every right
> But I know someday he'll find
> That the Nazis' cruel, cruel treatment
> Has taught him to be kind.

Then Adrienne, with tears in her eyes, reflects on her husband's life. She tells the reporter that it was hard at times, that Mitka's secrets "took a toll on the family." Referring to her children, she states, "They love their father deeply, dearly, and he would lay down his life for any of us. But there isn't the closeness. I wish there had been more closeness, but it wasn't possible. And we didn't know why."

The camera shifts to Mitka, who says, "I didn't have nothing to give them. I couldn't say, 'This is my family.' I couldn't say to them, 'This is your grandmother.'"

Adrienne acknowledges that the search for Mitka's identity is important, but she stresses that there are more important things than having a lineage. "All the hate that was shown to him through his childhood never shows." Again, her eyes fill with tears and her voice breaks as she adds, "He's a kind man."

The episode ends with Adrienne and Mitka holding hands and walking down the beach. The last words viewers hear are from him.

I heard what you said. I think that's about the nicest thing I've heard since we've been married for forty-two years. You never told me things like that.

Through simple, love-filled exchanges, the Kalinskis reveal the price paid for secrets. Mitka's bravado and humor and "I can do anything" facade were a kind of armor that kept those around him from seeing who he really was. He hid his shame, but he also hid his tender heart. Adrienne, no shrinking violet, matched his toughness with her own brand of the same. As secrets came to light, so, too, did new abilities to express their love.

Franzen's next episode begins with a poignant conversation with Kathleen Regan, one of the Quakers at Bad Aibling who meant so much to Mitka. She spoke of the deeply frightened boy who cried easily, found solace in music, and pulled at her heartstrings in powerful ways. The focus then shifts to the present and to Mitka's seemingly unending quest for identity. His words that close out not just this episode but also the entire three-part series encapsulate his life.

It's never going to end until I find out who I am. All I know is . . . my name is Mitka. That's what I know. All the rest has been given to me.

Franzen captured insights about Mitka and his experiences within the context of historical events. She also caught the significance of Adrienne and the love story the two shared. The news story brought minor celebrity to Mitka in the San Francisco area.

At the time, Mitka could not know that he was soon to meet someone who would unlock doors behind which lay answers he sought.

At Doran Beach in June 1996, Mitka told his story to a camper who worked for California's Department of Education as a computer programmer but whose avocation was that of a ham radio operator (call sign W6HZT). Like other amateur radio operators, he spent hours chitchatting across the globe in the ham radio network. A part of ham revolves around the pleasure of making contact with other operators. Using radio frequencies, operators experience something akin to what the social Internet would become for its users. This man also had computer skills, a passion for problem solving, curiosity, and indefatigable energy. More important, he decided that using his skills to help Mitka find his past was an endeavor worthy of his time. His name was Gary Nixon.

In short order, Gary attacked a search on multiple fronts. He emailed his ham radio contacts in eastern Europe, summarizing Mitka's story and asking for help in locating any clues to his past. Following Adrienne's example, he sent letters to editors of newspapers in several cities where some bit of evidence might be a connection to Mitka. He used computer searches to follow bread crumbs of knowledge about Mitka in the hope that some trail might lead to the disclosure of new information. The snippets of memory Mitka had from his "pre-Nazi" life—playing with a wooden boat, a beautiful woman who gave him a rubber band that he used as a makeshift musical instrument, people in black hats riding in wagons—these were among the feeble clues Gary employed. Letters from Eduard Gruschka, the only person in Rotenburg who claimed personal knowledge of Mitka's past, provided another starting point for his investigation.

Gary's first round of emails focused on a bit of concrete knowledge about Mitka's early years: his connection to a *Kinderheim* in Bila Tserkva. In July, only one month after he began to search, he obtained photographs of a *Kinderheim* in Bila Tserkva. The pictures matched Mitka's memories; it was where he'd been left as a small child.

These early emails produced another important result. Gary's work generated a swell of interest in Mitka's story among a small army of enthusiastic investigators in Europe. The quest had been joined.

Toward the end of 1996, Gary turned his attention to clues in Eduard Gruschka's letters. Piece by piece, he kept accumulating knowledge about Mitka. He was filling a file of tidbits, trying out one, then another, as he pursued answers to the riddles in front of him. In his search for sources, he discovered the Jozef Pilsudski Institute of America. Established in the United States in 1943, during a time when Poland was politically unstable, the Pilsudski Institute was and is "a major research archival and science institution for research of modern history of Poland."

He began to comb the archives, beginning with the name Kalinski and narrowing the search to a relevant time period. From Gruschka he had an additional scrap datum. In one letter Gruschka asserted that Mitka's father was a Polish military officer who had died in a prisoner-of-war camp.

Gary came upon one Wladyslaw Kalinski, a decorated Polish military officer whose history matched, in most particulars, the description of the man Gruschka had identified as Mitka's father. On one significant point, it diverged: Wladyslaw Zubosz Kalinski was born in 1892 and died in 1952 in London; this man had not died in a POW camp, as Gruschka had stated. Despite the discrepancy, Gary continued to accumulate biographical information about him.

Gary learned that Wladyslaw Kalinski served with honor in World War I and was wounded twice—once in 1915 and the second time in 1916. On January 1, 1932, Kalinski was promoted to the rank of colonel and for the remainder of his career commanded the Thirteenth Infantry Division, which was stationed in Rowne. He and his men fought heroically against the invading Germans but were eventually captured after the fall of Warsaw. From autumn 1939 (approximately the time that Mitka was left at the *Kinderheim*) until the end of the war in 1945, he was held in POW camps, first in Munich and later in Oflag VII-A in Dresden. After his liberation, he moved to London, where he died in 1952.

This discovery seemed promising to Gary and to Mitka and Adrienne. With the new information in hand, Gary turned, once again, to his fellow ham operators, especially those in Poland and Ukraine who might be able to locate and interpret regional records. One operator who responded to Gary's call for help was Marcin Michalack, a student at the AGH University of Science and Technology in Krakow.

In Marcin, Gary had found a sleuth whose enthusiasm for making sense of the jumbled clues to Mitka's origins matched his own. Marcin took up the investigation and proceeded to dig into various records, one of which was a peculiar book titled *Index of Poles Buried in London Cemeteries*. In an email sent to Gary Nixon on March 28, 1997, he noted that the book contained a record of Wladyslaw Kalinski buried in a London cemetery. From this find he located death certificates for a Colonel Kalinski and his widow, Maria.

An obscure detail in Maria's 1983 death certificate held promise of a breakthrough. On the document, Peter Holownia was listed as Maria Kalinski's grandson. Given that only fourteen years had passed since this certificate had been filed, Peter was, most probably, alive. Could he be found? It was this question that set Marcin off again. Using the search engine WhoWhere?, Marcin located a P. Holownia at the London Medical Center. Excited by this discovery and fully invested by now in the search for Mitka's origins, Marcin emailed Peter Holownia on April 10, 1997. No record of Marcin's email to Peter exists, but Peter's reply to Marcin does:

Dear Sir

Thank you for your E-Mail of April 10th.

I am indeed the grandson of Colonel Wladyslaw Kalinski.

Both daughters from his marriage to my grandmother, Maria Kalinski (maiden name Wejroch—now deceased), that is my mother, (Barbara Holownia) & aunt, (Lala Bartel) are both still alive. We are however all unaware that my grandfather had any other children?

I would be delighted to contact and help your friend Mitka Kalinski in any way possible.

Best wishes,
Peter Holownia

Perhaps a critical link had been found, perhaps not. Marcin had cc'd Gary Nixon on his email correspondence with Peter, which opened the door for Gary to join the conversation. On April 11, 1997, Gary sent Peter a lengthy email explaining his role and providing Peter with a brief but detailed summation of Mitka's situation. Gary explained several reasons they were now contacting him for assistance. He stated:

- That Mitka had been separated from his family since early childhood and that he not only had been in camps but also had suffered as a slave in the Gustav Dörr household.

- That "a man who knew Mitka's father [Gruschka] had told him 'Your father was above an officer in the army. He was given land (many acres) near Gatkowa for his efforts in the Polish/Russian war.'"
- That he (Gary) had read a book on Polish military medals and discovered that only one medal—the Virtuti Militari—included an award of land.
- That he found the name of Wladyslaw Kalinski when he searched for recipients of this medal and thought there was a chance he might be Mitka's father.
- That Marcin Michalack, a ham radio operator and a student in Poland, had located Colonel Kalinski's grave and his and his wife's death certificates.
- That because Peter Holownia's name was listed on Maria Kalinski's death certificate, they sought to contact him to see if he might be helpful.

Gary continued in the email to suggest ways in which Peter might be of assistance. For instance, he sent photographs of Mitka as a young man and asked that Peter and his family look at them to see if there might be a resemblance. He went on to ask if there might be "a family Bible or other book where family records might be kept."

The pace of the back-and-forth emails quickened. On April 14, 1997, Peter wrote that he had shared the story with his mother, one of Wladyslaw Kalinski's two daughters. He wrote:

> We were both extremely moved by Mitka's life history . . . my mother broke down in tears. She is slowly putting together the movements of our family from the years she was born to the outbreak of war so that we can precisely match locations to events. *There is no doubt in our minds that if my grandfather is Mitka's father then this was from a relationship with another woman (i.e. not my grandmother), and from what my mother can remember of her early family life this may well have been the case.* We strongly suspect that Mitka may have been born around 1932–3. Please bear with us for the reasons and explanations which my mother is putting together.

Gary responded that same day, supplying more detail of Mitka's earliest childhood memories:

I'm still not sure how much of Mitka's life story you know as I've not gotten a copy of the mail Marcin sent you. I believe you know he was kept as a child slave laborer seven years, including four AFTER the war! He was released in 1949. His treatment was beyond horrifying. These details should come directly from Mitka. While I know them (and I wish I didn't), I believe it is his place to share them, not mine. They are, unfortunately, one of the centerpieces of his life, and, as such, bear repeating. They are not for the weak, though, so if your mother has great empathy for Mitka, I might suggest you learn the details and act accordingly.

On to other matters . . . maybe some of these "random" things Mitka remembers will ring a bell with your mother. The two story house he remembers . . . was near some railroad tracks with hills behind it. On the other side of the tracks was a dance hall.

All of this is pretty fuzzy, but before the orphanage in Ukraine, he remembers being with an older grandmotherly-type woman in the house in the woods, where he slept above the stove (on a little ledge) to keep warm. He remembers the seasons turning a couple of times when he was at the orphanage. He wandered with other displaced Ukrainians for a couple of months before being picked up and sent to Babi Yar (a very bad place). He survived by being shorter than the people in front of him who were being shot. They fell on him. He was left for dead, and he escaped shortly thereafter, only to be picked up again. In all he was at four camps before being sent to the slave farm. The things he witnessed at these camps are hideous as well.

Gary continues in a second email:

He [Mitka] remembers a tiny (slight, small) lady leaving him in his crib. She was thin and had long dark hair.

He remembers being approached by a German soldier on a white horse and being asked, "Who set off the rockets?" He remembers nothing more about this but has great guilt feelings connected with it.

He remembers that his "father's" car (I use that term because he did. I am referring to the man of the house that had parties, fancy clothes, etc.) was sort of a sports-car looking thing, with a wheel on the back (trunk). . . .

He remembers a house with a "straw" roof (thatched I suspect) with a chimney in it. It was the (I sound it out) "pee-etch-kah" he used to sleep above. It was a clay unit used for baking bread. You could sleep above it to stay warm. Nearby was a door to a stable. This was in an interim house between his "happy" family times and the orphanage.

Finally, he remembers playing with two older girls. . . . They all used to play at a house. There was . . . a new house under construction. . . . He remembers playing in there with the girls and there being nothing for flooring besides floor joists (he was afraid he would fall through). The house was a split level on a small hill. He remembers these play times as "happy" times, i.e. before being sent to the orphanage or still with his family.

Gary then added information about Mitka and Adrienne's intentions.

I spent two hours with Adrienne and Mitka . . . this evening on their way home. [Mitka and Adrienne were traveling back to Sparks after spending time at Bodega Bay. Gary, at this time, lived in Sacramento.] He didn't get much sleep after hearing the contents of your letter! He has a zillion questions and would love to talk to you both, especially your mother, but I suggest that he wait to see what information she comes up with before calling. He's absolutely certain of one thing. The minute he gets on the phone, he'll be tongue-tied!

They both wanted me to make sure you know that, while he has spent a lifetime wondering about and searching for his family, he has absolutely no intention of invading the privacy of you, your mother, or anyone. He just wants some peace, that's all. God knows he's earned it. I guess that's another way of saying they're not gold-diggers either. I can vouch for that. I've only been involved with them for ten months, but their searching goes way back a long, long time before I came into the picture.

Peter responded with encouragement and grace. Among other things, he assured Gary and Adrienne and Mitka "that it never crossed our minds, in any way, that we regard this as any sort of intrusion on our privacy or whatever else and that we would like to share whatever we have regarding my Grandfather."

What followed was a sentence that, taken in isolation, could have discouraged them.

> My mother, aunt, and grandmother (who I knew very well and lived with us for many years before her death in 1983) never mentioned or knew of any other son, or, indeed, daughter of Wladyslaw Kalinski.

But the next passage contained a thread on which Mitka, Gary, and Marcin hung their hope. At that moment it was all they had.

> We were shocked to know that there may have been a son and what we presume must have been [from] another relationship. As far as we are concerned this is in the past and whatever extra-marital relationships/marital problems [my grandfather] may have had, it is really immaterial to the fact that if Mitka (as seems extremely likely) was my grandfather's son, then we are family—end of story.

Peter ended the correspondence with an overview of his mother Barbara's and the Kalinski family's lives during the years that were relevant to Mitka's quest. A portion of his email lists dates with events. The information proved nothing, but it did offer helpful pieces in the still-forming puzzle.

1928	Barbara (Basia) born in 18.4.1928 Berezwecz (where my grandfather stationed during this time)
1930	Lala born 17.7.1930
1932	Moved from Berezwecz (in Byelorussia) to Stanislawow (Polish Ukraine) sometime in the autumn

1933	My mother started prep school
1935	Death of Marshal Pilsudski
1936	Moved to Poznan (Western Poland) where my grandfather was transferred to and stationed
1936–1939	Lived in Poznan until outbreak of war. My Grandfather was then made commander in chief of the 13th Infantry Division which was then stationed in Rowne but was transferred to the western front in Torum which he only joined there. He said that he did not actually know anyone in this division. The imminent outbreak of war must have made things extremely urgent.

Peter ended the email by promising that he and his mother were continuing to organize her memories and that they would be sending photos of his grandfather and other family members. He concluded with "I would dearly like to speak with Mitka now, but I think it appropriate that I first finish off sending all the details. And I think my mother should be the first person he should speak to."

Peter kept his promise and sent pictures to Gary two days later. When Gary shared the pictures with Mitka and Adrienne, their reaction was instantaneous and overwhelming. Each saw "remarkable similarities" between Wladyslaw Kalinski and Mitka. But even more, as Adrienne pointed out, Jimmy, their second son, when he was a young adult, looked "exactly" like Wladyslaw.

Gary relayed their reactions to Peter. On Saturday, April 19, Peter responded. Again, his words were encouraging, but Adrienne thought it was important to guard against feelings getting too far ahead of evidence.

I am thrilled about the news that Mitka and Adrienne immediately recognized such close family similarities—I almost certainly have an uncle (& my mother says that when she was little she always wanted to have a brother to play with).

Peter added a seemingly disconnected fact about his grandfather. To Mitka, it was directly connected.

> One more thing regarding my grandfather's personal features— during the Polish-Soviet war of 1920, he was wounded and lost his left eye which was replaced by a glass one—apparently this made very little difference to his facial appearance. In fact, my mother says that nobody meeting him would have the slightest suspicion that he had a false eye unless told, and it obviously did not interfere with his subsequent army career.

One of Mitka's earliest memories had been of a man who wore a patch over his eye, a man who made a small toy boat for him, a man he had always believed to be his father. It was a memory that Gary had never shared with Peter. To Mitka, this fact was a powerful confirmation that he might have found his father.

In the same email Peter continued to offer more information about his grandfather. He noted that his grandfather had shared little about his family history with his wife and daughters. "My grandmother, mother, and aunt knew very little about my grandfather's side of the family; he never said much and would tend to avoid the subject as much as possible."

It seemed that, by sharing a detached memory, Peter was trying to understand and construct a rationale for his grandfather's suspected extramarital life. Circumstantial as the evidence was, all the stakeholders believed that coincidence could not explain what was happening.

Peter elaborated on further details from his grandfather's life that appeared to support the idea that Colonel Kalinski may have kept secrets and that one secret could have been that he had a son.

> My mother remembers her mother telling her of a curious incident during my grandparents' courting days in Warsaw. During their engagement, my grandmother quite by accident stumbled across my grandfather sitting in a café with another lady. . . . There could be many perfectly reasonable explanations, but what she couldn't forget was my grandfather's reaction. He apparently gave some trivial

reason to her, but she remembers that he was in a great state of inner turmoil which he was barely suppressing—his hands were gripping the sides of the table so powerfully that they were turning white, and my grandmother remembers seeing something like real fear in his expression, something that she never before or later ever saw again. Could this "mystery" woman have been an old flame or was this a still ongoing affair—perhaps—maybe—possibly this was the woman that he may have a relationship out of which Mitka was going to be later born from—I think we will never know.

Another thing my grandmother used to say was that throughout their marriage there were definite occasions when she could not account for his movements in Stanislawow, and my mother even herself remembers also later in Poznan where my grandfather would sometimes put on his civilian clothes and leave for a day or so without saying where he was going. My grandfather also traveled abroad, and he was away a lot on army business, so there was more than plenty opportunity to be in another relationship. Another thing was that family accounts were completely under the sole control of my grandfather—apparently he would never reveal his earnings or the financial state of the family to anyone—including his wife and simply provided her with housekeeping money—although the family was obviously well off. They lived in nice large houses and went on expensive holidays etc., my grandmother was sometimes going short and was puzzled that someone of the status of my grandfather could be short of money.

Peter included more biographical details about his grandfather and then concluded his email by stating,

I would also like to send my deepest and most sincere regards and best wishes (& from my mother) to Mitka who may very well be my Uncle. And please rest assured that will [*sic*] leave no stone unturned in our efforts to find Mitka's history.

Best wishes,
Peter Holownia

Sometime soon after April 17, Barbara became convinced that Mitka was, indeed, her half brother. Several things brought her to this conclusion. She, like Mitka, had limited early memories. Yet Mitka's memories matched her own to an uncanny degree. Also, she remembered a story about her father being seen with a woman who was not her mother, and his frequent, long, and unexplained absences, and that her parents' marriage was unhappy. Based on her reconstruction of her childhood, Mitka's story made sense. She found it not only plausible but utterly believable that her father was Mitka's father too. More than all this, one particular observation convinced her of the truth that she had a brother. In a picture of an adult Mitka, she saw her father. The physical resemblance extended beyond Mitka to his son Jimmy, who looked even more like Colonel Kalinski. Disinterested strangers, upon seeing photographs of the three men, believed them to be related.

In late April 1997, Barbara conveyed her sentiments to Mitka in handwritten notes. She wrote about her father in Polish and English. When Mitka heard the notes read to him, something happened that he still cannot explain. It was as if, for him, time and its passage collapsed into a single conscious moment of belonging. Barbara described Wladyslaw Kalinski as "our father." The word "our" was not lost on Mitka. By using those words, Barbara acknowledged a shared history with a man whose family tree had been nothing but a lone, detached branch—until that moment.

On May 4, 1997, Mitka placed a long-distance call to London and spoke with Barbara Holownia. The conversation remains a blur for him. He remembers that when she answered the phone, he tentatively said her name. Then she said two words: "My brother."

"Can you believe it?" Mitka reflects. "She said, 'My brother.' I couldn't talk anymore. I was all choked up."

Never had two words meant so much to a man as they did to Mitka in that moment. After fifty-eight years of longing for his family, Mitka heard the words that filled a hole in his heart.

CHAPTER TWENTY-TWO

Reunion

London, Summer 1997

With this milestone discovery of living blood relatives, previous designations used for Mitka, like "displaced" and "unattached," no longer applied. He had two sisters and a nephew. Hearing Barbara acknowledge him as her brother confirmed it. He couldn't contain himself. Just as he had felt compelled to tell anyone about his past in a pursuit of roots he might never unearth, now he felt, with equal fervor, the need to tell of the miraculous discovery of who he was.

On Saturday, May 3, 1997, Mitka left a message for Lyanne Melendez, a reporter for the ABC affiliate in San Francisco, providing an update on his search efforts.

When, in 1995, on the occasion of the fiftieth anniversary of the end of World War II, Ms. Melendez had interviewed Mitka, he had taken a special liking to her, as had Adrienne. This reporter grasped something about Mitka's life that many other journalists had missed. Many had, quite understandably, gravitated to the physical gruesomeness of his experiences. Ms. Melendez went beyond the obvious and focused on the pain inflicted on his personhood, on his soul. She saw his wounded spirit. In questioning him, she went straight to the isolation of his existence and elicited comments from him about his deepest longings.

"When I think of my mother and her arms around me and my arms around her . . . when I think of that, sometimes I fall to pieces," Mitka had told her on air.

For quite some time before the 1995 interview, the Kalinskis had been fans of Lyanne Melendez. Oftentimes they had watched her on television while they were in Bodega Bay. Meeting her had been a delight, rather like meeting a star. That a reporter, whom they already respected, should take an interest in Mitka's story put the interview on solid ground from the outset. The Kalinskis were comfortable and appreciative. There was trust. When the report aired, its quality further cemented the relationship.

When Lyanne Melendez returned Mitka's call on Monday, she had a proposal. Would Mitka be open to an arranged reunion with his sister in London? KGO-TV 7 would pay for airfare and lodging for Adrienne and him. It all seemed too good to be true.

Lyanne put a plan in place. She, Mitka, and Adrienne would fly to London on Friday, July 25. They would connect with a London-based film crew upon their arrival to document the reunion. On the Thursday before their departure, Mitka spoke to Lyanne about their lives up to that day. "After all we have been through, you don't give up. You go to the end, whatever that is."

The phrase "the end, whatever that is" sums up, in tidy fashion, the elusive target of Mitka's search. The transatlantic trip to London wouldn't be the end of the journey for Mitka, but it was the most meaningful stop up to that point.

Mitka boarded the Virgin Atlantic flight from San Francisco to London with no thought other than "I just wanted to meet my family." At the time he mused, "It doesn't seem real. It won't be real until I see my sister and put my arms around her. Tomorrow I will see her. I don't know what my reaction will be."

Peter Holownia stood where he could spot passengers getting off the airplane. He scanned the picture of Mitka he held in his hands. Would he know his uncle from the photograph? Then, across the crowd, Peter spotted him. He began pushing through people, and before he knew it, he and Mitka were face-to-face. It was Mitka's eyes that confirmed what Peter believed was true: this was his uncle. He extended his hand to shake Mitka's. Mitka ignored the hand and instead reached out to clutch the shoulders of the bookish, tall and slender young man with the shy smile.

"Peter. Peter, is that you? Is that really you?"

Mitka repeated the words, and then he drew Peter into his embrace. Adrienne stood by Mitka's side, silent, absorbed in the moment. She had no response other than to look into Peter's face and smile.

As Mitka and Adrienne made their way through customs and then waited for their baggage, Peter was there with them. Mitka tried, as best he could, to contain the joy he was experiencing. Adrienne reflected on all they had been through to arrive at this day. They got their luggage and loaded into Peter's car.

Mitka, who loved to drive, took notice of his nephew's skill in maneuvering "on the wrong side of the road" as they made their way to a small guesthouse on the outskirts of London. After the Kalinskis had settled into their quarters, they had some spare time before the reunion with Mitka's sister. They took the opportunity to explore a few of London's tourist sites.

The high point of their tours was a Holocaust museum. Just as he had done at Dachau thirteen years earlier, Mitka studiously examined each exhibit. One after the other, he saw portrayals of the lives of Jews in the camps—displays that mirrored his own experiences. Each picture, each artifact, carried him to places and incidents that were alive in his memory. As painful as they were, these tangible representations of his life were, in a strange way, also vindicating. His recall was accurate.

One particular photo stood out to Mitka. It depicted a row of bodies, each one suspended by arms tied behind. Dislocated shoulders framed heads bowed forward with chins at rest on lifeless ribs. At six years old, Mitka heard the wailing of those not yet dead. He smelled the stench of rotting flesh at Buchenwald. To see this picture from Buchenwald and the other exhibits was to page through the scrapbook of his youth.

"I was there," he said quietly. "I was there."

The day finally arrived, the day for which Mitka had waited a lifetime. On Saturday, July 26, Peter picked up Adrienne and Mitka and drove them to a small apartment. Kasha, Peter's Polish-born wife, greeted them at the door with a big hug. Conversation—mostly small talk—occupied the two couples for a time. It really didn't matter what anyone said. After each utterance, as if on cue, each person smiled. Another would say something, and again all smiled. At some point, Peter, needing to break the awkward tension, retrieved crystal flutes and a bottle of champagne. They toasted and drank. No one quite knew what to do with the emotion of the moment.

Mitka's mind raced. Snapshots of his life appeared before him in a random mental shuffle. His elevated anticipation overrode any conscious control of what was going on around him. There were happy toasts for the moment they shared but sadness too, for the lost years. Mitka spoke in a low voice, "It's been a long life and a long search. Now it's over."

With that, the small party drove from Peter's flat to what Brits refer to as a "bedsit"—a one-room apartment serving as both bedroom and living room.

Mitka walked through the door behind Peter, carrying a bouquet of flowers. A silver-haired woman sat on the bed. "She was like a fawn, so tiny," Adrienne recalls, "just sitting there with those big, sad eyes."

With two strides Mitka was standing before the woman. He knelt down and presented the flowers. "These are for you," he said. Then he leaned in to embrace her. Words deserted him as he rose and sat on the bed. It was a moment he had played out a thousand times, though he could never visualize with whom. Now the object of his longing sat next to him. He first put his hand on her shoulder and kept moving it as if to confirm that she was real. He reached for her hand and held it with both of his. The two sat close. Enclosed in the nest of Mitka's hands, her hands disappeared from view. Neither could speak. Peter, Kasha, and Adrienne watched in silence. After a time—too long for ordinary circumstances, but not awkward in this instance—Mitka spoke.

"All my life I had nothing—nothing—and now this. In that cattle wagon train I thought, 'I will never find my way home.' I go further and further away and finally, here, I find something here—my sister."

Barbara responded to her brother, and a river of conversation flowed between the two. The three others present were mere bystanders.

The next day, Sunday, July 27, was uncommonly warm and sunny for London. The day began with a drive to Saint Mary's Roman Catholic Cemetery, located in an area called Kensal Green in Northwest London. Peter and Adrienne accompanied brother and sister for the short trip. The trip passed silently. Mitka was lost in thought. The others, aware of the solemnity of the occasion, left him alone to reflect.

When they arrived at the main gate to the cemetery, Lyanne Melendez and two cameramen joined the party. Though trained to maintain a detached, professional bearing, the cameramen let show on their faces that this was no run-of-the-mill story. Mitka had pierced their practiced neutrality.

When the caravan of a news crew and family entered the cemetery, they turned left and made their way to a parking area beside the section A plots. The party proceeded on foot to section G, the "Garden" plots.

Barbara, steadied by a cane in her left hand and by the strong arm of her brother on her right, walked slowly along the path until they arrived at a long, rectangular white stone over a grave. The attached headstone was engraved with the name "Wladyslaw Kalinski."

Mitka and Barbara held hands and stood in silence before their father's grave. They didn't move. Minutes passed before Mitka released his sister's hand. He placed his right foot on the stone slab covering the grave, then bent from the waist to lower his forehead onto the stone that marked his father's final resting place. Standing beside him, Barbara, with head bowed, placed her hand on Mitka's back.

After a time, Mitka stood and stepped back to stand beside his nephew and sister. Peter put his arm around his uncle's shoulder. Mitka remained calm, though his face had the ashen appearance of grief, according to Adrienne.

Later Mitka spoke with Lyanne Melendez. The usual energy in his voice was replaced with quiet resolve. The time spent at his father's gravesite gave him something he never expected. He knew where he came from.

"I am satisfied," he said. Then he repeated, "I am satisfied."

Lyanne returned to San Francisco ahead of the others. The Kalinskis remained in London for a few more days. Both were emotionally drained. They took advantage of the off days to do some light sightseeing around London. But the highlight of each day's agenda was time spent with Barbara. She had been in ill health before the visit and was exhausted by the emotional impact of the reunion. Mitka wondered if it would be the last time he would see his sister, which turned out to be the case.

Caught between a desire to stay with his newfound family and the reality that he was returning home, he wrestled with long-dismissed wishes that had resurfaced. "If only I had a brother," he often said. Other times, he lamented, "If only I knew my mother and father." On August 4, Adrienne and Mitka bid tearful farewells to Peter, Kasha, and Barbara. The next day, they flew back to the United States.

Back home in Sparks, the story on Mitka's lips was the miracle of meeting his sister in London. The joy didn't last. Soon after returning to Nevada, Adrienne was hospitalized with a blood clot in her lung. Coming, as it did, on the heels of finding his sister, the health scare replaced Mitka's joy with dread. He couldn't bear the thought of losing Adrienne.

Not surprisingly, Adrienne remained tough, realistic, and optimistic throughout her hospitalization. While convalescing at home, she wrote a letter to Barbara expressing her great joy over what had transpired and describing their time together as "those days of 'wine and roses.'" She also reported on Mitka, noting that he was "surviving all of the unexpected that has happened recently" and that there is great "pride and happiness in his face when he talks about 'his family.' He has so much love for all of you."

Barbara responded with a lovely handwritten note. She echoed Adrienne's sentiments about the "happy events that took place just only few weeks ago." Barbara also hinted, though, at the emotional toll the past months had taken, noting that "many moments from my childhood, also my relations to my parents in the past, still distant in my memory and subdued by day-to-day events [and] current problems, . . . have been evoked by meeting you both." The meeting with the Kalinskis in London was, it seems, a prized but difficult time for Barbara.

Mitka had two half sisters. Barbara accepted him. His sister Lala, who lived in Edmonton, Alberta, had a different reaction. She refused any contact with Mitka. At Peter's suggestion, Adrienne had written to Lala prior to the trip to London, telling her, with great gentleness, of the discovery that they were "relatives" and imploring her to contact her nephew to learn more. Adrienne reiterated that they only wanted to know her and that she and Mitka recognized that this letter and their insertion into her life was stressful. There was no response. A second letter, written in January 1998 and hand-delivered by a Catholic priest traveling to Edmonton, also drew no response from Lala. Again, there was only silence.

Adrienne, based on things she inferred from conversations with Peter and Barbara, believes the marriage between Mitka's father and his legal wife was never good and that they, in fact, led separate lives after Colonel Kalinski was released from the POW camp. "Barbara was closer to her father. And Lala stuck with her mother. That's what I think from what they have told me. Maybe that's why she won't see Mitka today. I bet Lala thinks Mitka's mother was part of the problem there."

Mitka ached with grief and frustration at Lala's refusal to meet or speak with him. He still does.

"I want to get in my car and drive there and knock on her door. I want to say, 'I am your brother.'"

Whenever Mitka's family comes up in a discussion, the subject of his unmet sister pricks him with longing not dissimilar to what he felt as a child. The feelings are powerful, intrusive, and persistent.

Most of the time Mitka accepts that he will always live with ghosts lurking in the shadows. Some of the time, the ghosts come into the light, demanding his attention. Nightmares continue for Mitka, though they happen less often. When his nightmare is over, his bedroom appears as if a tornado touched down.

Mitka's way of dealing with his unsettled state is to talk and talk. He repeats what he said moments before—not so much for his immediate audience but rather, it seems, to grapple with these ghosts and demons he cannot kill. At best he can push them back into the shadows.

With Adrienne, Mitka feels free to fully rehash his life. With others, he tends to present parts of his story that he believes will captivate them. His delivery is full of humor and anecdotes, each one skillfully presented. What his audience hears keeps them hooked. But there's something more going on beneath the surface. By his own admission, in telling stories Mitka is working out reconciliation with a past he cannot change. His storytelling is a means of making peace with a life he would not have chosen, but, of course, he had no choice. The battle to make a separate peace is a battle he expects to fight until his dying day. He may never win the war, but in the course of his life he has defeated many enemies.

Mitka's painful memories did not disappear in some magical moment of liberation when he knelt at his father's grave. The graveside visit did, however, instill a measure of peace in him. It also brought a stinging reality to the forefront: as yet he could not say where he was born, or on which day or year. But the main mystery that preoccupies him, a mystery he knows he may never solve, is the identity of his mother. There are credible clues but no proof of who his mother was.

In July 1997, Mitka had found his sisters, a nephew, and his father. Neither Hitler nor anyone else could take this away. "I am satisfied" are words his family never thought they would ever hear from him. He, too, was surprised.

Mitka had arrived at one destination that brought him sorrow, comfort, and joy: he found his father. He fulfilled that quest. But another quest still remained: to find his mother.

CHAPTER TWENTY-THREE

Bar Mitzvah

Mineola, Long Island, 2001

When Mitka stood at his father's grave, he felt as though he stood on holy ground. He clung to his sister's hand and gazed at a stone that honored the man who had given them life. They knew a kinship that linked them across time and distance.

Although Mitka still shouldered the accumulated weight of his life, it didn't buckle his knees as it had on past occasions. What had once been heavy was no less so. Rather, he had renewed strength to bear it. In the silence of that moment, memory weighed no more than a feather.

Mitka had said, "I am satisfied." It was and was not true. He had been granted fulfillment of a long-denied need. He had found his father and sisters. Still, he had no one to call "Mother." If there was to be an end of searching, he had to persist beyond this way station. Peace was still elusive, somewhere beyond his grasp. He wanted his mother.

Mitka and Adrienne returned to the Nevada desert and to their usual habits and rhythms. But neither home nor patterns could quiet Mitka's mind.

By this time Mitka had learned that, if only for his own sanity, he couldn't live in a constant state of limbo. He had to sleep and eat and walk and work and play and be present. Sometimes he succeeded at living without the intrusion of events long past; more often he did not.

Over the next four years, reporters, most of a local variety, took a renewed interest in Mitka. The lengthy news segment about Mitka by Lyanne Melendez aired on KGO in August 1997. The feature story caught the attention of Louise Bobrow.

Louise was a nurse from Long Island, New York, who loved stories. One expression of this passion was coaxing others to tell her their stories, which led to professional work as a writer and documentary filmmaker. When she came across Mitka's story, she was working with the Shoah Foundation to record the stories of Holocaust survivors.

Louise sought out Mitka and recorded hours of him telling of the events of his childhood. Deeply touched by his story, she also shared it with Rabbi Anchelle Perl, rabbi of the Orthodox Jewish synagogue Chabad Mineola on Long Island. He was especially moved by Mitka's late-in-life discovery and confirmation that he was, indeed, a Jew. At the urging of Bobrow, the ebullient, gregarious rabbi called Mitka to welcome him to the "family."

Rabbi Perl's first call to Mitka began a telephone friendship. Other calls followed. In one of these conversations the rabbi asked him if he'd ever had formal bar mitzvah.

Mitka, of course, had never had his bar mitzvah. When he was thirteen, the age at which Jewish boys undergo the ceremony to take on the rights and responsibilities of a Jewish adult, the Dörrs were enslaving him and had not even told him he was Jewish.

Rabbi Perl was inspired to act. He wanted to meet Mitka, and he had a proposal for him. Would he celebrate his bar mitzvah at Chabad Mineola? At once, the question opened a door for Mitka that he didn't even know was there. Was this possible?

Mitka reflects on Rabbi Perl's invitation.

Of my mother, there were still no records. That's why it became important to explore the one connection I had to her: our faith. I learned that a Jewish boy does not truly come of age until he has his bar mitzvah. Could I become a man so late in life?

Mitka knew he wanted to be bar mitzvahed. He hesitated, though. Uncertainty and shame overwhelmed him—for a few reasons.

With Adrienne handling the paperwork, he had tried at various times to apply for reparations from the German government. In fact, he received a few small checks because of the unreported—and uncompensated—labor he did for the Dörrs. He was, however, never able to receive anything from the Child Survivor Fund of the Conference on Jewish Material Claims against Germany. "The criteria for eligibility specify, among other things, that compensation be limited to Jewish Nazi victims." Despite overwhelming evidence, Mitka did not have *official* birth records that could establish his Jewish identity. He could not meet the standard of proof that the bureaucrats required. He believed that this lack of official records, coupled with his inability to read and study the Torah in a traditional way, would surely disqualify him from a bar mitzvah.

"I don't have no official documents proving I have Jewish roots," Mitka recalls telling Rabbi Perl. He then beams as he remembers the rabbi's response: "What matters is that you have a Jewish soul."

Mitka then raised his other fear. "How could I, who can't even read or write, do this? I feel so ashamed somehow. You are supposed to read and study for this, but that I cannot do."

Mitka's illiteracy was not, however, a disqualifier, at least as far as Rabbi Perl was concerned. "He taught me the traditional prayers and the parts of the Torah I needed. When I heard the words, they were familiar to me. Especially if they were more sung than said. If I sort of sang them . . . I could, for sure, remember them that way."

He adds, "And he taught me that you do not say the name of G-d. Out of respect, Orthodox Jews say, 'Hashem.' That's what they say instead of his name."

In a 2010 interview, Rabbi Perl elaborated on his thinking as he worked to prepare Mitka for the bar mitzvah:

The purpose of studying the Torah was to learn to read the Hebrew language, to be able to sound the letters, explain what they look like, how to read it, and how to sing it. . . . The way we read and the way we sing, the way we look at something, is not just applicable to the actual letters, but a lesson in life. [When] you look at something, you can read it one way or another. You have to learn to apply the song of life. . . . Mitka didn't have the preparation of six to eight months [of study], but Mitka didn't need that preparation because his life's experience and his being able to overcome—that was the best experience, the best preparation we'd never wish on anyone.

His bar mitzvah has historical dimensions because he came from an era where there were those who were determined to destroy him, to destroy his kind with a vengeance. . . . He had survived that and survived it without a hook on his shoulder, a chip on his shoulder. He never expressed a hatred of his background; he just expressed appreciation for what he was.

He continued, contrasting Mitka with a typical thirteen-year-old who might prepare for months prior to the ceremony.

The difference between Mitka and the typical bar mitzvah boy? The answer is very little different outside of the height and outside of his age. His spirit is as young as a thirteen-year-old today. The symbolism of a bar mitzvah is an open manifestation of a below-the-surface holiness that develops with age.

Mitka had survived such an amazing background. . . . Others had been killed, but he lived and became a slave. . . . Then, these many years later, it was time for him to have bar mitzvah.

Adrienne was elated. So was the entire family. This was a ceremony that would fill a hole in Mitka's heart. In planning the trip to New York, it was agreed that grandson Michael and son-in-law Mike Bland would accompany Mitka and Adrienne. On August 18, 2001, the party of four boarded a flight to the Big Apple.

Louise Bobrow had graciously invited Mitka and Adrienne to stay with her on Long Island. Mike and Michael found lodging at a nearby hotel. The family spent Sunday, August 19, riding the subway, an activity Mitka insisted on because "I really like that subway," and walking along the boardwalks of a nearby beach. It was a quiet day for them, one for rest before the important event planned for the next morning.

Monday, August 20, the day of Mitka's bar mitzvah, was not hot by Long Island standards, but the humidity made it seem so to the Kalinskis, who had grown used to the dry, high desert climate of Sparks. Adrienne, Mitka, Michael, and Mike headed to the synagogue early so that Mitka could have time with Rabbi Perl prior to the ceremony.

The much-anticipated moment had arrived. As custom required, Adrienne took her seat in the synagogue on the left side of a six-foot-high *mechitza*, a curtain that separates men and women in Orthodox prayer services. She wore a small pendant that she wears to this day: a Star of David enclosing a Christian cross at its center, which she had purchased years before at a Holocaust museum in London. For Adrienne, who is not a Jew, the pendant is an important representation of her unity of faith with her husband. Grandson Michael and son-in-law Mike, both wearing yarmulkes, sat on the front row on the right. To honor and support Mitka, 150 members of the congregation gathered on that special Monday morning.

When all were seated, Mitka entered the synagogue wearing a black-and-white *tallit* (prayer shawl) and his yarmulke and carrying the Torah scroll. Joy radiated from him as, with each deliberate step, he took in the faces of those who were there to celebrate with him. He saw Rabbi Perl waiting at the podium, a sight that calmed his nerves. As he stepped forward, he gently placed the scroll on the podium. Rabbi Perl, though only five foot four, should have looked small next to Mitka; on this day he did not. Perhaps it was his exuberance in welcoming his congregation to this sacred moment, or maybe it was the humility and deference Mitka displayed. Regardless, it was clear to all the authority and respect that Rabbi Perl commanded.

Rabbi Perl began the service by raising his fist in a jubilant gesture like a runner who had just crossed the finish line in first place.

"Let's hear it for Mitka Kalinski at his bar mitzvah," he shouted. As one, the congregation applauded, in random clapping that synched into unison.

When the jubilation subsided, the rabbi continued. "In Nazi Germany you would never see such a bar mitzvah like this taking place. I would like to thank and give recognition to all of the public officials who made an effort to be here this morning." Then, looking directly at Mitka, he said, "Never—never could you imagine back then the public support of judges and public officials attending your bar mitzvah."

In the moment, Rabbi Perl did not mention that he had sought support for Mitka from other officials outside the Long Island congregation, and that many wrote warm, personal, congratulatory letters to honor Mitka. Among them were New York Governor George Pataki, Senator Hillary Clinton, and Vice President Dick Cheney.

Reflecting on the experience, Mitka opens a scrapbook and notes with pride, "How about that? These people know about me."

Pointing to the impressive signatures and the official stamped seals, Mitka conveys the validation these letters assign to his life. No mere perfunctory tokens, the letters have become cherished expressions of what was so long denied: official recognition both of what he had suffered and, perhaps more importantly, of what he had achieved.

Once Rabbi Perl acknowledged the public support for Mitka, he shifted gears. Turning to the congregation with a playful grin, he stated, "Now I think this is one of the most difficult bar mitzvahs I have ever had to officiate. Typically the rabbi is taller than the bar mitzvah boy." To demonstrate his point, the rabbi rose on his toes, bouncing in a vain attempt to reach Mitka's height.

Then, with the timing of a polished comedian, Rabbi Perl continued, "Typically the rabbi is older than the bar mitzvah boy. And typically the rabbi has more experience than the bar mitzvah boy." Laughter erupted before a hushed solemnity settled over the sanctuary.

"Never can we imagine the challenges that dear Mitka has had throughout his life. And, therefore, what we have to give you, Mitka, is 'Thank you.' Thank you for your courage. Thank you for being an example of hope. We appreciate you and give thanks for what your life gives to us."

Next, Rabbi Perl turned to Louise Bobrow. It was her introduction of Mitka to Rabbi Perl that had culminated in this day. He invited her to address the congregation.

She beamed as she spoke. "When I first met Mitka, I was deeply moved by his story—in the camps and then a slave for seven years, including four years after the war. And I could tell, more than anything, that he wanted to be fully Jewish.

"When I met Mitka, I was struggling with my own spirituality. And he"—she paused and smiled at Mitka—"has brought me closer to Hashem. So I want to say thank you to you, Mitka, and *mazel tov.*"

The time had come for Mitka to do what was required of a soon-to-be bar mitzvah. In Hebrew, as Rabbi Perl had taught him, he prayed.

The words—words that, when sung, rang clear and familiar from his long-ago childhood—spilled from his mouth. Faintly but distinctly, he knew this language of his people from a time before he was left at a *Kinderheim* in Ukraine.

Then in English Mitka spoke.

In an interview later published in *Guideposts*, Mitka recalled the moment.

> I recited the prayers the Rabbi had taught me and talked—a little, in English—about what I was feeling after all these years. For so long I carried this weight around, the weight of my past, of knowing too much and yet not enough. Now I feel such lightness inside, in the place where I had felt it that long-ago night Hashem spoke to me in the rustle of the leaves . . . in my soul.

When Mitka concluded his brief remarks, a shofar (ram's horn) sounded. The joy of the event was trumpeted for all to hear. Rabbi Perl picked up the resounding call.

> May Hashem bless you, Mitka Kalinski . . .
> **Amen** came the congregation's response.
> . . . With a life of peace.
> **Amen.**
> . . . With a life of goodness.
> **Amen.**
> . . . With a life of blessings.
> **Amen.**
> . . . With a life of good sustenance.
> **Amen.**
> . . . With a life of good, physical health.
> **Amen.**
> . . . With a life in which you never, ever suffer shame
>   and humiliation.
> **Amen.**

With each "Amen" (Let it be so), this gathering of Jews had offered their assent to the calls from the rabbi.

One last command had to be fulfilled. Rabbi Perl placed two *tefillin*, small leather boxes that hold parchments with teachings from the Torah, on Mitka—one on his forehead, one on his arm. This was in obedience to Deuteronomy 6:8: "You shall bind [the commandments] as a sign upon your hand, and they should be for a reminder between your eyes."

With that, the man-boy had become a man, with all the responsibilities and privileges of that holy station. There was only one more thing to do: celebrate.

"Rabbi Perl told me, 'You better wear your dancing shoes.' I had no idea what to expect," Mitka recalls. "The rabbi—oh, he just jumped up. He was a little guy, but he was so happy, he jumped up so that his head was as high as mine."

Mitka was lifted high on the shoulders of men and carried into the room as music played. It was the traditional music associated with the hora. People clasped each other's hands and danced.

Eventually Mitka broke away to greet participants, who told him, "*Mazel tov.*" Some wanted to talk at length, to tell their stories or to hear more of his.

"Oh, those people—they were so nice to me. And everyone wanted to talk to me." He laughs, "They had a wonderful lunch, but I missed it. There was so much talking that I couldn't get to lunch."

Missing lunch didn't matter to Mitka. The pleasure of speaking one on one with his newfound brothers and sisters trumped any consideration of eating.

As he and Adrienne were preparing to leave, Mitka spoke what was in his heart.

I know it's possible now. Every time they said that blessing, I was thinking about the time when I was a nobody. I was just a *Judenfresse* in those years. That's what I was called. And I hear the beautiful rabbi's voice, and I just can't believe it. How would someone do something like this for me, for somebody they didn't even know?

I want to thank the rabbi. I want to thank him so much. He lifted
me up. He gave me courage. I have found my people. It's like I have
known them all my life. I have found my people.

Years later, Rabbi Perl, in a 2012 broadcast, stated,

Even as many years have passed, we all continue to speak proudly
of the special bar mitzvah ceremony celebrated with Mitka. He is a
very humble and sincere individual whose life story as a child slave
during the Holocaust continues to inspire us on a daily basis. He
approached his long-overdue bar mitzvah ceremony with us here on
Long Island with the same open eyes of wonderment and joy found
on the face of every young thirteen-year-old becoming bar mitzvah.
Mitka remains in our hearts and souls a beacon of light and hope,
proving beyond all doubt that while the Nazis may have controlled
his body, Mitka's soul was forever awake and free, connected to the
infinite Almighty under all circumstances.

That Mitka was invited to have his bar mitzvah in New York was
a providential closing of a circle. Fifty years before, in 1951, Mitka had
first touched American soil at a synagogue in the Bronx. His first subway ride had taken him out to Long Island, close to where he had now
come home to his faith. Nostalgia welled in Mitka as each memory
rushed forward.

The day had carried a glut of memories, expectations, and emotions. Mitka was touching all that had, at one time, been painful,
together with precious few fond recollections. He remembered, as a
child, encountering so much death and not knowing what it meant.
He thought about learning English and the ways of work, manhood,
love, marriage, parenting, calamity, and recovery. He thought of teaching himself to play the accordion and of learning to fix clocks and
machinery and of the animals he loved and of treasured movies that
were his "teacher." Also, there was the ever-nagging question of who
he was.

At some point on the morning of his bar mitzvah, the security of belonging to a family beyond just his immediate family took hold. He had, for so much of his life, been unsure of how to be a Jew, even denying it on occasion. In his bones, he knew he was, but to survive, he often tried to divorce himself from this inescapable part of his being. On this day he didn't tug at the anchor; he let it hold. He was not adrift. What once had been necessary detachment now became attachment.

Before he returned to Nevada, Mitka wanted to visit one more site in New York. He wanted to go to the Museum of Jewish Heritage near Battery Park. At some point during their visit, he slipped away from Adrienne to be alone.

"I walked to a place where I was by myself, and I just looked out at the Statue of Liberty. I remember I seen her when I first came to New York back in 1951."

In those moments, sitting alone on a bench in Battery Park, Mitka spoke to "that beautiful statue" on the small island in New York Harbor. It wasn't enough to silently think his words. It wasn't enough to whisper them. He had to address "the Lady" out loud. "When I came here before, I didn't know who you were. But now I know. And I just want to thank you."

Mitka reflects on that solitary occasion. "I don't mind telling you. I was full of tears at that moment."

Freedom wasn't an abstract concept to Mitka; it was a visceral reality. On this day he felt the same emotion that had overtaken him in 1949 when, after American GIs freed him from slavery, he jumped for joy, shouting, "I am free!" This time around, his freedom came, paradoxically, by his binding himself to the Jewish covenant with God.

Mitka tells his story in simple words. "I didn't know . . . now I know . . . I just want to thank you." Settled in America with a family that loves him and now welcomed into a faith community that connects him with the parents he never knew and with the Presence that once spoke to him, Mitka feels beyond blessed.

The Jewish orphan, so often in the line of Hitler's homicidal intentions, had won. The prisoner, little Mitka, had left the camps alive—

broken, but alive. The Nazis had taken his family, his faith, his name, and his freedom.

But every one of these things he reclaimed. His name is Mitka, and he is proud to be Jewish—he has even survived to see some of his children embrace Judaism. What the locust had eaten had been restored.

Mitka is an unabashedly cheerful man, a man who loves, who seeks no revenge, who trusts, who delights in the moment, who embraces truth, and who trudges forward expecting to find answers to mysteries yet unsolved.

But he is also a man who lives with an ache in his heart, a man who manages his lifetime of trauma, in part, by telling and retelling all that happened to him. He determined not to forget, and in his storytelling he remembers.

When Mitka was at his lowest, locked in his cold room at the Dörrs', he heard a voice. He believed what he heard then, and he believes it now. What he had heard—"Am Ende findest du dein Ziel"—means "In the end you will find your purpose." That voice and those words kept him going through dark years and lonely times. It was his bar mitzvah that had confirmed to him what his purpose was.

When he had come to America, for the next thirty years Mitka desperately tried to escape the boy who so long ago had been left behind at a *Kinderheim* in Ukraine. He tried to bury the orphan who rode crowded cattle cars and to deny the slave who was beaten, starved, and frozen at Badegasse 14. He never forgot the voice, but, at times, he tried to do so. He strained to keep his past, his shame, a secret.

He could not.

The newly minted Mitka came from his bar mitzvah to boldly engage the Statue of Liberty. He spoke to her as a child would, but he told the hard-won truth of an old man.

From the beginning there had been promise within the boy. There was love and grace, there was laughter and music, there was tenacity and resilience, there was stubbornness and fearlessness, there was letting go and holding on, there was hurt and agony, and there was hope and faith. Then, at his nadir, there was a promise given to the boy that his purpose would be realized. Time and again it was almost snuffed out.

But he clung to the promise. The man with reasons to hate chose love. He refused bitterness and found happiness. He, the victim, rejected victimhood. The grace he received became the grace he gave.

The man who could not write his name made joy his unforgettable signature. Now through bar mitzvah the boy became the man. The promise was realized.

Afterword

Now, in the spring of 2020, as I write these words, the world marks the seventy-fifth anniversary of the Allied liberation of the concentration camps. One way we memorialize such epochal events is to tell stories—stories like Mitka's. To tell his story is to lob another salvo against a fortress of ideas that bring only madness, destruction, and death.

Back in the summer of 2016, Robert Lucchesi introduced Lynn and me to the Kalinskis. Joel had met them earlier—again, through Robert.

It was Robert who, for more than twenty years, persisted in trying to get Mitka's story told. He pressed forward without encouragement that it would ever happen. Now he has the reward of things once unseen yet believed.

Today, I reflect on the work of writing this story and the unflagging assistance of Lynn and Joel—the hundreds of hours of interviews and phone calls, the thousands of documents and pictures studied and archived, the dozens of books used in research. Especially, I remember cherished time spent with Mitka and Adrienne and with most of their extended family in Sparks, Nevada.

The story told in this book concludes with Mitka's bar mitzvah in 2001, when, for the first time, Mitka put on a pair of *tefillin*, boxes containing pieces of parchment that proclaim, "Hear, O Israel! The LORD is our God, the LORD alone."

Throughout his life Mitka longed for ties to bind him to family and to something more. In the ritual of becoming a bar mitzvah, he experienced a bond with his Jewish faith and with his past that satisfied this longing.

In the nineteen intervening years, much has happened. Mitka is in his mideighties; Adrienne is ninety. He continues to live with one haunting grief and most likely will until the day he dies. He does not know who his mother was or the date and place of his birth.

Since meeting Mitka and Adrienne in 2016, we continue to be amazed by remarkable qualities they have in common. At their advanced age, they still possess alert, curious, and engaged minds. They listen, laugh, converse, question, tease, reflect, and fully participate in life as much younger folk would. Often the exchanges are funny, raucous, and sometimes messy, but always there is an undercurrent of loyalty and love. They are fully present in living day to day. Yet, despite all these good things, Mitka still struggles, tooth and nail, with his past.

In 2005 Mitka and Adrienne experienced the loss of their son Jimmy. Since his accident in 1974 and the brain injury he suffered, he never regained full use of his body. For most of his adult life he lived with the effects of multiple sclerosis, often confined to a wheelchair. He lived a productive life, however, and he gave his parents two grandchildren.

Three living children—Mike, Cheryl, and Donna—and grandson Michael, who, in most regards, is a son, look to Mitka and Adrienne not merely as aging seniors but as the active, in-charge leaders of the clan, which in fact is true. It's a balancing act that they pull off in nimble and effective ways, despite inherent chaos and some physical limitations for Adrienne. Days are filled engaging with one or another member of the family, which now includes seven grandchildren and seven great-grandchildren. They direct and negotiate family matters in ways that would tire those half their age. The newest great-grandchild, Aiden Mitka, born in 2017, was named for both of them. They babysit him one to three days a week.

One way the Kalinskis occupy their days is with shopping. These excursions are less about buying something than they are about getting out of the house. When they shop, the ever-gregarious and irrepressible Mitka makes friends of clerks, managers, and other shoppers. He walks alongside Adrienne, helping her navigate with a walker, opening doors, and carrying packages. While this is happening, a stream of good-natured banter continues unabated between them. It feels a bit like watching a comedic film.

One of their favorite activities is dining at casino buffets. Adrienne loves a plateful of mussels in the shell cooked in lots of garlic and butter. Mitka still devours amazing amounts of his favorite foods—roasted chicken, corn on the cob, and potatoes.

Mitka has become a minor celebrity in Sparks and Reno. The Reno Philharmonic Orchestra has honored him, and he speaks occasionally at schools, Rotary and Kiwanis lunches, and other community events. Sometimes, when they walk down a store aisle, he and Adrienne are recognized. They stop and talk to anyone.

Adrienne is virtually blind with advanced macular degeneration. You might not notice this unless you saw her reading, keeping the family books, or writing checks and letters. Sitting in the same seat she has occupied for sixty years—her throne as the family matriarch at the end of the dining room table—she is surrounded by a collection of magnifying glasses. Reading and writing are painstaking tasks for Adrienne, yet she keeps at it day after day. Sometimes it means her eyes are inches from the text. She misses nothing. She presses on despite how her world has contracted because of her limited sight. She won't have anyone's pity. And her sometimes biting, sardonic wit still finds its way into conversations. It's an ingrained tendency that reveals a keen perception of human nature and life's vicissitudes. "Wise realist" seems an apt description of her.

Mitka spends his days tinkering and watching television. In the former, he is fixing all manner of appliances or cars or solving all sorts of plumbing and electrical problems for family and friends. He watches local and national news, through which he satisfies his hunger to know and learn. At the center of his daily viewing is the Jewish Broadcasting Service (JBS). Although he and Adrienne do run errands, neither feels able to make the drive from Sparks to Reno to participate in services and activities at Congregation Temple Emanu-El. Instead, Mitka worships every Friday evening by watching a livestream on JBS of Shabbat services at New York's Central Synagogue. For entertainment, Mitka watches movies. He has seen most of what he watches hundreds of times. He recites the year the film was made and the names of the director and actors, and he gives any captive listener a plot description and shares his memories of when he first viewed the film. His repertoire spans from 1930 to 1970 but consists mainly of those movies that played such an important role in his early life.

To spend any time with Mitka and Adrienne is to clearly understand one thing. Intuitive, natural, seamless, and unself-conscious, each serves the other in a dance of love. Oh, they do bicker and mock. While this patter may be jarring to someone hearing a spat between them for the first time, it quickly becomes apparent that tenderness and affection control their interaction. In a flash, laughter ensues.

Though only snippets of memory of his father and mother remain, he is an exemplar of the biblical commandment to honor your parents. He has done all he can to know them and to make them proud.

I conclude with a couple of impressions from our time with Mitka.

As we talked with people about Mitka and his story, the word "survivor" came up most often. Adjectives like "persevering," "resilient," "courageous," and "inspiring" also kept cropping up in our conversations. His children regularly called him a hero.

All of these words are telling, and true. There was, however, one word that seemed to encompass all that Mitka has become in his long, amazing life. That word is *Mensch*.

English speakers have borrowed this word from Yiddish, which roughly translates as "a good person." A fuller sense of what it means to be a *mensch* suggests character, integrity, dignity, and authenticity. Interestingly, the word *mensch* literally means "human." To be a *mensch*, we might say, is to embody what we think of as the *ideal* human, someone who lives life to the fullest, as we wish we could. It is a high compliment, therefore, to call someone a *mensch*.

Mitka is a *mensch*.

Today Mitka lives a humble existence. He lives joyfully without bitterness. He is a loving man full of hope. He laughs often. When I see his eyes, I cannot help but smile.

As Lynn, Joel, and I, with our editors, worked through a final draft of Mitka's story, Lynn reminded me of a Scripture, one that captures what I have come to know about this man. In Deuteronomy 30:19, Hashem speaks: "I have put before you life and death, blessing and curse. Choose life."

Mitka chose life.

Acknowledgments

To write Mitka's story has been a lesson in humility. Throughout the process, we felt the weight of responsibility that comes with trying to tell this important story. We wanted to be faithful to the truth, the historical truth and that of Mitka's experiences. Also, we wanted to keep our promise to Mitka and Adrienne that his story would be told. None of this could have been accomplished without the help of others. To each one who helped we are indebted, and thankful.

It is not an overstatement to recognize that without Robert "Bob" Lucchesi's persistence this book would not have come to be. Since the spring of 1994, when Bob first learned Mitka's story in a Bodega Bay campground, he has pursued his dream of getting the story told through a book and a film. There were many setbacks, but he would not quit. Without Bob, Mitka's story would have been a saga shared only among family and friends.

When we finished part 1, we asked several readers for their comments and criticism. Anthony Arnold, Barry and Laurie Gillespie, Joel Kaminsky, Archie Lohr, Teresa Lohr, Lisa Lucchesi, and Lois "Bonnie" McVeigh each offered helpful insights. Professor Frank Benyousky gave us the benefit of his careful reading of the text, which profoundly changed our early work and influenced our writing throughout the book.

Long before the first word was written, Gary Nixon's investigative work unlocked secrets that changed Mitka's life. His contributions were invaluable to our work.

Professor Grant Leneaux, Mitka's friend since 1981, provided us with keen insights and recall of specific events critical to the story.

Jacob Wheeler at one time had set out to write Mitka's story. Had circumstances allowed him to do so, it would have been an excellent book. His act of generosity in sharing his original research with us was a true gift.

Richard Briggs, of Briggs Photography in California, went above and beyond to help us with the delicate and at times tedious task of digitizing the hundreds of pages of photographs and historical documents related to this project. We owe him our utmost thanks. Thanks are also due to Mahmoud Elsheikh and Alondra Lara for their kind assistance with the www.mitka.life website.

There are others, too many to list, who have helped us and the Kalinskis in telling their story. At the risk of inadvertently leaving individuals out, we must mention Dr. Xabier Irujo, Rabbi Anchelle Perl, and Nicolette Tiller. We also thank Dr. Heinrich Nuhn for his kindness and hospitality to Joel Lohr while in Rotenburg conducting research for this book.

Our agent, Claudia Cross, believed in this story from the start. Over and again, she calmly and wisely counseled us. Her patience with us is only exceeded by her consummate professionalism.

To the entire publishing team at Eerdmans we offer thanks. We must mention Victoria Jones, who so carefully and professionally edited the manuscript. Her work, undoubtedly, made this a better book. Further, Andrew Knapp, our acquisitions editor, deserves special commendation. He believed in Mitka's story and has championed the book throughout the publishing process. We followed his guidance, which was a good decision.

Finally, to Mitka and Adrienne, who have given us their trust and shared intimate details of their lives in countless hours of interviews, we are deeply grateful. Our task was made easier by their unfailing hospitality and hard work. We marvel at their energy and focus. We came to know their entire family, each of whom contributed to different aspects of the story. To Mike, Cheryl, Donna, and Michael, and their children, we offer special thanks. We are privileged to have shared so many meals, so much laughter, and such affection with the whole family.

Notes

Kinderheim

6   *At the time Bila Tserkva could be described as a religious city*   For more information, refer to "History of Jewish Communities in Ukraine: Belaya Tserkov," http://jewua.org/belaya_tserkov/; "Welcome to Ukraine: Bila Tserkva City, Ukraine," http://ukrainetrek .com/bila_tserkva-city; and "History of the Jews in Ukraine," http://berdichev.org/history_of_the_jews_in_ukraine.html.

7   *"A schoolhouse in Bila Tserkva"*   Wendy Lower, "From Berlin to Babi Yar: The Nazi War against the Jews, 1941–1944," *Journal of Religion and Society* 9 (2007): 4.

8   *"Judeo-Bolshevism"*   Lower, "From Berlin to Babi Yar," 9. Lower makes the point, supported by Doris L. Bergen in *The Holocaust: A Concise History* (New York: Rowman & Littlefield, 2009), 20, that Hitler and other Germans tended to conflate Bolshevism and Judaism, thus placing blame for Communism squarely on the heads of Jews.

8   *The killing of Jewish children*   Lower, "From Berlin to Babi Yar," 5; see also Bergen, *Holocaust*, 157.

8   *"Alternative accommodation for the children was . . . impossible"*   Bo1 Report by Lieutenant Colonel Helmut Groscurth, from a translation provided by EHRI Online Course in Holocaust Studies, Institute for Contemporary History, https://training.ehri -project.eu/sites/training.ehri-project.eu/files/B1_IfZA_F_45_8

_71x-75_translation_0.pdf. For additional discussion of the Bila Tserkva massacre, see Lower, "From Berlin to Babi Yar," 4–5, and Bergen, *Holocaust*, 157–58.

8   *"I went to the woods alone"*   Report by SS Obersturmführer August Häfner titled "On the Killing of the Children," quoted in Ernst Klee, Willie Dressen, and Volker Riess, eds., *"The Good Old Days": The Holocaust as Seen by Its Perpetrators and Bystanders*, trans. Deborah Burnstone (New York: Macmillan, 1988), 154.

10   *Watching the History Channel years later*   Bergen, *Holocaust*, 156. For an in-depth discussion of Babi Yar and its antecedents, refer to Lower, "From Berlin to Babi Yar."

10   *As with the Bila Tserkva massacre*   Bergen, *Holocaust*, 156.

Camps

13   *Official SS regulations proposed 50 deportees per car*   For a fuller picture, see Simone Gigliotti, *The Train Journey: Transit, Captivity, and Witnessing in the Holocaust* (New York: Berghahn, 2009), especially chapter 4, "Immobilization in 'Cattle Cars.'" Compare with the shorter account in Abraham J. Edelheit and Hershel Edelheit, *History of the Holocaust: A Handbook and Dictionary* (Boulder, CO: Westview, 1994), 70.

13   *It was not uncommon for guards to find*   See "Deportation to the Camps," http://www.aish.com/ho/o/48970811.html.

14   *"As a temporary settlement for seasonal workers"*   Nikolaus Wachsmann, *KL: A History of the Nazi Concentration Camps* (New York: Farrar, Straus & Giroux, 2015), 200. Wachsmann describes the arrival of a prisoner-bearing train around the time of Mitka's arrival in the autumn of 1941:

> On October 7, 1941, a freight train pulled up at a ramp near the Auschwitz main camp and slowly came to a halt. Inside were 2,014 men, the first Soviet POWs dispatched to the camp for forced labor. The doors were flung open and the prisoners, dazed and dirty, staggered out of the stifling carriages into the bright light, gasping for air. Among them was twenty-eight-year-old infantry lieutenant Nikolaj Wassiljew from Moscow. "We did not know

where we had arrived," he said later, "and what kind of camp this was." The SS guards soon showed them: screams and blows rained down on Wassiljew and others. Some feared that they would be shot straightaway. Instead, the SS forced them to strip and jump into a vat filled with disinfectant. Wassiljew recalled that those "who did not want to jump were kicked and pushed with sticks." Then the bone-thin POWs had to crouch naked on the floor.

15   *There are pictures of clay pits and brickmaking operations*   See Wachsmann, *KL*, 166–68, for a description of the brickmaking attempts at Sachsenhausen-Oranienburg. For Buchenwald brickmaking, see Debórah Dwork and Robert Jan van Pelt, *Auschwitz* (New York: Norton, 1996), 171–72. For more on the overall operations of the SS-owned and -operated German Earth and Stone Works Company (Deutsche Erd- und Steinwerke GmbH), or DEST, which had granite quarries, brick and tile plants, and a stonecutting plant, see www.gusen.org/gudest1x.htm.

15   *"Relatively healthy young men were taught"*   Martin Goldsmith, *Alex's Wake: A Voyage of Betrayal and a Journey of Remembrance* (Philadelphia: El Capo, 2014), 298.

15   *Based on descriptions of drainage projects*   See Dwork and van Pelt, *Auschwitz*, 191–93.

16   *"Hangman of Buchenwald"*   For this epithet and more on Sommer, see David A. Hackett, *The Buchenwald Report* (Boulder, CO: Westview, 1995), 35, 60, and the truly gruesome prisoner accounts on 152ff.

16   *"The unofficial camp executioner"*   Wachsmann, *KL*, 221.

17   *"Sommer was a man of exceptional cruelty"*   Wachsmann, *KL*, 221.

17   *"Strict but fair"*   Quotes by Heinrich Himmler are from "Speech on the Day of the German Police [January 29, 1939]," in Nikolaus Wachsmann and Christian Goeschel, eds., *The Nazi Concentration Camps, 1933–1939: A Documentary History* (Lincoln: University of Nebraska Press, 2012), document 274. For more on the idea that "work makes free," see the column by the late Barry Rubin, "How the Auschwitz Sign Claiming That 'Work Makes Free' Embodies Current Western Thinking and Policy," available at www.rubincenter.org/2009/12/auschwitz-sign/.

17   *"Mystical declaration"*   Otto Friedrich, *The Kingdom of Auschwitz*
      (New York: HarperCollins, 1982), 3.

17   *"There is a path to freedom"*   Wachsmann, *KL*, 100, citing Harry
      Naujoks, *Mein Leben in KZ Sachsenhausen: Erinnerungen des ehe-*
      maligen Lagerältesten (Cologne: Dietz Verlag, 1987), 136.

19   *To be murdered*   Susanne Hohlmann, "Pfaffenwald: Sterbe- und
      Geburtenlager, 1942–1945" (University of Kassel thesis, 1984).

21   *He also believes the incisions were made*   See Hohlmann, "Pfaffen-
      wald," 83, 193.

22   *Rotenburg an der Fulda*   After World War II, the town name
      Rotenburg an der Fulda was officially changed to Rotenburg a.d.
      Fulda, but the original name is still widely used in writings today.
      For simplicity's sake, we use "Rotenburg an der Fulda" throughout
      the book.

Iron Gustav

23   *Second, he was assigned a date of birth*   The minimum age for con-
      scripted labor in Germany changed as the war went on, reduced to
      ten years old by the time Mitka was taken into the Dörr household.
      See "Conscript Labor," in *World War II: The Definitive Encyclope-*
      dia and Document Collection, ed. Spencer C. Tucker, 5 vols. (Santa
      Barbara, CA: ABC-CLIO, 2016), 1:449–51.

24   *"His head was shaven bald"*   This sentence appears in a newspaper
      article written after Mitka returned to Rotenburg an der Fulda in
      1984. The title of the article is translated as "Out of Nobody, Slowly
      There Comes a Somebody," and the line above the headline reads,
      "A Former Inmate of Pfaffenwald Returns." See "Aus dem Niemand
      wird ganz langsam ein Jemand," *Bad Hersfeld Newspaper*, Novem-
      ber 22, 1984, 19, for the actual article.

24   *From its beginning, the picturesque village was home to Jews*   "Roten-
      burg an der Fulda," in *The Encyclopedia of Jewish Life: Before and*
      during the Holocaust, ed. Shmuel Spector and Geoffrey Wigoder
      (New York: New York University Press, 2001), 2:1095.

25   *Ester Einhorn was born and brought up*   Ann Beaglehole, *A Small*

Price to Pay: Refugees from Hitler in New Zealand, 1936–1946 (Wellington, New Zealand: Allen and Unwin, 1988), 18.

25   *Gustav was an active member of the Sturmabteilung (SA)*   The quotation and information in this paragraph are drawn from the "SA: Nazi Organization" article in the 2017 online *Encyclopædia Britannica*, www.britannica.com/topic/SA-Nazi-organization. Compare to Wolfgang Peter's "Sturmabteilung," in *The Encyclopedia of the Third Reich*, ed. Christian Zentner and Friedemann Bedürftig (New York: Da Capo, 1997), 928–32. For a comprehensive treatment, see Daniel Siemens, *Stormtroopers: A New History of Hitler's Brownshirts* (New Haven: Yale University Press, 2017).

26   *On that Monday night, and stretching into the wee hours of Tuesday morning*   These and many of the following details about Kristallnacht in Rotenburg are drawn from Heinrich Nuhn's extensive work on the subject. For English content, see his archives at http://www.hassia-judaica.de/eng_places.html, as well as his article "'Like Hunted Animals.' The November 1938 Pogroms in Rotenburg an der Fulda: Henny Rothschild's Letter from 18 October 1939," trans. Judith N. Levi, *Leo Baeck Institute Year Book* 60 (2015): 1–25. The original article, in German, was published in *Zeitschrift des Vereins für hessische Geschichte und Landeskunde* (ZHG), Band 117/118 (2012/13), S. 215–36. The quotation that "not a single pane of glass nor any window crossbar remained" is from Nuhn, "'Like Hunted Animals,'" 7.

26   *Thus, infamously, November 9, 1938, became known as* Kristallnacht   Tim Cole, *Holocaust Landscapes* (London: Bloomsbury Continuum, 2016), 11–13. For more on Kristallnacht, especially how the events in Kassel, Rotenburg an der Fulda, and Bebra gave rise to and served as templates for the actions that happened throughout Germany, see Alan E. Steinweis, *Kristallnacht 1938* (Cambridge, MA: Belknap Press of Harvard University Press, 2009), 16–35.

27   *Home ceased to be a safe place for them*   Again, see Cole, *Holocaust Landscapes*.

27   *"Around 3 p.m. Lotte came by"*   Nuhn, "'Like Hunted Animals,'" 8.

27   *"You can imagine all that was stolen"*   Nuhn, "'Like Hunted Animals,'" 19.

28   *"After the war, dean Hammann of the Rotenburg-Neustadt Lutheran congregation"*   Nuhn, "'Like Hunted Animals,'" 19n95. Italics original.

28   *"Horst Mainz, the chief SA squad leader"*   Nuhn, "'Like Hunted Animals,'" 19n95. Italics original.

28   *"A lot has happened everywhere"*   Nuhn, "'Like Hunted Animals,'" 25.

29   *"The biggest Nazi in Rotenburg"*   "Aus dem Niemand wird ganz langsam ein Jemand," 19.

29   *Locally, Gustav was known by the sobriquet*   From a letter written by Eduard Gruschka to Demitro (Mitka) Kalinski, January 21, 1984. Gruschka describes Gustav Dörr as "an active Nazi participant" known for "torturing the Jews." He notes that, for these reasons, "He was called 'der Eisene Gustav.'"

Moly

33   *A typical metal milk can of the era*   To understand some of Mitka's experiences with dairy farming and the transport of milk, see the video "German Dairy Farm 1930s," https://www.youtube.com/watch?v=66RqgoQEb9M.

35   *"My brother is missing in Russia"*   The term *Judenfresser* is a difficult one to translate, especially since it seems to have two meanings, depending on context. Literally, it means Jew-gobbler, or Jew-eater, and it was sometimes used of anti-Semites who were out to destroy the Jewish people, especially in the early 1900s (for one example, see the classic newspaper comic depicting Karl Lueger, the infamous anti-Semitic mayor of Austria who inspired Adolf Hitler). However, when used of a Jew it may actually be *Judenfresse* (as we have written). Literally translated "Jew eat," it seems to carry the sense of "Jewish pig," or Jew-pig—clearly a derogatory term. Given the long history of anti-Semitic associations between the Jewish people and pigs, including the sickening "Judensau" located at the

Wittenberg church where Martin Luther preached, the term is particularly stinging. For more on "Judensau," see Daniel N. Leeson, "Judensau 2010," *Journal for the Study of Antisemitism* 2, no. 2 (2010): 393–409.

36   *They made no attempts to get to know the* Stoppelrusse   The reference to Mitka as a *Stoppelrusse*, or "Bald Russian," is taken from "Aus dem Niemand wird ganz langsam ein Jemand," *Bad Hersfeld Newspaper*, November 22, 1984, 19.

36   *Looking at a published photograph of one of Gustav's wagons*   In Peter Green, *The March East 1945: The Final Days of Oflag IX A/H and A/Z* (Stroud, Gloucestershire: History Press, 2012), 107.

The Voice

41   *In part, Mitka's relationship with the Dörr family*   For helpful discussions of Stockholm syndrome, see M. Namnyak, N. Tufton, R. Szekely, M. Toal, S. Worboys, and E. L. Sampson, "'Stockholm Syndrome': Psychiatric Diagnosis or Urban Myth," *Acta Psychiatra Scandinavica* 117, no. 1 (January 2008): 4–11; and Joseph Carver, "Love and the Stockholm Syndrome: When the Abused Loves the Abuser," http://counsellingresource.com/therapy/self-help/stockholm/.

41   *It was the work Mitka did and the relative independence it gave him*   For a thorough analysis of Germany's practices and policies in regard to conscripted labor during World War II, see Edward Homze, *Foreign Labor in Nazi Germany* (Princeton: Princeton University Press, 1967). Homze asserts that the use of forced labor was common in the Third Reich. It had been conceived by Nazi leadership as a way to reduce rampant unemployment, further their ideological vision, rebuild Germany's infrastructure, and—in defiance of the Treaty of Versailles—rearm the country by ramping up munitions factories. In its earliest iterations, it involved complex social engineering efforts, such as removing women from the workforce so that they could bear Aryan children, destroying labor unions, implementing wage controls, and more. Over time, though,

it became clear that Germany had neither the material nor human resources to meet the demands of a full-blown military campaign. The 1938 passage of the Compulsory Labor Decree (*Dienstverp-flichtyeverdonunung*) provided clear sanction to conscript prisoners as laborers.

41   *Indeed, his life had all of the characteristics associated with slave labor*   Conditions associated with slavery in Nazi Germany receive thorough treatment in Cord Pagenstacher, "We Were Treated Like Slaves. Remembering Forced Labor for Nazi Germany," in *Human Bondage in the Cultural Contact Zone: Transdisciplinary Perspective on Slavery and Its Discourses*, ed. Raphael Hormann and Gesa Machekthun (Berlin: Waxman, 2010), 281–97, and Pankkos Panavi, "Exploitation, Criminality, Resistance: The Everyday Life of Foreign Workers and Prisoners of War in the German Town of Osnabruck, 1939–1949," *Journal of Contemporary History* 40, no. 3 (2005): 483–91.

41   Arbeitsbuch*, a workbook required for all laborers as a way to document and regulate them*   Homze, *Foreign Labor*, 10.

42   *"In addition to rationing, these systems included . . . periodic animal censuses"*   Jill Stephenson, "Nazism, Modern War and Rural Society in Wurttemberg, 1939–45," *Journal of Contemporary History* 23, no. 2 (1997): 348.

45   *Nazi national anthem, the "Horst-Wessel-Lied"*   Named for its SA author Horst Wessel, this piece was also known as "The Flag on High."

46   *Am Ende findest du dein Ziel*   We have chosen to translate the German word *Ziel* as "purpose," though a more literal translation might be "destination" or "goal." Since Mitka often speaks of this as a kind of "end goal," or final destination in life, we feel that "purpose" captures the meaning of this word best, in context.

A White Flag

50   *Another prominent sign of the war that Mitka encountered was flak guns*   For more on Germany's *Fliegerabwehrkanone* ("flak") weaponry, see "Anti-aircraft Defence," in *A Dictionary of the Second*

World War, ed. Elizabeth Anne-Wheal, Stephen Pope, and James Taylor (New York: Peter Bedrick Books, 1989), 16–18.

50   *In 1939 the Nazis commandeered the Jakob-Grimm-Schule*   For a thorough and detailed discussion of Oflag IX A/H and Oflag IX A/Z, refer to Peter Green, *The March East 1945: The Final Days of Oflag IX A/H and A/Z* (Stroud, Gloucestershire: History Press, 2012). Green, whose father was a prisoner in Oflag IX A/Z, also has a blog, *Oflag IX A/H and Oflag IX A/A*, that focuses on the prison in Rotenburg an der Fulda, among other things, located at https://oflag1945.wordpress.com.

50   *Records from Oflag IX A/Z do, in fact, show that prisoners escaped*   Green, *March East*, 29–30. Green notes, "Escape attempts occurred at both camps. The only successful one from Rotenburg was in early 1943 by two Indian Army officers who reached Switzerland." He describes attempts at both camps but focuses on two unusual ones at the Rotenburg facility. The first occurred in September 1944. "Seven men, disguised as orderlies under the supervision of two other prisoners disguised as German guards, walked out of the main gate having made a copy of the key to the gate. . . . The 'guards' had wooden rifles and uniforms made by the prisoners. The men were all back in the camp in October." A second attempt "was a tunnel at Rotenburg that started above ground, on the first floor. The tunnel went into an outside wall in an upstairs toilet and then down inside the rubble-filled core of the wall." Green notes that the Germans discovered the material that had been dumped as the tunnel was constructed but that "it took them a month to find the [actual] tunnel." He further comments that, "when the Jakob-Grimm-Schule was renovated in the 1980s, there was still rubble from the tunnel lying on the rafters in the roof."

51   *Hitler Youth, the Nazis' mandatory youth organization*   Though thirteen was the age at which German boys entered the Hitler Youth, they would have entered Deutsches Jungvolk (German Young People) first, at age ten, before graduating into the program. Female youth joined the Jungmadelbund (League of Young Girls) at age ten and then graduated to the Bund Deutscher Madel (League of Ger-

man Girls) at fourteen. For more information, see the essay "Hitler Youth," https://www.britannica.com/topic/Hitler-Youth.

51   *Though it's hard to imagine youth persuading local officials to lock up a boy*   See Tilman Allert, *The Hitler Salute: On the Meaning of a Gesture*, trans. Jefferson Chase (New York: Metropolitan Books, 2008).

53   *The Allies were in the final stages of bringing Germany and its Nazi war machine to its knees*   See Victor Davis Hanson, "Ends: Winners, Losers, Neither, and Both," in *The Second World Wars: How the First Global Conflict Was Fought and Won* (New York: Basic Books, 2017), 503–29, for a discussion of the end of the war in Europe. Also refer to Doris L. Bergen, "Death Throes and Killing Frenzies, 1944–1945," in *The Holocaust: A Concise History* (New York: Rowman & Littlefield, 2009), 215–32. Bergen's focus is on the Holocaust, but she does an able job of situating her discussion in the larger context of the end of the war in Europe.

53   *"Even Nazi true believers had to see that the war was lost"*   Bergen, *The Holocaust*, 221.

53   *Kassel, a much larger city with significant munitions factories and a concentration of Nazi personnel*   According to "The 10 Most Devastating Bombing Campaigns of World War II," "The City of Kassel . . . was subjected to an ongoing bombing campaign that began in early 1942 and went on almost until the end of WWII in 1945. . . . The city was targeted so vehemently largely because of its important military-industrial sites: the Fieseler aircraft plant, Henschel tank-making facilities, railway works and engine works were all based there." http://www.onlinemilitaryeducation.org/posts/10 -most-devastating-bombing-campaigns-of-wwii/.

53   *The American soldiers, referred to by the Germans as "Amis"*   This slang term is a contraction of "Amerikaners." See Gordon L. Rottman, *FUBAR: Soldier Slang of World War II* (Oxford: Osprey, 2007), 205.

55   *"I heard that he run away"*   Mitka's guess about Gustav's running away may have been close to the truth. Green, *March East*, focuses on the evacuations of Oflag IX A/H and A/Z, which were in response to orders from the German Military High Command, who

(a) "wanted to keep their prisoners from being liberated" (47) and (b) viewed the prisoners as "too valuable a military resource to be abandoned" (48). Green provides detailed information about the evacuation that began on March 29, 1945. He reports that most prisoners were forced to march out of camp with the goal of reaching a camp at Mulhausen and that provisions were made to transport the sick and to move camp equipment. "Rotenburg had two carts provided by Gustav Dörr, a carrier in Rotenburg. Along with the wagons, he supplied sixteen horses and two Russian POWs as drivers. Gustav Dörr joined the evacuation. Perhaps not just to look after his property; did he feel safer surrounded by Allied prisoners?" (56).

57   *A gaping hole was all that remained*   Bergen, *Holocaust*, 221.

Amis

59   "Bap . . . bap, bap . . . bap—*they put up this pontoon bridge*"   Pontoon bridges played a critical role in the Allied victory in Europe. For detailed information on the variants of this structure and on key uses during World War II, see Alfred Beck, Abe Bortz, Charles Lynch, Lida Mayo, and Ralph E. Weld, *The Corp of Engineers: The War against Germany* (Washington, DC: United States Army Center of Military History, 1985).

59   *As troops moved through the region, some remained behind*   For a description of the work and roles of US troops, especially in areas in and around Rotenburg, in 1945, see chapter 9, "Kaput," in Robert S. Allen, *Lucky Forward: Patton's Third US Army* (New York: Manor Books, 1947, 1977), 258–94.

60   *As Mitka's life changed, so did the world*   Numerous sources provide an overview of the end of World War II in Europe. See the now dated but still helpful Louis L. Snyder, *The War: A Concise History, 1939–1945* (New York: Julian Messner, 1960), as well as the helpful online summaries of Alan Taylor, "World War II: The Fall of Nazi Germany," https://www.theatlantic.com/photo/2011/10/world-war-ii-the-fall-of-nazi-germany/100166/; "World War II in Europe, 1945," http://www.historyplace.com/worldwar2/time

line/ww2time.htm#1945; and "May 7, 1945: Nazi Germany Surrenders in World War II," https://learning.blogs.nytimes.com/2012/05/07/may-7-1945-nazi-germany-surrenders-in-world-war-ii/.

60   *Mitka was one of the "lost children"*   Christian Höschler, *Home(less): The IRO Children's Village Bad Aibling, 1948–1951* (self-pub., eplubi, 2017), 14.

60   *A relatively small group within the larger tribe of displaced persons after the war*   Ben Shepard, *The Long Road Home: The Aftermath of the Second World War* (New York: Anchor, 2012), 4.

60   *In the early months after the war's end, Mitka overheard a story*   Green, *March East*, 56. See also Green, "Oflag IX A/Z Rotenburg an de Fulda: Research News 2," https://oflag1945.files .wordpress.com/2011/01/newsletter2-1.pdf, for additional information about Gustav Dörr's role in the evacuation of prisoners from Oflag IV A/Z.

61   *An American soldier spoke to him—in Yiddish*   For more on Jewish soldiers who served in WWII, see "Jewish Soldiers in the Allied Armies," http://www.yadvashem.org/holocaust/about/combat -resistance/jewish-soldiers.

63   *"4.5 million of whom were roaming the Western Zones of Germany alone"*   Höschler, *Home(less)*, 10.

63   *"International relief agencies to take on the enormous task"*   Höschler, *Home(less)*, 10–11.

65   *"This is to advise you"*   F. Przylusky memo to UNRRA, District Office, No. 2, Bad Wildungen, Child Welfare Officer, December 10, 1946.

66   *From under the bed he snuck in the dark to find a wallet*   Mitka cannot recall the date of his adventure with Willi at the Lullusfest. It was likely before summer 1948 because Mitka has a distinct memory of Willi's saying that he had lifted a *"Hundert Reichsmark."* In late June 1948, the Western Allies, as part of a "currency reform," helped to replace the swastika-adorned *Reichsmark* with the Deutsche Mark. See "Mark: German Currency," https://www.britannica .com/topic/mark-German-currency.

66   *Lullusfest, a carnival of sorts*   Lullusfest dates back to 852. It commemorates the life and death of Archbishop Lullus of Mainz, who

reestablished a Benedictine monastery that came to be associated with the founding of Bad Hersfeld. The Lullusfest is generally regarded as the oldest folk festival in Germany.

66 *"16 years of age or under; outside of their countries of origin or that of their parents"* Louise W. Holborn, *The International Refugee Organization: A Specialized Agency of the United Nations: Its History and Work, 1946–1952* (London: Oxford University Press, 1956), 503–4.

67 *In Kassel, at district court, Gustav faced a reckoning with the law* Heinrich Nuhn, "'Like Hunted Animals.' The November 1938 Pogroms in Rotenburg an der Fulda: Henny Rothschild's Letter from 18 October 1939," trans. Judith N. Levi, in *Leo Baeck Institute Year Book* 60 (2015), 8n21, offers insight into the trial of Gustav Dörr:

> In the proceedings of the state court of Kassel (judgment of 26 May 1948), Gustav Dörr (b. 1906), the owner of a trucking company, escaped sentencing, on the grounds that for medical reasons, he could not be held responsible for his actions (Section 51, paragraph 1 of the German Strafgesetzbuch, or criminal law statutes). The charges against him, however, were found to be fully justified: "Besides, the main trial has proven that D. was one of the most active participants in the activities. The accused should not be considered the main instigator or leader. However, he has violated the laws relating to civil disorders and rioting (Section 125, paragraph 2 of the German criminal law statutes)."

68 *"Child was living in a Kinderheim"* "Information Obtained from Tracing Bureau Checked with Child," n.d. The memo offers the following time line, one that indicates that, for several years, UNRRA and then IRO were attempting, with what appears to be diligence, to resolve Mitka's situation.

> 30.11.46 [Nov. 11, 1946] Letter from Mr. Przyluski advising result of examination by Field Tracing Officer.

> 22.3.47 [Mar. 22, 1947] Submitted to the Soviet Repatriation Center for authentication of nationality.

> 8.10.47 [Oct. 8, 1947] Letter from Zone ITS with attached original DP2 and DP2a.

16.11.47 [Nov. 16, 1947] Letter from Mr. Vorobiov. The child does not want to be removed and the foster parents do not want to keep him any longer.

8.12.47 [Dec. 8, 1947] Original documentation from Mr. Vorobiov. As the foster parents do not want to keep him any longer.

23.12.47 [Dec. 23, 1947] Letter from Lt. Col. Soviet Army requesting the repatriation.

19.1.48 [Jan. 19, 1948] Submitted to the Military Government requesting authorization from removal.

19.2.48 [Feb. 19, 1948] Refused by the OMG [Official Military Government].

19.2.48 [Feb. 19, 1948] Letter to the Chief Soviet Repatriation Officer stating that the removal request was refused.

26.2.48 [Feb. 26, 1948] Letter to the Chief Soviet Repatriation Officer informing that the case has been sent to the Tracing and Child Search Officer for further investigation.

14.4.48 [Apr. 4, 1948] Letter from Mr. Vorobiov with attached letter from Mr. Madurowicz.

The time line and other documents hint at the fact that US officials did not accept the Dörrs' story that Mitka was their foster child and, further, that these officials believed the child had been mistreated.

69   *A memorandum on December 23, 1947, lists "KALINSKI, Mitka"* T. Hantsyrev, Lt. Col., Soviet Army memo to Mr. Jean L. Bailly, Field Representative for Greater Hesse, Tracing and Child Search Division, December 23, 1947.

69   *A month later, an official letter was submitted* Mr. Jean L. Bailly, Field Representative, Tracing and Child Search Division, APO 633, US Army memo to Mr. Sharon L. Hatch, Chief Public Welfare and D. P. Division, Office of Military Government for Greater Hesse, Wiesbaden, January 19, 1948.

69   *"Prefers to stay with present family"* Memo to International Refugee Organization, Tracing and Child Search Division, Wiesbaden, February 19, 1948.

69   *This case does not concern a girl* Mr. Jan W. Madurowicz, Tracing/

Search Officer, ITS, Fulda, Jossfstr.15 memo to Mr. Nick Vorebicv-Pokcevsky, Senior Tracing/Search Officer, IRTS, Wetzler, Weingartenstr. 50, April 13, 1948.

70   *On September 27, 1948, ITS issued an official "Transfer Slip"*   International Tracing Service, US Zone Headquarters, Transfer Slip for Kalinski, Dimitro (Mitka), September 27, 1948.

70   *Three days later, on September 30*   Mr. Sharon L. Hatch, Chief PW [Prisoners of War] and DP [Displaced Persons] Branch memo to Mr. Jean L. Bailly, US Field Representative, APO 633, US Army, September 30, 1948.

70   *A letter from A. M. Jacobsen, a child-care officer in Fulda*   A. M. Jacobsen, Child Care Officer, Sub-Area Fulda memo to Area Child Care Officer, Area 1, Frankfurt, February 16, 1948.

71   *"The boy could not be transferred Tuesday 22/2, 1949"*   Memorandum from A. M. Jacobsen, Child Care Officer, Sub-Area Fulda, February 23, 1949.

72   *Kalinski, Demitro (Mitka). The boy has been located*   Memorandum from A. M. Jacobsen, Child Care Officer, Sub-Area Fulda, February 25, 1949.

Bad Aibling

74   *Mitka arrived in Hanau on Saturday, February 26, 1949*   The camp at Hanau was focused on serving displaced persons from Baltic countries, especially Lithuania, Latvia, and Estonia. For more information, refer to "Camps in Germany for Refugees from the Baltic," http://www.archiv.org.lv/baltic_dp_germany/index.php?lang=en&id=417, and "The Baltic Displaced Person Experience," http://www.draugas.org/news/the-baltic-displaced-person-experience/.

74   *Hanau was only a temporary placement for Mitka*   IRO Resettlement Registration Form for Unaccompanied Children, March 12, 1949.

75   *When Mitka arrived at the Children's Village*   Christian Höschler, *Home(less): The IRO Children's Village Bad Aibling, 1948–1951* (self-pub., eplubi, 2017), provides an excellent overview of the Children's

Village at Bad Aibling. See especially the introduction for a helpful general description of this facility and its work.

75 *On November 22, 1948, the Children's Village at Bad Aibling officially opened* Höschler provides vivid details about the challenging early days of the Children's Village and about the various agencies involved in creating and implementing its mission in his first chapter, "'The First Days Were Grim': Setting Up the Children's Village, 1948–1949."

75 *When Mitka came in March 1949, he was one of 389 residents* Höschler, *Home(less)*, 42–43.

76 *"To this day, all the particulars of our arrival in B. A. remain a big black smudge"* Kathleen Regan, quoted in Höschler, *Home(less)*, 31. Regan was a member of the AFSC team and the director of the program at the Reception House.

76 *The residents of Bad Aibling's Children's Village* Höschler, *Home(-less)*, 34–36.

77 *"There was something about Mitka"* Kathleen Regan, "The Holocaust at 50," interview by Michelle Franzen, KFTY-50 Santa Rosa, Summer 1995.

78 *He had a name that belonged to him* As mentioned, Mitka is a common nickname for Demitri and other spellings of that name.

78 *"His deep and inscrutable singular name"* T. S. Eliot, "The Naming of Cats," from *Old Possum's Book of Cats*, in T. S. Eliot, *The Complete Poems and Plays: 1909–1950* (New York: Harcourt, Brace, 1971), 149.

79 *"My name is Mitka"* This phrase appears in Reg Green's *The Nicholas Effect: A Boy's Gift to the World* (self-pub., Booktango, 2012), 103. Green's book tells of the murder of his son, Nicholas, and of the transformational effect of Nicholas's life and death. He describes a telephone conversation that began with the words "My name is Mitka." This call was, of course, initiated by Mitka Kalinski, who was moved by Nicholas's story. His reaching out to Green and their subsequent friendship were sources of comfort to both men. This phrase also provides the title for an orchestral composition by Jordan Roper, which was performed by the Cheyenne Wyoming Symphony and the Reno Philharmonic Orchestra; see https://

soundcloud.com/jordansroper/mitka-live-concert-recoring-2017 and https://www.mitka.life/mitka-concert.

79   *"He doesn't remember anything about his identity"*   Kathleen Regan, quoted in Höschler, *Home(less)*, 31.

79   *Dr. Margaret Hasselmann, chief medical officer at the Village*   Höschler, *Home(less)*, provides a photograph of Margaret Hasselmann and others (67) and includes a description of her medical and academic work with the Children's Village (93–94).

79   *"THE BOY, KALINSKI, DIMITRO BORN 14.12.32"*   Quoted from a memo/report from Dr. Margaret Hasselmann, dated November 2, 1950, and addressed "To Whom It May Concern." The report is reproduced here verbatim, including the use of all caps.

79   *"There were no documents whatsoever available to prove his age"*   "Social History" for Dimitri Kalinski prepared by L. Wijsmuller, Child Care Officer, dated August 25, 1950.

80   *The self-appointed teen leaders of the Village residents were skilled*   Höschler, *Home(less)*, 41–51.

81   *The Village's deputy administrator and program director, Nora Ryan*   Höschler, *Home(less)*, 51.

82   *"Smoked, drank, cussed like a GI"*   Quotation is from Frances Berkeley Floore's *The Bread of the Oppressed: An American Woman's Experience in War-Disrupted Countries* (Hicksville, NY: Exposition Press, 1975), 263; cited in Höschler, *Home(less)*, 34.

82   *"Not only difficult, but impossible to handle"*   Quotation is contained in Joseph A. Walker's report "Field Inspection Trip," Munich Military Post, Archives Nationales AJ/43/93, December 17, 1948, 3; cited in Höschler, *Home(less)*, 34.

82   *"Unfortunate as the mascot [Johnny Daussy]"*   Quotation is from a referral to R. Sprengel, camp psychiatrist, by L. Wijsmuller, dated March 9, 1950.

82   *"He's painfully self-conscious and supersensitive"*   This quotation and those in the next paragraph are from a report by L. Wijsmuller, dated October 18, 1949.

83   *"Daussy had been around a great deal"*   Quotations and other information about the break-in at the Quaker House are drawn from an undated report by L. Wijsmuller, titled "KALINSKI, Demitro."

84   *"I have been here for a few days already"*   This dictated letter from "Kalinski Demitro" to "Miss Wijsmuller" was written in Piusheim on November 1, 1949. A handwritten note indicates it was translated by Geo. Sedgin on November 9, 1949.

85   *Dr. Renate Sprengel, the resident psychiatrist*   In a letter to "Mrs Lefson," dated November 11, 1950, Dr. L. Renate Sprengel writes, "He [Mitka] at the beginning of our guidance showed much sympathies for [the German family] and he considered to go back and stay with them. I proposed to let him visit this family, what he wished to do, as I expected that this would clear his inner situation."

85   *"Also, the IRO and the Children's Village staff had the mandate to do one of three things"*   Lynne Taylor, *In the Children's Best Interests: Unaccompanied Children in American-Occupied Germany, 1945–1952* (Toronto: University of Toronto Press, 2017), 198–222, 250–56, discusses the complex policies regarding decisions about resettlement and repatriation.

86   *After Hansen's visit, she typed a two-page, single-spaced report*   "Report on a visit paid to Kalinski, Demitro, born December 1932 and his foster parents, Mr. and Mrs. Dörr, Badegasse 14 in Rotenburg/Fulda on April 26th, 1950" by Carla Hansen, Child Care officer, Field Office, Kassel.

Demitro

89   *For all children who passed through the Children's Village*   For more information about the complexities faced by international organizations working with displaced persons, see Christian Höschler, *Home(less): The IRO Children's Village Bad Aibling, 1948–1951* (self-pub., eplubi. 2017), 10–17, and Lynne Taylor, *In the Children's Best Interests: Unaccompanied Children in American-Occupied Germany, 1945–1952* (Toronto: University of Toronto Press, 2017). Chapter 9 of Taylor's book, "The Residual," has special relevance for Mitka's situation in that it examines the particularly thorny issues that surrounded children whose circumstances were still unresolved four or five years after the end of World War II.

89   *In Mitka's case, advertisements placed by the IRO in Ukrainian newspapers*   Efforts to determine Mitka's nationality and to find any

relatives are detailed in a memo written by Sheila Collins on behalf of Herbert W. Meyer, Chief Child Search Officer, to "The Director, Children's Village (13B) Bad Aibling," dated July 6, 1950.

90 *Since Mitka could not be repatriated, resettlement was the only choice* See Taylor, *Children's Best Interests*, 242–53.

90 *"Numerous national governments, especially the United States"* Taylor, *Children's Best Interests*, 243.

90 *While a number of governments agreed* Taylor, *Children's Best Interests*, 244.

91 *There was little apparent concern about his role in the break-in at the Quaker House* The staff's belief in Mitka's relative innocence in the incident at the Quaker House and their faith in his good character are verified in many documents, including a memo addressed "To Whom It May Concern" from M. L. Wijsmuller, dated June 23, 1950, and the "Social History," detailing information staff had gathered or perceived about Mitka, prepared by L. Wijsmuller on August 25, 1950.

91 *As did regular changes in teachers* Höschler, *Home(less)*, reports that in its early stages the Village suffered from a shortage of qualified teachers and that "as a result, no proper schooling took place until the end of 1948" (102). Eventually adult DPs were found who could serve as teachers, but, in the view of some staff, this was not a satisfactory solution. "According to Quaker Natalie Kent, many of the DPs employed as teachers were 'very skilled, but still with the DP attitude of not really wanting to be here, just waiting'" (102–3). Some German teachers who were more stable were eventually located; "however, most of the teachers continued to be DPs, who in one way or another were only in transit in Bad Aibling" (103).

92 *"They made me a Mensch"* Mitka's comment that he became "a *Mensch*" is part of a report written by L. Wijsmuller, labeled "Referral to Dr. R. Sprengel" and dated March 9, 1950. Though literally translated "man," the German word *Mensch* often carries with it the sense of "a good person" or "a person of honor."

92 *"If only I had an older brother"* Dr. Renate Sprengel, in a memo to Mrs. Lefson dated September 13, 1950, is among those noting Mitka's longing for a brother or some other male figure who could serve as a role model for him.

92   *The Village had been influenced by the work of Anna Freud*
        Höschler, *Home(less)*, 94–100.

93   *One example of this came when the Village established a kind of token*
        economy   Höschler, *Home(less)*, 75–76.

94   *"Would gain considerable satisfaction and recognition"*   Report by
        Emmy Garvey Lefson, April 4, 1950.

94   *At Bad Aibling, Mitka also grew physically*   Dr. Margaret Hassel-
        mann, chief medical officer at the Children's Village, memo "To
        Whom It May Concern," November 2, 1950.

94   *"At the time I saw him, I thought he was quite a disturbed boy"*
        Quotations are from a letter to Mr. Douglas Deane from Miss
        Theodora Allen, European representative of the US Committee
        for the Care of European Children, written September 25, 1950.
        Taylor, *Children's Best Interest*, 253–66, writes at length of Allen's
        role on the committee, suggesting that she was among the most
        vocal members of the organization and that her concerns were that
        decisions be made that were truly in the best interest of each child.
        It is likely that her memo, expressing doubts about Mitka's readi-
        ness to immigrate to America, was born out of genuine concern for
        finding the best placement for a boy who, in her words, appeared
        to have serious "interdisturbance."

96   *Lefson, for example, writing with the support of Deane*   The first
        quotation is from a memo addressed "To Whom It May Concern,"
        written by E. G. L. (Emmy Garvey Lefson) and dated October 31,
        1950. The second is from a memo to "Miss Th. Allen," dated No-
        vember 6, 1950. Emmy Lefson signed both memos, indicating that
        she was writing for Mr. Deane.

96   *In the end, when time was running out and the few remaining chil-*
        dren had to be placed   In the November 6 memo, Lefson reported,
        "Dimitri still has his ups and downs and is inclined from time to
        time to cut classes." She then shifted to a number of positive qual-
        ities of the boy: "Something most positive in the boy is his lively
        interest in a number of subjects. His utmost interest is in music....
        Dimitri also spends a lot of time in participating in all sorts of sport
        activities and has been the leader of the softball team in the Village.
        Since the weather is now getting worse, he has started to play chess

in which he is reasonably good. Our YMCA sports leader is his great friend and he talks most highly about him." Others also supported Mitka's immigration to America, including Dr. Hasselmann, who on November 2, 1950, wrote, "I BELIEVE THAT THE BOY IS PHYSICALLY AS WELL AS MENTALLY READY FOR SPEEDY EMIGRATION." Dr. Sprengel, the psychiatrist who saw him and who had concerns about his maturity, added her support, noting that even though Mitka was not yet fully mature, "he is eager to learn and to live with other kids on a higher knowledge level. This signifies that he is going to make further steps to activity." She further stated, "I don't think Dimitri needs analytic help in US."

America

101   *Including Mama and Papa Bonderowska*   Mitka remembered them as Papa and Mama Rosa, probably an easily pronounced, affectionate nickname. It is likely that they were DPs who lived as house parents at Bad Aibling.

103   *Today the onetime synagogue is a charter school*   At the time of writing, 718 Bryant Street is occupied by the Hyde Leadership Charter School. Information in this paragraph regarding the synagogue was gleaned from "Remembrance of Synagogues Past: The Lost Civilization of the Jewish South Bronx," http://www.bronxsynagogues .org.

105   *"Remember that you were a slave in the land of Egypt"*   All translations of the Hebrew Bible (or Tanakh/Old Testament) are from *Tanakh: The Holy Scriptures, The New JPS Translation according to the Traditional Hebrew Text* (Philadelphia: Jewish Publication Society, 1985).

108   *A cease-fire in the Korean War was signed in November 1953*   "How Many Americans Died in Korea?," CBS News, June 5, 2000, https:// www.cbsnews.com/news/how-many-americans-died-in-korea/.

108   *"bitch of Buchenwald"*   Ilse Koch was the wife of Otto Koch, commandant of Buchenwald. See Hackett, *Buchenwald*, 43.

109   *For the most part, these were "'feel-good' tunes"*   "A Brief History

of the Early Years of Rock and Roll," https://fiftiesweb.com/music/1950-1954-music/.

Tim

110   *"In Baltimore, at Mount Royal, I reconnected with Wasyl"*   Mitka is referring to Wasyl Palijczjuk, a friend he met while hospitalized for appendicitis while he was at Bad Aibling. Wasyl immigrated to Baltimore at approximately the same time Mitka immigrated to the Bronx. For information about Palijczjuk, see Carol Sorgen, "A Refugee's Artistic Journey," *Beacon,* November 19, 2012, https://www.thebeaconnewspapers.com/a-refugees-artistic-journey/.

111   *William Painter, the Baltimore-based inventor of the bottle cap*   A Baltimore resident, William Painter invented the bottle cap in 1891. Shortly thereafter, in 1892, he founded Crown Cork and Steel to mass-produce the caps. The company was housed at two sites. Mitka (Tim) worked in the manufacturing plant on Eastern Avenue. For more information, see Sierra Hallman, "Crown Cork and Seal on Eastern Avenue," https://explore.baltimoreheritage.org/items/show/513, and "History and Timeline: Crown Cork," https://www.crowncork.com/about-crown/history-and-timeline.

114   *"I took the physical. My draft card was 1-A"*   Mitka may have been referring to the Selective Service College Qualification Test (SSCQT). This test, which was actually 150 items, was developed by the Educational Testing Service in 1950 and was used to evaluate more than 500,000 Selective Service registrants. Its primary function was to determine eligibility for student deferment. For more information on the history of selective service and the draft, see "In Pursuit of Equity: Who Serves When Not All Serve?," a report by the National Advisory Commission on Selective Service (Washington, DC: Government Printing Office, 1967). For information on the SSCQT, see "Student Deferment and the Selective Service," https://www.ets.org/research/policy_research_reports/publications/report/1983/icfq.

115   *"The song 'Shrimp boats is a-coming'"*   Paul Mason Howard and Paul Weston wrote "Shrimp Boats." The version Mitka heard on the boat was most likely recorded in 1951 by Jo Stafford.

Adrienne

120   *"I believe that this was the first plastic in the United States"*   Mitka's
       assertion that Durez was the first plastics manufacturer in America
       is not quite accurate, but it was, apparently, one of the earliest. For
       a brief history of the development of plastics in the United States,
       see the Scientific History Institute, "The History and Future of
       Plastics," https://www.sciencehistory.org/the-history-and-future
       -of-plastics.

121   *"And Joe Katzenberger got a job there"*   Asbestos exposure and
       illnesses such as mesothelioma have been linked, specifically, to
       Durez Plastics in North Tonawanda. See, for example, Sweeney
       Payne, "Only in North Tonawanda: Mesothelioma Cancer Heri-
       tage in NT," *Niagara Reporter,* January 27, 2016, http://niagarafalls
       reporter.com/only-in-north-tonawanda-mesothelioma-cancer-her
       itage-in-nt/.

121   *"One thing was, we could sleep on the job"*   Though perhaps hard
       to believe, sleeping while on duty, especially during night shifts,
       was not uncommon in some industries during this time, including
       factory work. As Mitka explained to us when asked, this was only
       allowed for short periods, usually as part of a break or after the crew
       had completed its work for the night.

122   *"I had a form to fill out"*   Though it may seem hard to imagine an
       American home donning a swastika flag, especially so soon after
       the war in which the Nazis were defeated, Mitka tells the story
       matter-of-factly. Further, history shows that Nazi supporters were
       alive and well during this period in the United States. See Freder-
       ick J. Simonelli, *American Fuehrer: George Lincoln Rockwell and the
       American Nazi Party* (Urbana: University of Illinois Press, 1999),
       which shares the story of the 1959 formation of the American Nazi
       Party.

122   *"And the job I got was at American District Steam Company"*   Ac-
       cording to historical notes archived in the Social Networks and Ar-
       chival Context Cooperative, "The ADSCO Mfg. Co. was formed
       in the 1870's in Lockport, N. Y. as the American District Steam Co.
       In 1957 ADSCO became a wholly owned subsidiary of Yuba Indus-
       tries. ADSCO was acquired from Standard Prudential Corporation

in 1973 by a group of local investors. The company manufactured pipe line expansion joints, pressure vessels, weldments, large industrial heaters and other custom products." "Yuba Consolidated Industries: ADSCO Division," http://snaccooperative.org/ark :/99166/w6966jvs.

124 *In today's dollars, $150 per week is equivalent to $1,400* "Inflation Calculator," http://cpiinflationcalculator.com.

129 *"Here he was—this big guy"* Mitka's description of Wee Willie as a "big guy" is accurate, perhaps even understated. According to https://www.cagematch.net/?id=2&nr=9511, the professional wrestler was six-foot-five and weighed 290 pounds.

130 *"Jim Vona, he owned practically everything in town"* Mitka's perception of Jim Vona as someone who did not always operate within the strict limits of the law seems to have been accurate. According to articles in the *Buffalo News*—for example, "N. Tonawanda Merchant Convicted of Bribery" (October 14, 1994) and "Bribe Brings Jail Sentence for Man of 79" (May 5, 1995)—Vona was convicted of bribing a city council member and sentenced to a year in jail and a $1,000 fine.

130 *Mitka starts singing a Perry Como lyric* "Round and Round" was written by Joe Shapiro and Lou Stallman and recorded by Perry Como in January 1957.

Marriage

135 *Adrienne, together with her "sisters"* As noted in the previous chapter, Verna and Hilda were Adrienne's cousins, the daughters of her great-aunt and great-uncle, Matilda and Louis. She was raised with them from infancy and considers them to be her sisters.

142 *This one was with Union Concrete, a company based in West Seneca, New York* Union Concrete, founded in 1950, is still thriving in New York today. We have found an April 23, 1999, obituary in the *Buffalo News* for an Elmer J. Nobilio and several mentions of a Richard Hoefer and an Al Hoefer in lists of Cornell University alumni but could not locate specific information about either of the companies that provided Mitka with work after he left ADSCO.

143 *One hundred twenty-four inches of snow* "Buffalo Monthly Snowfall," https://www.weather.gov/buf/BuffaloSnow.

Heading West

148 *He went downtown and asked to talk to the sheriff* According to his obituary in the *Reno Gazette Journal*, June 16, 1996, 16, Bud Young served as sheriff of Washoe County from 1952 to 1971.

149 *So he took a job with Jim Brussa* Jim Brussa died in 2012. Brussa Masonry, the company for which Mitka worked, is apparently still in existence in Reno. See "Masonry Licensed Contractors in Reno, Nevada," http://www.uslicensecontractors.com/masonry/nevada/reno/.

The Sixties

160 *"I got all of the neighbors to sign a petition"* See "Sidewalk Shuffle Bugs Kalinski," *Sparks News Tribune*, May 5, 1978, for insight into Mitka's engagement with local issues in Sparks.

The Seventies

169 *Her son Jimmy had suffered a traumatic brain injury* Traumatic brain injury, or TBI, is defined by the Centers for Disease Control and Prevention as "a disruption in the normal function of the brain that can be caused by a bump, blow, or jolt to the head, or penetrating head injury." Jimmy Kalinski's symptoms were among those that are identified as "danger signs" by the CDC.

169 *"The sheriff's department flew us to San Francisco"* The *Reno Gazette Journal* obituary for Sheriff Bud Young, June 16, 1996, notes that, among other things, he started an "aero squadron" that used private planes and pilots to assist law enforcement as they worked in the geographically large Washoe County. It is likely that it was a private plane from this aero squadron that flew Adrienne and Jimmy to San Francisco.

171 *Reagan described "billions of dollars of waste"* Ronald Reagan, televised campaign address, "A Vital Economy: Jobs, Growth, and Progress for Americans," October 24, 1980, https://www.reaganlibrary.gov/10-24-80.

171 *"In the sights of both the president and Congress were tens of thou-*

sands of disabled individuals"   For a thorough discussion of the
Social Security Disability Act of 1956 and its amendments in 1958,
1960, 1965, 1967, and 1972, refer to John Kearney, "Social Security
and the 'D' in OASDI: The History of a Federal Program Insur-
ing Earners against Disability," https://www.ssa.gov/policy/docs
/ssb/v66n3/v66n3p1.html. Also helpful in clarifying the range of
policies linked to Social Security Disability Insurance (SSDI) and
related benefits, such as those involving Supplemental Security Income (SSI), is "Legislative History of the Social Security Disability
Insurance Program," https://www.ssa.gov/legislation/DI%20legis
lative%20history.pdf.

171   *Eliminating federal social support programs where "real need cannot
be demonstrated"*   Ronald Reagan, "Address before a Joint Session
of Congress on the Program for Economic Recovery," February 18,
1981, https://www.reaganlibrary.gov/21881a.

The Phone Call

179   *The modern word "crisis" comes from a Greek word*   Robin Burk,
"The Rethink We Need to Avoid America's Collapse," *American
Mind: A Publication of the Claremont Institute*, October 3, 2019,
https://americanmind.org/essays/the-rethink-we-need-to-avoid
-americas-collapse/.

179   *"Vitally important or decisive state of things"*   "Crisis," https://www
.etymonline.com/word/crisis.

180   *Rabbi Irnie Nadler*   Yitzchak Irnie Aaron Nadler was born in
1984 in Youngstown, Ohio, and died in 2004. At the time of his
death he was the rabbi of the North Tahoe Hebrew Congregation.
Rabbi Nadler, who described himself as "reconservadox," was someone whose "warmth" made congregants and others "feel at home."
For more on Irnie Nadler, see Alix Wall, "North Tahoe's Reconservadox Leader Dies at 50," *Jewish News of Northern California*,
https://www.jweekly.com/2004/05/28/north-tahoe-s-reconserv
adox-congregational-leader-dies-at-50/.

181   *"Rabbi Nadler told me that a former student of mine"*   This and all
subsequent quotes attributed to Professor Grant Leneaux are from
Grant Leneaux, "German Lessons" (unpublished manuscript), n.d.

181   *An English translation of the January 2, 1982, call transcript*   All quotations from the phone conversation are taken from a transcript translated by Grant Leneaux. Present in Nevada during the call were Rabbi Irnie Nadler, Professor Grant Leneaux, Adrienne Kalinski, and Mitka Kalinski. Other information about the call, such as the tones of voices, appearances, and attitudes of participants, comes from interviews with the Kalinskis and Professor Leneaux.

185   *"Now we had leads"*   Adrienne Kalinski, "Mitka: Lost and Forgotten Child of the Holocaust" (unpublished manuscript), 9. This manuscript was originally written in 1984 and was updated in 2002, 2005, 2008, and 2015. This and all subsequent quotations are from the 2015 version.

185   *"How long, O LORD, shall I cry out . . . ?"*   These words are from Habakkuk 1:2. Similar words are found in other passages in the Hebrew Bible, especially the Psalms. See, for example, Psalms 6 and 13.

185   *"Mitka—the little* Stoppelrusse*"*   "Bald Russian"; see chapter 3.

185   *"Had actually dared not only to call Gustav, but to question him"*   Adrienne Kalinski, "Mitka," 9.

186   *"Mitka was in an almost continuous state of depression"*   Adrienne Kalinski, "Mitka," 10.

186   *"A Roman Catholic priest, a Jewish rabbi, a psychiatrist"*   Adrienne Kalinski, "Mitka," 11.

187   *"We are determined to learn about Mitka's background"*   June 22, 1982.

Citizenship

191   *"Immediately Mitka began to tell Charlie"*   Adrienne Kalinski, "Mitka," 12.

191   *"A map or some postcards from the Rotenburg area"*   Adrienne Kalinski, "Mitka," 15.

191   *"With Mitka's help, I had—months earlier—sketched a map"*   Adrienne Kalinski, "Mitka," 15.

193   *"Once there at Gustav's farm"*   Adrienne Kalinski, "Mitka," 18–19.

193   *Gruschka called himself Gustav's "prisoner of war"*   Eduard Grus-

chka to the Reiprich family, October 1983; translated by Grant Leneaux, November 12, 1983.

196   *"I kept thinking about Michael [their grandson]"*   Adrienne Kalinski, "Mitka," 27.

197   *"Unable to sleep one night, I got up"*   Adrienne Kalinski, "Mitka," 27.

Back to Germany

199   *"Poor Mitka was shaking"*   Adrienne Kalinski, "Mitka," 30.

199   *"Immediately Mitka was on alert"*   Adrienne Kalinski, "Mitka," 32.

201   *"A first glimpse of a human lifestyle"*   Adrienne Kalinski, "Mitka," 41.

201   *"Where the big arched sign had once read 'Bad Aibling's Children's Village'"*   Adrienne Kalinski, "Mitka," 39.

201   *"Too soon it was time for us to leave this quaint little Bavarian town"*   Adrienne Kalinski, "Mitka," 43–44.

202   *"Michael Jason Biesel—nine-year-old grandson of Dimitri Kalinski"*   Adrienne Kalinski, "Mitka," 48.

203   *"The sound of this name hit me like a stroke"*   This quotation is from an "embargoed" article written by Reinhard Renger in December 1984 and intended for *Stern* magazine. Translated by Helena Chambers, May 23, 1985.

203   *"It also created in him a kind of imperative"*   The moments when Mitka learned that Pfaffenwald was a real place are described in Adrienne Kalinski, "Mitka," 56–57.

205   *"Oma Deist embraced Mitka like a long-lost son!"*   Adrienne Kalinski, "Mitka," 65–66.

206   *"Rosemarie led us to the entrance"*   Adrienne Kalinski, "Mitka," 67.

207   *"As if to shield herself from an oncoming blow"*   Adrienne Kalinski, "Mitka," 68.

208   *At the time, Anna Jakob (not to be confused with Tante Anna)*   According to the Kalinskis, when Charlie Viney knocked on the door of Badegasse 14, the woman who answered was Anna Jakob. Charlie had shown her a photo of Mitka as a young boy. When she saw this, she directed him to Burgasse 14, to the home of Frau

Deist. She also, apparently, called Gustav's home to warn them of an American who was seeking information about Mitka. When Charlie knocked on the door of the Dörr home, Lisa, Gustav's wife, met him and simply said, *"Nein, nein, nein"* and refused to let him enter. Charlie suspects he was rebuffed at the door, even before he attempted to question Gustav, because the warning from Anna had enabled the Dörrs to prepare.

209 *"My first impression of her"* Adrienne Kalinski, "Mitka," 85.

Fobianka

211 *Indeed, the transcript of Fobianka's words* All quotations are translated from a transcription of "The Fobianka Tape of November 13, 1984."

212 *Susanne Hohlmann, who he knew had written a soon-to-be-published thesis about Pfaffenwald* Hohlmann, *Pfaffenwald*.

213 *A reporter from the local Bad Hersfeld newspaper* "Aus dem Niemand wird ganz langsam ein Jemand," *Bad Hersfeld Newspaper*, November 22, 1984, 19.

213 *Local citizens planned a* Volkstrauertag, *or National Day of Mourning, ceremony* The National Day of Mourning, or *Stiller tag* ("Silent Day"), was established in 1922 to honor the World War I dead. Although not an official state holiday, it is a time when Germans remember and honor those killed in both world wars and under other conditions. For more information, see "National Day of Mourning in Germany," https://timeanddate.com/holidays/Germany/volkstrauertag.

213 *Sunday, November 18, was cold and dreary* Adrienne Kalinski, "Mitka," 90.

214 *"Als zehnjähriger Junge habe ich mit dir vergeblich gelitten"* Adrienne Kalinski, "Mitka," 108.

214 *"We're all just standing around waiting for whoever would be there"* Adrienne Kalinski, "Mitka," 108.

215 *After the ceremony, the* Stern *reporter, Reinhard Renger* Adrienne Kalinski, "Mitka," 110.

215   *"Print absolutely nothing about Gustav or her family"*   Adrienne Kalinski, "Mitka," 110.

215   *"Pfaffenwald was a good camp"*   Adrienne Kalinski, "Mitka," 110. It is again worth noting that Fobianka's statements are unproven and in direct contradiction to records of deaths and to the eyewitness testimony of several individuals, including Mitka, who reported clearly on abortions and other operations done with "pocketknives" ("Operationen konnten bestenfalls mit einem Taschenmesser durchgeführt warden"; see Susanne Hohlmann, "Pfaffenwald: Sterbe- und Geburtenlager, 1942–1945" [University of Kassel thesis, 1984], 83), deaths of adults and infants, beatings, starvation, and the like.

216   *"All these years—nobody even bothered"*   Adrienne Kalinski, "Mitka," 112.

"My Brother"

218   *She asked Anna to release the paperwork*   Adrienne Kalinski to Anna Dörr Krause, July 4, 1985.

219   *"Now, on behalf of Mitka and his family"*   Adrienne Kalinski to Anna Dörr Krause, August 30, 1985.

219   *With this new approach, Adrienne penned a letter*   Adrienne Kalinski to the editor of *Hersfelder Zeitung*, November 11, 1987. The letter was published in January 1988.

220   *In his January 21, 1988, letter, he asserted four points*   Wolfgang Both to Dimitri Kalinski, January 21, 1988.

220   *"The years following our trip to Germany"*   Adrienne Kalinski, "Mitka," 127.

222   *Out of this came a three-part series*   "The Holocaust at 50," Summer 1995.

222   *"Yes, Mitka was robbed of every right"*   Adrienne Kalinski, "Mitka" (unpublished poem, 1984).

223   *At Doran Beach in June 1996*   Information about Gary Nixon was supplied by Mr. Nixon himself in an email to Andrew Bukin on August 28, 1997.

224   *"A major research archival and science institution"*   https://www
.pilsudski.org/en/about-us/history/609-history-of-the-institute.

225   *Gary learned that Wladyslaw Kalinski served with honor*   The information in this paragraph is from an email Peter Holownia sent
to Gary Nixon on April 19, 1997.

225   *A peculiar book titled* Index of Poles Buried in London Cemeteries   We have not yet located this out-of-print book, so we are re-
lying on Gary Nixon's report of its contents.

226   *"Dear Sir"*   Peter Holownia to Marcin Michalack, April 10, 1997.

227   *"A man who knew Mitka's father"*   Gary is quoting from a letter
from Eduard Gruschka to Adrienne and Mitka. In it, Eduard reports on things he knew or learned about Mitka's father, including
the fact that "he received 140 acres of land" because of his service
in the war between Poland and Russia.

227   *"We were both extremely moved"*   Peter Holownia to Gary Nixon,
April 14, 1997. Italics added.

228   *"I'm still not sure how much of Mitka's life story you know"*   Gary
Nixon to Peter Holownia, April 14, 1997.

228   *"He [Mitka] remembers a tiny (slight, small) lady"*   Gary Nixon to
Peter Holownia, April 15, 1997.

Reunion

235   *On Saturday, May 3, 1997, Mitka left a message*   Gary Nixon to
Peter Holownia, May 5, 1997.

236   *"After all we have been through"*   Virtually all the direct quotations
related to the Kalinskis' trip to Europe are drawn from the two-part
KGO-TV 7 special hosted by Lyanne Melendez, filmed July 24–26,
1997, and aired in August 1997. The Kalinskis own copies of this
broadcast and share it with permission of the station.

240   *"Those days of 'wine and roses'"*   Adrienne Kalinski to Barbara Holownia, August 29, 1997.

240   *"Happy events that took place just only few weeks ago"*   Barbara Holownia to Adrienne Kalinski, n.d.

240   *"At Peter's suggestion, Adrienne had written to Lala"*   Adrienne
Kalinski to Lala Bartel, June 8, 1997.

240   *"A second letter, written in January 1998"*   Adrienne Kalinski to Lala Bartell, January 29, 1998.

241   *"The battle to make a separate peace"*   We are aware that we have borrowed the phrase "a separate peace" from John Knowles's novel *A Separate Peace* (New York: Scribner's Sons, 2003).

Bar Mitzvah

244   *Louise sought out Mitka*   The Shoah Foundation interview with Mitka/Dimitri Kalinski, #41151, was conducted by Louise Bobrow on May 11, 1998. It is housed in the Visual History Archive at the USC Shoah Foundation: The Institute for Visual History and Education. Access requires completing a simple, free application in order to log in.

244   *Rabbi Perl's first call to Mitka began a telephone friendship*   Interview with Rabbi Anchelle Perl conducted by Jacob Wheeler, February 14, 2010, in Mineola, New York.

244   *"Of my mother"*   Traditional Jewish law stipulates that a child of a Jewish mother is Jewish. Modern challenges to the principle of matrilineal descent are not uncommon, with patrilineal descent now the norm in some branches of Judaism, notably Reform. See Joseph Telushkin, "The Law of Return: Who Is a Jew?" and "Patrilineal Descent," in *Jewish Literacy*, rev. ed. (New York: Morrow, 2001), 358–59, 481–82; compare Sarah Lyall, "Who Is a Jew? Court Ruling in Britain Raises Question," *New York Times*, November 8, 2009, A8. All evidence of Mitka's origins confirms that his mother was a Jew and that, before he was left at the *Kinderheim*, he was raised as a Jew. He had been circumcised as an infant or young child at a time in eastern Europe when only Jewish boys were circumcised. And he had vague memories of traveling on horse-drawn wagons with men in black hats with curls of hair at their temples. He was placed in—and ran from—a *Kinderheim* in Bila Tserkva that was the home of Jewish orphans in the town and region. And he knew Yiddish. After Mitka came to the United States, he recognized the hymns—Hebrew Scripture set to music—that were

chanted in the Bronx synagogue where he lived. Years later, when he again attended Shabbat services, he would sing along with the congregation, unaware of where or how he knew the words but recognizing them nonetheless. Others also recognized Mitka as a Jew. He had been forced to wear a yellow star while in Dachau, a circumstance that created a sense of fear in him because "everyone who had a yellow star disappeared." Finally, the Dörrs, his captors for seven years, believed him to be a Jew and, even as they tried to hide this fact from outsiders by giving him a German name, privately cursed him as a *Juden* or *Judenfresse.*

244   *"Could I become a man so late in life?"*   Mitka Kalinski, "The Day I Became a Man: A Child of the Holocaust Faces the Past He Tried to Forget and Finds the Faith He Never Really Knew," interview by Amy Wong, *Guideposts*, March 2002, 35. Compare the retelling of Alice Sparberg Alexiou, "A Survivor's Faith Rekindled," *Washington Post*, August 25, 2001, https://www.washingtonpost.com /archive/local/2001/08/25/a-survivors-faith-rekindled/7abe22c6 -8fc2-4418-8c73-37a7ea71eb73/.

245   *"The criteria for eligibility specify"*   Letter from Leonard Orland on behalf of the Conference on Jewish Material Claims against Germany, Inc., September 20, 2019.

245   *"The purpose of studying the Torah"*   Interview with Perl conducted by Wheeler.

246   *Son-in-law Mike Bland*   Mike (Michael Bland) was married to Donna Kalinski. Prior to his trip with Adrienne and Mitka to Long Island, he had been, according to Donna, an avowed atheist. He was, however, so deeply moved by his father-in-law's story and bar mitzvah and by the deep faith of the men and women he met that he converted to Judaism soon after his return to Sparks. He became a serious student of the Torah and the Talmud. At the time of his death from a heart attack in 2010, he was, in fact, studying to be a rabbi. He is buried in Israel.

247   *A six-foot-high* mechitza, *a curtain that separates men and women*   For more about the practice of separating men and women during worship, see Norma B. Joseph, "Mechitzah: Sep-

arate Seating in the Synagogue," https://www.myjewishlearning
.com/article/mehitzah-separate-seating-in-the-synagogue/.

247   *On that special Monday morning*   A bar mitzvah can take place
on any day the Torah is read. In addition to Shabbat (Saturday),
the Torah is read on Mondays and Thursdays in traditional synagogues. August 20, 2001, also happened to be Rosh Chodesh Elul
(the beginning of the Hebrew month of Elul), which likely added
to the festivities.

249   *"I recited the prayers the Rabbi had taught me"*   Mitka Kalinski,
"Became a Man," 35.

250   *"I know it's possible now"*   Personal video, Mitka Kalinski Bar Mitzvah, Chabad Mineola (Mineola, Long Island, New York), August 1,
2001.

251   *Even as many years have passed*   Rabbi Anchelle Perl, Chanukah
Telethon, shown on various regional networks in the Tri-State area
(New York, New Jersey, Connecticut), December 16, 2012.

253   *What the locust had eaten had been restored*   In Joel 2:25 God says,
"I will restore to you the years that the locust hath eaten . . ." (KJV).
This passage refers to restoration after great loss and destruction.

About the Authors

Steven W. Brallier is both a collector and a teller of stories, qualities he developed in his childhood on the western highlands of Kenya. After life in Kenya, Steve had a long career in the entertainment industry as a promoter, agent, and writer, which exposed him to many people with amazing stories. None was more compelling than Mitka's. Almost immediately a deep trust developed between Steve and the Kalinskis, a trust that provided the essential foundation for the powerful story that is *Mitka's Secret*.

Joel N. Lohr is president of Hartford Seminary, a leading interfaith graduate school. He is an award-winning author, scholar of religion, and passionate leader in interreligious relations and higher education. His teaching and research have focused on the Bible, specifically the Torah (or Pentateuch), as well as Jewish-Christian relations and dialogue. He has published ten books, with both academic and popular publishers.

After receiving her PhD in 1991, *Lynn G. Beck* held faculty positions at UCLA and the University of Alabama before becoming academic dean at Pacific Lutheran University and the University of the Pacific. She is the author or coauthor of eight books and a number of articles and has had leadership roles on national, state, and local boards.